Sabbats
ALMANAC

Llewellyn's Sabbats Almanac:
Samhain 2015 to Mabon 2016

Cover art © Carolyn Vibbert/Susan and Co.
Cover design by Ellen Lawson
Editing by Ed Day
Interior Art: © Carolyn Vibbert/Susan and Co., excluding illustrations on pages
37, 75, 110, 149, 184, 218, 221, 259, and 295, which are © Wen Hsu

You can order annuals and books from *New Worlds*, Llewellyn's catalog. To
request a free copy call toll free: 1-877-NEW WRLD, or order online by visiting
our website at http://subscriptions.llewellyn.com.

ISBN: 978-0-7387-3398-2

Llewellyn Worldwide Ltd.
2143 Wooddale Drive
Woodbury, MN 55125-2989
www.llewellyn.com

Printed in the United States of America

2015

JANUARY
S	M	T	W	T	F	S
				1	2	3
4	5	6	7	8	9	10
11	12	13	14	15	16	17
18	19	20	21	22	23	24
25	26	27	28	29	30	31

FEBRUARY
S	M	T	W	T	F	S
1	2	3	4	5	6	7
8	9	10	11	12	13	14
15	16	17	18	19	20	21
22	23	24	25	26	27	28

MARCH
S	M	T	W	T	F	S
1	2	3	4	5	6	7
8	9	10	11	12	13	14
15	16	17	18	19	20	21
22	23	24	25	26	27	28
29	30	31				

APRIL
S	M	T	W	T	F	S
			1	2	3	4
5	6	7	8	9	10	11
12	13	14	15	16	17	18
19	20	21	22	23	24	25
26	27	28	29	30		

MAY
S	M	T	W	T	F	S
					1	2
3	4	5	6	7	8	9
10	11	12	13	14	15	16
17	18	19	20	21	22	23
24	25	26	27	28	29	30
31						

JUNE
S	M	T	W	T	F	S
	1	2	3	4	5	6
7	8	9	10	11	12	13
14	15	16	17	18	19	20
21	22	23	24	25	26	27
28	29	30				

JULY
S	M	T	W	T	F	S
			1	2	3	4
5	6	7	8	9	10	11
12	13	14	15	16	17	18
19	20	21	22	23	24	25
26	27	28	29	30	31	

AUGUST
S	M	T	W	T	F	S
						1
2	3	4	5	6	7	8
9	10	11	12	13	14	15
16	17	18	19	20	21	22
23	24	25	26	27	28	29
30	31					

SEPTEMBER
S	M	T	W	T	F	S
		1	2	3	4	5
6	7	8	9	10	11	12
13	14	15	16	17	18	19
20	21	22	23	24	25	26
27	28	29	30			

OCTOBER
S	M	T	W	T	F	S
				1	2	3
4	5	6	7	8	9	10
11	12	13	14	15	16	17
18	19	20	21	22	23	24
25	26	27	28	29	30	31

NOVEMBER
S	M	T	W	T	F	S
1	2	3	4	5	6	7
8	9	10	11	12	13	14
15	16	17	18	19	20	21
22	23	24	25	26	27	28
29	30					

DECEMBER
S	M	T	W	T	F	S
		1	2	3	4	5
6	7	8	9	10	11	12
13	14	15	16	17	18	19
20	21	22	23	24	25	26
27	28	29	30	31		

2016

JANUARY
S	M	T	W	T	F	S
					1	2
3	4	5	6	7	8	9
10	11	12	13	14	15	16
17	18	19	20	21	22	23
24	25	26	27	28	29	30
31						

FEBRUARY
S	M	T	W	T	F	S
	1	2	3	4	5	6
7	8	9	10	11	12	13
14	15	16	17	18	19	20
21	22	23	24	25	26	27
28	29					

MARCH
S	M	T	W	T	F	S
		1	2	3	4	5
6	7	8	9	10	11	12
13	14	15	16	17	18	19
20	21	22	23	24	25	26
27	28	29	30	31		

APRIL
S	M	T	W	T	F	S
					1	2
3	4	5	6	7	8	9
10	11	12	13	14	15	16
17	18	19	20	21	22	23
24	25	26	27	28	29	30

MAY
S	M	T	W	T	F	S
1	2	3	4	5	6	7
8	9	10	11	12	13	14
15	16	17	18	19	20	21
22	23	24	25	26	27	28
29	30	31				

JUNE
S	M	T	W	T	F	S
			1	2	3	4
5	6	7	8	9	10	11
12	13	14	15	16	17	18
19	20	21	22	23	24	25
26	27	28	29	30		

JULY
S	M	T	W	T	F	S
					1	2
3	4	5	6	7	8	9
10	11	12	13	14	15	16
17	18	19	20	21	22	23
24	25	26	27	28	29	30
31						

AUGUST
S	M	T	W	T	F	S
	1	2	3	4	5	6
7	8	9	10	11	12	13
14	15	16	17	18	19	20
21	22	23	24	25	26	27
28	29	30	31			

SEPTEMBER
S	M	T	W	T	F	S
				1	2	3
4	5	6	7	8	9	10
11	12	13	14	15	16	17
18	19	20	21	22	23	24
25	26	27	28	29	30	

OCTOBER
S	M	T	W	T	F	S
						1
2	3	4	5	6	7	8
9	10	11	12	13	14	15
16	17	18	19	20	21	22
23	24	25	26	27	28	29
30	31					

NOVEMBER
S	M	T	W	T	F	S
		1	2	3	4	5
6	7	8	9	10	11	12
13	14	15	16	17	18	19
20	21	22	23	24	25	26
27	28	29	30			

DECEMBER
S	M	T	W	T	F	S
				1	2	3
4	5	6	7	8	9	10
11	12	13	14	15	16	17
18	19	20	21	22	23	24
25	26	27	28	29	30	31

Contents

Introduction

NEARLY EVERYONE HAS A favorite sabbat. There are numerous ways to observe any tradition. This edition of the *Sabbats Almanac* provides a wealth of lore, celebrations, creative projects, and recipes to enhance your holiday.

For this edition, a mix of writers—**Magenta Griffith, Dallas Jennifer Cobb, Eilidh Grove, Suzanne Ress, Elizabeth Barrette, Diana Rajchel, Susan Pesznecker,** and **Natalie Zaman**—share their ideas and wisdom. These include a variety of paths ranging from traditional Celtic to Eclectic as this diverse group of authors take a personal approach to each sabbat. Each chapter closes with an extended ritual, which may be adapted for both solitary practitioners and covens.

In addition to these insights and rituals, specialists in astrology, history, cooking, crafts, and family impart their expertise throughout.

April Elliott Kent gives an overview of planetary influences most relevant for each sabbat season and provides details and a short ritual for selected events, including New and Full Moons, retrograde motion, planetary positions, and more.

Blake Octavian Blair explores the realm of old-world Pagans, with a focus on customs such as ritual bread baking for Lammas and lesser-known facets of well-known symbols like the pumpkin and the maypole.

Doreen Shababy conjures up a feast for each festival that includes an appetizer, entrée, dessert, and beverage.

Tess Whitehurst offers instructions on craft projects that can also be incorporated into your practice.

Linda Raedisch focuses on sustainable activities the entire family can share in conjunction with each sabbat.

About the Authors

Elizabeth Barrette has been involved with the Pagan community for more than twenty-five years. She served as the managing editor of *PanGaia* for eight years and Dean of Studies at the Grey School of Wizardry for four years. She has written columns on beginning and intermediate Pagan practice, Pagan culture, and Pagan leadership. Her book *Composing Magic: How to Create Magical Spells, Rituals, Blessings, Chants, and Prayers* explains how to combine writing and spirituality. She lives in central Illinois where she has done much networking with Pagans, such as coffeehouse meetings and open sabbats. Her other public activities feature Pagan picnics and science fiction conventions. She enjoys magical crafts, historic religions, and gardening for wildlife. Her other writing fields include speculative fiction, gender studies, social and environmental issues. Visit her blog *The Wordsmith's Forge* http://ysabetwordsmith.livejournal.com or website *PenUltimate Productions* http://penultimateproductions.weebly.com. Her coven site with extensive Pagan materials is Greenhaven Tradition, http://greenhaventradition.weebly.com.

Blake Octavian Blair is an eclectic Pagan, ordained minister, shamanic practitioner, writer, Usui Reiki Master-Teacher, tarot reader, and musical artist. Blake blends various mystical traditions from both the East and West along with a reverence for the natural world into his own brand of modern Neopaganism and magick. Blake holds a degree in English and Religion from the University of Florida. He is an avid reader, crafter, and practicing vegetarian. Blake lives with his beloved husband, an aquarium full of fish, and an indoor jungle of houseplants. Visit him at www.blakeoctavianblair.com or write him at blake@blakeoctavianblair.com.

Life is what you make it, and **Dallas Jennifer Cobb** has made a magical life in a waterfront village on the shores of great Lake Ontario. Forever scheming novel ways to pay the bills, she practices manifestation magic and wildlands witchcraft. She teaches Pilates, works in a library, is an elected official, and writes to finance long hours spent following her heart's desire—time spent in nature and on the water. She lives with her daughter and an ancient cat in a huge, happy home. Contact her at jennifer.cobb@live.com.

Magenta Griffith has been a Witch more than thirty-five years and a High Priestess for more than twenty-five years. She is a founding member of Prodea, which has been celebrating rituals since 1980, as well as being a member of various Pagan organizations such as Covenant of the Goddess. Magenta, along with her coven brother Steven Posch, is the author of *The Prodea Cookbook: Good Food and Traditions from Paganistan's Oldest Coven*. She presents classes and workshops at a variety of events around the Midwest. She shares her home with a small black cat and a large collection of books.

Eilidh Grove, also known as Ellen Coutts Waff, FSA Scot, is a folklorist, singer, and herbalist in the ancient Celtic tradition. She sings with Fol-de-Rol, a British folk trio, performing yearly at the Maryland Renaissance Festival. She has lived in Middlefield, Connecticut, for thirteen years; previously she lived in the Baltimore/Washington area where she was a staff nurse at the Baltimore Birth Center. She has a particular interest in "enchantment"—the art of magical singing/poetry—and has been active in the Wiccan, Pagan, and Druid community since 1978. Ellen is a Druid with Ord na Darach Gile, Celtic Reconstructionist Druids, and founding member of The Druid Grove of Two Coasts. She is working on the gardens at Talcott House, her 1742 home in Connecticut. Ellen and her daughter, Meg, own Laurel Brook Studios, which specializes in art clothing, costuming, and beading.

April Elliott Kent has been a professional astrologer since 1990. She is the author of *Astrological Transits* (Fair Winds/Quarto, 2015), *The Essential Guide to Practical Astrology* (Alpha/Penguin, 2011), and *Star Guide to Weddings* (Llewellyn, 2008). April's writing has also appeared in the *Mountain Astrologer* and *Dell Horoscope* magazines and in Llewellyn's Moon Sign and Sun Sign books. She lives in San Diego, California. Her website is BigSkyAstrology.com.

Susan Pesznecker, aka Moonwriter, is a mother, writer, college English teacher, nurse, and hearth Pagan living in northwestern Oregon. She holds a master's degree in nonfiction writing and loves to read, watch the stars, camp with her wonder poodle, and work in her own biodynamic garden. Sue is a cofounder of the Ars Viarum Magicarum, an online school of magick (http://magicalconservatory.com/), and cofounder of the Druid Grove of Two Coasts (https://www.facebook.com/groups/DruidGroveofTwoCoasts/). She's the author of *Gargoyles* (New Page, 2007), *Crafting Magick with Pen and Ink* (Llewellyn, 2009), and *The Magickal Retreat: Making Time for Solitude, Intention & Rejuvenation* (Llewellyn, 2012). She also regularly contributes to many of the Llewellyn annuals. Visit Sue on her Facebook page: http://www.facebook.com/susan.pesznecker.

Linda Raedisch lives and writes in northern New Jersey. Her favorite time of year is Yule, followed by late spring and early fall. All the rest are either too hot, too cold, or too humid. Linda's first book, *Night of the Witches: Folklore, Traditions and Recipes for Celebrating Walpurgis Night*, has been translated into French. (Linda really ought to be able to read it, but she's forgotten a lot since high school.) Her second book, *The Old Magic of Christmas: Yuletide Traditions for the Darkest Days of the Year,* is the result of a lifelong search for all that is untoward about her favorite holiday. Linda is currently at work on her third book for Llewellyn, due out in August 2017. (If you've guessed it's about Witches, you're not on the wrong track.)

Diana Rajchel has practiced Wicca, and alongside it witchcraft, for close to twenty years. Ever a pragmatist, she believes magic can and should be used to make life happier, healthier, and sometimes even a little bit easier. She has most recently written two books for Llewellyn, on Mabon and Samhain. She is located in the San Francisco Bay Area where she pursues magic, ecstatic dance, belly dance, and urban spirit work.

Suzanne Ress has been practicing Wicca for about twelve years as the leader of a small coven, but she has been aware of having a special connection to nature and animal spirits since she was a young child. She has been writing creatively most of her life—short stories, novels, and nonfiction articles for a variety of publications—and finds it to be an important outlet for her considerable creative powers. Other outlets she regularly makes use of are metalsmithing, mosaic works, painting, and all kinds of dance. She is also a professional aromatic herb grower and beekeeper. Although she is an American of Welsh ancestry by birth, she has lived in northern Italy for nearly twenty years. She recently discovered that the small mountain in the pre-alpine hills she and her family and animals inhabit was once the site of an ancient Insubrian Celtic sacred place. Not surprisingly, the top of the mountain has remained a fulcrum of sacredness throughout the millennia, transforming from Celtic "Dunn" to Roman fortress to its current form—Catholic chapel, and this grounding in blessedness makes Suzanne's everyday life especially magical.

Doreen Shababy lives a witchy, rural lifestyle near a blink-of-an-eye town in northern Idaho. She is the author of *The Wild & Weedy Apothecary: An A to Z Book of Herbal Concoctions, Recipes & Remedies, Practical Know-How & Food for the Soul*, published by Llewellyn. Before that she produced a small but widely circulated "kitchen-table" journal by the same name, focusing on wild plants for food and medicine. Doreen's work has also appeared in many Pagan publications. She has led weed-walks and demonstrations for all ages and has forever worked with natural foods in both career and on the domestic scene, from teaching preschool cooking classes and developing a series of gluten-free baking lessons to fixing soup for anyone who will have some. Doreen loves creating with fabric, and is occasionally known to pick up a crochet hook. She has been a student and practitioner of hands-on healing arts for over twenty years, including Source Connection Therapy, Reiki, and other intuitive therapies. Doreen's approach to magick is practical and spontaneous, and she is devoted to feminine spirituality. She is primarily a soloist requiring frequent doses of social contact for fun and recreation. Doreen and her husband produce and sell herbal extracts, healing balms, and other products from their kitchen apothecary.

An award-winning author, feng shui consultant, and intuitive counselor, **Tess Whitehurst** presents ancient, sacred, and highly empowering wisdom in an extremely friendly and accessible way. She's written six books that have been translated into nine languages, and her articles have appeared such places as *Writer's Digest, Whole Life Times*, and *Law of Attraction* magazine. She's appeared on morning news shows on both Fox and NBC, and her feng shui work was featured on the Bravo TV show *Flipping Out*. Tess lives with her longtime boyfriend, Ted Bruner, and their magical black cat, Solo, in a cozy, incense-scented, twinkle-light-lit country house near Columbia, Missouri. Visit her at www.tesswhitehurst.com.

When she's not on the road or chasing free-range hens, **Natalie Zaman** is trying to figure out the universe. She is the coauthor of the *Graven Images Oracle* deck (Galde Press), and the YA novels *Sirenz* and *Sirenz Back In Fashion* (Flux) and *Blonde Ops* (St. Martin's Press). Her work has appeared in Llewellyn's *Magical Almanac, FATE, Sage-Woman*, and *newWitch* magazines, and she currently writes the recurring feature "Wandering Witch" for *Witches and Pagans* magazine. Find Natalie online at http://nataliezaman.com or at http://broomstix.blogspot.com, a collection of crafts, stories, ritual, and art she curates for Pagan families.

Samhain

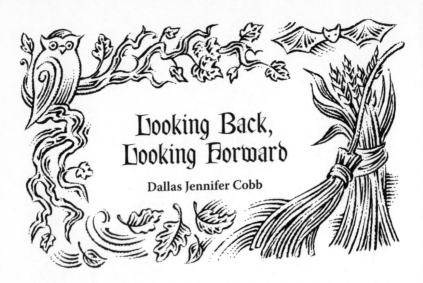

Looking Back, Looking Forward

Dallas Jennifer Cobb

SAMHAIN IS A TIME to journey to the dark side. I don't mean into "black magic" or the so-called "dark arts," but a journey to the shadow side of self—that place of repressed emotions, suppressed expression, blocked memories, and forgotten purpose. We journey to the shadowlands to commune with the ghosts of our past, visit what has died in us, express our longing and loss, and through that expression find healing and a way back to love. We know that it is only through love that we can move forward in the circle dance.

Tradition

Also known as Festival of the Dead, Ancestors Night, Hallowmas, All Hallow's Eve, Feast of the Dead, Remembrance of the Dead, Hallowe'en, and the Third Festival of the Harvest, Samhaim is celebrated by Pagans worldwide. It is renowned as a time when the veils between the worlds are thought to be thinned: people could more easily commune and communicate with their departed ancestors, and souls could cross back to earth, seeking the warmth of hearth and home fires, or warm-blooded humans.

Old and sacred, Samhain is celebrated as the most important of the eight sabbats; not just the end of summer and the beginning of winter, Samhain was the Celt's New Year's Eve. Traditionally, Samhain stretched from sunset on October 31 to midnight on November 1, but somewhere along the line, the two got separated into Hallowe'en and All Saints/All Souls Day, respectively.

But let's reunite them and consider the whole of Samhain, a time of grieving, mourning, and loss; of the practice of slaughter and sacrifice; of taking stock of harvest's abundance; of celebratiing abundance; and looking forward with clarity.

At the end of the old year, we take time for a quiet, dark pause. While November 1 was technically the New Year, the solar new year didn't arrive until the Sun was reborn at Yule. The time between Samhain and Yule really is "a time out of time," malleable and ethereal, as if we live between the worlds—we are able to look within, look back, and then look forward.

Life Cycle

Samhain is a time of endings and beginnings: of inventorying riches, celebrating abundance, and planning for depleted stores—when time seems to warp and slow down, yet rush with a sense of urgency too. Indeed, it feels like we are between the worlds.

Historically, Samhain was the traditional "summer's end." Livestock came home from summer pasture, back to the village green or homestead barn where winter shelter was easier. In this time of blood, death, and endings, meat animals were slaughtered and hung, and sick or injured animals were culled so that scarce resources could be devoted to the winter-long care of healthy breed stock. Root cellars were stocked with root crops, apples, nuts, and seeds. Dried grains were ground and prepared for feeding both people and animals.

In tune with Gaia's cycles, villagers knew their survival depended on storing, taking inventory, and preparing. After taking stock of their resources, traditional villagers planned celebrations of the third harvest, enjoying a feast on November 1. Knowing what stores they had laid in for the winter ahead, villagers knew what could be spared to celebrate fruition, maturity, abundance, and immortality.

Intertwining the energies of death and abundance, Samhain provided a focus on resurrection and the third phase of the Triple Goddess, the Crone. Honoring age, death, and the dearly departed, villagers honored the past and cleared the way forward. In Mexico, on Dia de los Muertos, families gather at ancestral graves to clean them, say prayers, and make offerings of sugar skulls. In Ireland and England, Cailleach's Reign is celebrated on All Saint's Day in honor of the Celtic Crone Goddess.

The God and Goddess

With the final harvest of the year, the God has died and descended to the underworld, where he rests and awaits his reincarnation/re-birth. The Goddess is alone and grieving, mourning the loss of her lifelong companion. Shrouded in grief, she turns inward and leaves the world in increasing darkness.

Celebrated as Morrigan, the Irish Goddess of death, she is also known as Hecate, Oya, Cerridwen, Eurydice, Hel, Inanna, Kali, Nephthys, Samia, Sedna, Tara, and Vanadis.

Now in her third phase as Crone, the Goddess is a wise woman, insightful as she looks back over her fruitful life. Filled with wisdom and intuition, she is adept at divination. Casting runes, reading cards, or guided by her pendulum, the Crone draws from her long experience, and divines. In the present, she looks to the past to help interpret and foretell the future.

Symbols, Rituals, and Rites

Think of the modern vision of Hallowe'en—a witch/crone stirring a cauldron set over a fire while a black cat and raven look on. She is surrounded by pumpkins carved into jack-o'-lanterns, fallen leaves, and even costumed/masked children scurrying nearby, begging for treats. You'll realize you already know the symbols traditional to Samhain.

The practice of lighting large fires to draw the spirits was practiced by the Celts who stoked the fires in memory of their ancestors, who were believed to gather to warm themselves.

Ravens and crows are symbols of Samhain because they feed on carrion flesh and feast on the bodies of the dead. The cauldron representing the Goddess's womb was also used to catch the blood dripping from the freshly slaughtered animals. The pumpkin, symbolic of fall harvest, was traditionally used to shelter candles, creating a lantern to see in the dwindling light. The pomegranate is associated with Samhain because of the six pomegranate seeds ingested by Persephone, which necessitated her six-month residence in Hades.

Food and drink were laid out as an offering, left by the fires to honor the dead and appease the spirits. Inside the houses, it was customary to leave a small feast on the table for the nourishment of the dead or lay a plate of food outside the door. When sitting to eat, many families prepared an extra plate and laid it at an empty spot, so their ancestors knew they were always welcome. The practice of going door to door begging for "soul cakes" may have been the precursor of trick-or-treating, as poor people begged for food in exchange for saying prayers for a family's departed ancestors.

The colors associated with Samhain come from nature: the resonant ochre, brown, and scarlet of trees and vegetation turning color as their life force dwindles; the vibrant gold, red, dark green, and orange of harvested grains, squash, pumpkin, apples, and pomegranate; the deep, rich blood of slaughtered animals; the blazing orange and gold of the fire that warms and protects; and the black of the creeping long nights.

Quiet contemplation and personal inventorying were traditional practices undertaken at Samhain. The "dark pause" was used to inventory not only food and fuel needed to get their household through winter, but to look at personal accomplishments in the spiritual and emotional realms. People took stock of the unseen sources of nourishment and fuel for the spirit and emotions, and set goals for the year ahead. While they asked "Where was there growth? What was learned? What provided comfort? What is needed to move ahead?" the work of the next cycle was usually put off until after the solstice, reinforcing the feeling of a "dark pause."

Tools used for the planning process were those that were common to the Crone Goddess—scrying with water or mirrors, casting runes, reading cards, throwing bones or stones, throwing an apple peel over the shoulder and observing the shape it fell into, observing the shapes formed as blood first splattered into the bucket below a slaughtered animal, and placing hazelnuts by the fire and asking a yes/no question. If it pops, the answer is yes; if it doesn't, the answer is no. Images and metaphors gained from divination were used to interpret the past and envision the future.

With a sense of what one's next spiritual undertakings were, it was customary to stand before a mirror, look deep within and beyond "self," and make a secret wish or vow for the future based on the wisdom that arose from an assessment of the past year.

The Inner Journey

Embodying both the God and Goddess at Samhain, our inner journey is one of metaphorically both dying and grieving our lost love. We both rest and await reincarnation, while simultaneously weeping, mourning, and turning within. Focused on the dark terrain of the inner world, the shadowland, the world around us is left in darkness.

We must weep and grieve, releasing the heavy emotions, so we can resurrect ourselves ready to love and live again. From experience we know that the God will be reincarnated or resurrected, and the Goddess will once again be young, fertile, and productive. But this will happen only if we do the work needed now to move us through these dark times.

Preparing for the future, we examine the past and use our focused intent in the present to ensure our survival. Carefully looking forward we ask: What do I need to sustain me? What parts of me are healthy and strong? What parts of me are old and dying, and need to be released?

At Samhain, we ebb into darkness and turn within to set sights on the big picture, the work of the soul. We contemplate the end of the season; the finality of flesh; the symbolic death of spirit. Note what aspects of self are ready to be shed, to whither and die. Observe the process of emotional healing: What wounds have repaired? What bones knit? Where has our heart healed? And ask of each wound: "Could this kill me?" Now steel yourself, ready to sacrifice your frail, wounded, and sick parts so that the healthy may survive, for the greater good. So mote it be.

Only by letting go can we continue forward without falling, failing, or dying. Our careful preparation means we can survive the coming darkness and cold, readying the soul for its next spiritual lesson. We keep our sights on the big picture while attending to the daily tasks.

Many of us have repressed and suppressed emotions and memories because they felt too overwhelming at the moment. Because our society discourages tears, fear, and emotionality, many of us stuff them away. But at Samhain, you are invited to curl into the arms of the Crone, the wise mother, be enveloped in her safety and explore your dark side. Revisit the vampire feelings that suck the life out of you and the ghoulish memories that haunt your dreams. Commune with your wailing childhood soul, and allow all your ghosts to be heard.

Great mother Gaia is ever loving and protective. And tonight, realign with her ever-flowing cycle of seasons (birth, life, death, and rebirth) to find your way forward. Look to her larger metaphors of seasonal transitions to make sense of your own journey. In her arms, we find nurturing and wisdom.

With the safety of a cast circle, the support of loving community, and the sanctity of the sabbat, I invite you to journey into your darkness, release your stuck pains, let the tears, anger, and grief flow, and know that Gaia supports you. Gnash your teeth, wail and grieve, and let the song of the soul soak into the soil.

Because, here in Gaia's arms, we safely look inside and look back, in order to look forward.

Cosmic Sway

April Elliott Kent

WELCOME, THE DARKENING SEASON! As Samhain begins, a Disseminating Moon in home-loving, clannish Cancer is in harmonious aspect to the Sun in Scorpio; it is time to set down our tools and let our soil rest. A luminous grouping of Venus, Mars, and Jupiter in Virgo twinkles in the evening sky and blesses the harvest table. It's the season of darkening, but we are warm, well-fed, and nestled safely among our loved ones.

On November 12, the warrior planet Mars enters Libra, the sign of relationships, balance, and fairness. Mars last visited Libra between December 7, 2013, and July 25, 2014; here is your chance to revisit any conflicts that were left unresolved then. Mars in Libra avoids conflict, but when pushed too far—as is likely when Mars squares Pluto (December 6) and opposes Uranus (December 10)—its scales tip decidedly toward open warfare. Mark it on your calendar, for this will be an eventful week.

Neptune turns direct on November 18, and for a day before and after you may feel as though all you want to do is sleep. Then, on November 26, there is a wake-up call as Saturn squares Neptune. When Saturn is in Sagittarius, there is pressure to feel as though there is a right way to do things (ours) and a wrong way (everyone else's). This leaves little room for Neptune's gentler "live and let live" approach. Expect livelier-than-usual conversation around the Thanksgiving table, especially if the focus shifts to politics or religion.

Mars in Libra

Mars, the planet of conflict, is ill at ease in peaceful, genteel Libra (November 12, 2015 to January 3, 2016). What does a fighter do when he is asked to wear his morning suit for breakfast and eat with his pinkie sticking out? He picks up his butter knife and starts fidgeting with it. A bored Mars, forced to be polite, is an extremely edgy Mars. Tension and frustration build as Mars transits here. It is time to clear the air and restore balance to your life, particularly in your relationships. It's not just romantic relationships that need recalibrating, either, but all the important relationships in your life—with friends, family, neighbors, and coworkers.

New Moon in Scorpio – Nov. 11, 2015

This is one of the most magical, transformative New Moons of the year. The Sun and Moon make a sextile aspect to cheerful Jupiter, lightening Scorpio's brooding darkness. This is an excellent New Moon for summoning both practical help and magical intercession. Your friends or social connections present enticing opportunities that promise improved prosperity and adventure—you need only reach out your hand and take them.

Scorpio's modern ruler is Pluto, the wealthiest of all the Gods, so this is one of the year's best New Moons for prosperity spells, rituals, and affirmations.

Prosperity Ritual for Scorpio New Moon

Astrologer Simone Butler has invented a marvelous system for combining astrology and feng shui, which she calls Astro Feng Shui. Part of her method calls for matching your New Moon affirmations and rituals with the part of your house associated with that New Moon's sign. Since Scorpio is a financial sign, this is the New Moon to strengthen the wealth "gua" of your home, or the area in the farther back left corner from the front door.

Our bedroom lies in this part of our house, and here's what I do at every Scorpio New Moon. First, I clean this room thoroughly, tackling cobwebs, dust bunnies, and the detritus that collects in the closet and bedside tables. Absolutely everything is dusted, wiped down, vacuumed, and polished. I throw open the windows and smudge with sage, imagining all financial worries flying out the window and prosperity flying in. Then I simply write down a financial goal for the coming twelve months, set it on the bedroom altar, and light a tall green candle on top of it.

This ritual has had unexpected and powerful effects in our household. The first time I performed it, our ancient car and a series of old household appliances fell apart within days. Wherever we had been cutting corners and making do, the universe insisted that we make investments and bring our lives "up to code." The next time I performed the ritual, I was offered a book contract by a major publisher, with an advance equal to my total earnings for the previous year!

Full Moon in Gemini – Nov. 25, 2015

This will be a bumpy Full Moon, with the Moon opposed Saturn and square Neptune. In the United States, Thanksgiving falls the day after this Full Moon. Holiday gatherings with family can tap wellsprings of old hurts and grievances, and there are likely to be wounded feelings, particularly among siblings. Fortunately, the Full Moon in Gemini, the sign of communication, makes a good aspect to Mars in Libra. Honest but diplomatic conversations can help restore harmony to these important relationships. This can be an extremely effective Full Moon for releasing negative thought patterns and forgiving harsh words and broken promises.

New Moon in Sagittarius – Dec. 11, 2015

The New Moon in Sagittarius is one of the best moments of the year to set intentions that are designed to open up your life and move you in a fresh, new direction. This New Moon's beneficial aspects to Mars and Uranus bring a spirit of tremendous vitality and excitement to anything you try. However, the New Moon point is square Jupiter in prudent Virgo, so don't throw all caution to the wind. Laying practical groundwork first will make it easier to embrace adventure later on.

Jupiter is the planetary ruler of Sagittarius, and its current transit through conscientious Virgo brings blessings to work-related travel or trips that have a humanitarian purpose.

The Old Ways:
Memento Mori

Blake Octavian Blair

THE SAMHAIN SABBAT IS likely one of the most revered in the wheel of the year by modern Pagans. Samhain has ancient Celtic roots, chosen as the date for the new year, thusly also marking the official death of the old year. Death and dying are primary themes associated with and thoroughly examined at this time of year in seasonal celebrations. The season itself is a potent memento mori. Memento mori are objects that serve as visual and conceptual reminders of mortality. The term *memento mori* itself loosely translates from the Latin for "remember you must die." The use of the term for the concept is said to date back to medieval Christianity; however, we will see that the concept and examples of it far predate the term's origins. Fittingly, it is thought by many that the name Samhain is thought to have possibly stemmed from the name Samanna, who was the Aryan god of death. Let us take this opportunity to explore the realm of memento mori at this most-fitting sabbat.

In the Middle Ages, death was an all-too common part of everyday life. Numerous traditional memento mori symbols from that era have become staples of Western funerary art. Many of these can be observed in the art of funeral programs as well as carvings etched into headstones. The next time you are taking a stroll through your local graveyard (let's admit it: it's a favorite pastime of magickal folk), take a look at the stones. I find the older the cemetery, the better. Images such as books, barren trees, crowns, and skulls will likely appear on at least a few of the stones as well as in the more "communal" art displayed at the cemetery gates, in the landscaping, or in the architecture and trim of any buildings present. Skulls are a classic memento mori and, while they may not be popular in modern funerary or cemetery art, later on we'll look at a few cases where the skull continues as a potent memento mori through modern day. While some of these images may admittedly have Christian connotations, their symbolism as it relates to death surpasses the bounds of a specific cosmology. A book, while it can be seen as a biblical reference, can be used to denote any number of religious texts depending upon one's particular faith. The symbol can also refer to the Book of Life or the Book of the Dead, both are symbols and concepts that appear cross-culturally in many world faiths and even into more modern Pagan and New Age beliefs, as texts dealing with the journey of the soul through the cycle of birth, life, death, and the afterlife. The crown can represent triumph over and surpassing beyond physical death. Barren trees and sometimes the image of a tree stump is occasionally used to represent a loss of life, dormancy, or a life cut short (just as the stump was cut).

Barren trees and dead stumps are symbols that take their cue from nature. A vast majority of modern Pagans and magick makers strive to live with and align to the seasons of nature. With our affinity for the natural world, let us not forget that the autumnal season is in and of itself a potent memento mori. As autumn descends upon the earth, we are literally surrounded by a world that is a living memento mori. It may sound a bit of an oxymoron to say "living memento mori," however, it is fitting as death is but one phase in the cycle of life, death, and rebirth celebrated by so many spiritual traditions. The leaves drop from trees and begin to decay, the days are noticeably shorter, and we can visually watch the death of the vibrant summer. Beautiful but decaying leaves crunch under our footsteps. A person who is quite elderly and in declining health is sometimes even said to be in the "autumn of their life." If there ever was a need for proof of the season as a memento mori, look no further.

As mentioned, skulls are another potent and traditional memento mori. However, it need not be all doom and gloom, as sometimes the morbid is mixed with the festive as in the sugar skulls that are an iconic part of Mexican Dia de los Muertos celebrations. Made of hard, compacted white sugar and bedecked and trimmed with colorful icing designs, they adorn festive altars welcoming the ancestors to visit once again. Part of the festivities include removing the skulls from the altars and then delivering them as offerings to cemeteries on the date of November 2. In the case of the sugar skull, the memento mori is not only a reminder of the pervasive nature of death, but also of the continuance of spirit into the afterlife. The sugar skull tradition is a powerful example of the skull surviving as a memento mori, even if an especially festive one, into modern day.

Religious art and deity imagery from the world's religions also provide us many memento mori. The Buddhist deity Mahakala and the Hindu goddess Kali both sport adornments made of skulls. One of the lessons Kali brings to us as a goddess of both destruction and creation is that of impermanence. She wears a garland of skulls as a necklace—reminding us of the impermanence and fleeting nature of life. Mahakala wears a crown adorned with skulls, and while the symbolism is deep and multifaceted, it too serves as a memento mori of the impermanent nature of our physical incarnations.

The Victorian era brought with it one of the more, shall we say, literal examples of memento mori. Brace yourself... or perhaps in Victorian times, the corpse of a loved one. That's right, during this time it became fashionably popular to brace, prop up, and pose the bodies of deceased loved ones, as if living, and take photographs for a last remembrance of them. The phenomenon has been referred to as "mourning photography." Of course they had to act quickly so as to complete their photo shoot before rigor mortis and decay set in.

It was a common practice (and decidedly less complicated than mourning photography) in the Middle Ages and Victorian era to carry a small token of a memento mori symbol. Some examples would be a small carving or piece of jewelry with an image such as a skull or hourglass on it. However, the practice has somewhat fallen by the wayside in modern mainstream culture. However, a few subcultures, including modern Pagan folks as well as those in the goth movement, have carried the practice on in the present day. I believe that if we look with a critical gaze, we can see signs that perhaps the practice of reincorporating these symbols and the concept as a whole is starting very slowly to subtly reintegrate itself even among the mainstream.

Death is but a part of life! Contemplate if and how you engage with the concept of memento mori in your own practices. Perhaps in looking at the practices of yesteryear, you will find new ways to interact with the spirit of memento mori in our modern times! I wish you a blessed Samhain and I'll leave you with a classic memento mori reminder to make the most of life... Carpe diem! Seize the day!

Bibliography

McCoy, Edain. *Sabbats: A Witch's Approach to Living the Old Ways.* St. Paul, MN: Llewellyn Publications, 1994.

Nelson, Sara C. "Memento Mori: How Victorian Mourning Photography Immortalised Loved Ones After Death." Huffington Post, January 30, 2013, http://www.huffingtonpost.co.uk/2013/01/30/memento-mori--victorian-mourning-photography-immortalising-loved-ones-death_n_2580559.html.

Belanger, Michelle. *Walking The Twilight Path: A Gothic Book of the Dead.* Woodbury, MN: Llewellyn Publications, 2008.

"History of Day of the Dead & The Mexican Sugar Skull Tradition." MexicanSugarSkull, accessed July, 18, 2014. http://www.mexicansugarskull.com/support/dodhistory.html.

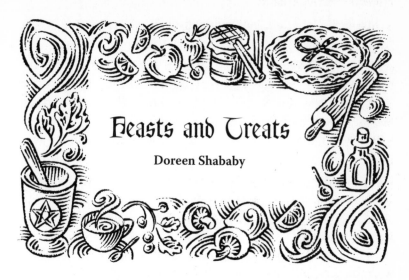

Feasts and Treats

Doreen Shababy

SAMHAIN IS LIKE HOMECOMING for me. No, I haven't been away; it just feels cozy and warm and familiar, and I love it, especially the colors up in the high country. It gives me the opportunity to look inward and think about my ancestors, and consider my loved ones. I like seeing the pantry full and the smell of the wood stove burning. And candy. I like candy too.

Oven-Fried Chicken

Meat is often a central dish at end-of-harvest feasting, whether from the forest, field, or barnyard. Irish custom also includes the winged ones, and chicken was commonly served either stewed or fricasseed. This recipe for oven-fried chicken may not be traditional Celtic fare, but it works so well and tastes so good. If you want to use a whole chicken cut up, figure on 2 pieces per person, and feel free to add your favorite herbs and spices to the mix. (I like Cajun.)

Prep time: 10 minutes
Cook time: 1 hour
Serves: 6

6 chicken hindquarters, cut up or left whole
1 teaspoon salt
½ teaspoon black pepper
1 cup all-purpose flour
½ cup cornmeal
½ teaspoon garlic powder
Olive oil pan spray

Line a rimmed baking sheet with parchment, then place a rack on the sheet to raise the meat off the bottom of the pan. (An ovenproof grill pan would work too.) Heat oven to 425 degrees F.

Season chicken generously with salt and pepper. In a sturdy paper bag, mix the flour, cornmeal, and seasonings, then place 2 pieces of chicken at a time in the bag, shake to coat, then place on rack on baking sheet; continue with the rest of the chicken. Lightly spray chicken with olive oil pan spray.

Place in oven and bake for 15 minutes, turn heat down to 350 degrees F, and bake 30 to 45 minutes, or longer, basting occasionally, until golden brown and juices run clear. Serve hot or cold.

Colcannon

Colcannon is an Irish original. So is Halloween. The secular celebration in the United States is often accompanied by candy, but in Ireland colcannon was sometimes used on Halloween as a divination tool. Special charms were hidden in the diners' bowls and, if you were lucky enough to find the right one (a ring perhaps), it was a portent of marriage.

Prep time: 15 minutes
Cooking time: about 30 minutes
Serves: 6

2 pounds red boiling potatoes
3 teaspoons salt, divided
4 cups (about 2 bunches) thinly sliced kale (any type), ribs and stems
    removed

1 large leek, thinly sliced, white and light-green part only
½ cup (1 stick) butter, divided
½ cup whole milk
¼ teaspoon ground black pepper

Peel potatoes, cut into quarters, then place in a saucepan with enough water to cover and 1 teaspoon salt. Bring to a boil, turn down to simmer, then cover and cook until fork-tender, 15 to 20 minutes. Drain and return to pan at low heat, cover to keep warm.

While the potatoes cook, cover kale with water in another saucepan, add ½ teaspoon salt, and bring to a boil. Cook about 5 to 10 minutes until tender as desired. Drain well, and leave in colander.

In the same (kale) saucepan over medium heat, sauté leeks with 2 tablespoons butter until soft, about 10 minutes, stirring occasionally. Add milk and ½ teaspoon salt and bring to a boil. Reduce heat to a simmer and cook, uncovered for about 10 minutes. Mash potatoes in their pan with 4 tablespoons butter, 1 teaspoon salt, and the pepper. With a wooden spoon, vigorously stir the leek-infused milk in with the potatoes until mixed.

Stir the cooked kale into the potato-leek pan and return to low heat for 5 minutes. Place in a serving bowl making a well in the center for the remaining 2 tablespoons butter. You can reduce the amount of butter used in this dish if desired, but all recipes traditionally call for a great big gob of the stuff melting on top. Who are you to argue with tradition?

Irish Whisky Cake with Icing

In keeping with the Irish-Celtic theme of Samhain, this cake is sure to spice up your evening with its spirited flavoring. Instead of the alcohol, you may add a teaspoon of vanilla and replace the whisky with apple juice, and use lemon juice to replace the whisky in the icing.

Prep time: 20 minutes
Cook time: 45 minutes, including simmering raisins
Serves: 8–10

1 cup raisins (or currants)
1½ cups water
8 tablespoons (1 stick) butter, room temperature
½ cup brown sugar
1 egg
1½ cups all-purpose flour
2 teaspoons baking powder
1 teaspoon baking soda
½ teaspoon salt
1½ teaspoons pumpkin pie spice
1 cup chopped walnuts
¼ cup Irish whisky

For the icing:
1 cup confectioners' sugar
¼ cup Irish whisky

Preheat oven to 350 degrees F. Grease and flour a 9 × 13-inch baking dish and set it aside.

Place the raisins and water in a small saucepan and bring to a boil. Turn down heat and let simmer uncovered, for 15 minutes. Drain the raisins, reserving the liquid; let cool.

In a large bowl, cream the butter and sugar until light and fluffy. Add the egg, blending well. Sift the flour, baking powder, baking soda, salt and spice into another bowl, then add to butter mixture. Stir in ¾ cup of the reserved raisin liquid (add water if necessary), the raisins, then the walnuts and the whisky. Pour into prepared pan. Bake until nicely browned and done in the center, 30 to 35 minutes. Let cool in pan before icing.

To make the icing: mix the sugar and whisky in a bowl until smooth. Pour over cooled cake to serve.

Ginger Ciders

While the preparation for this quaff takes longer to describe than to actually accomplish, I will take this opportunity to advise you to choose quality ingredients for this and all your food choices, organic and locally grown whenever possible, especially for your kids. Even some sodas are more "natural" than others. Read the ingredients!

Prep time: 2 minutes

Serves: 2

1 12-ounce bottle apple cider, hard or soft
1 12-ounce bottle ginger ale

Have two tumblers ready and pour half of the cider into each glass, then half the ginger ale in each to top them off. Stir and enjoy.

Notes from Cook to Cook: As you look over the recipes throughout this book, you will see a few packaged items amongst the ingredients for convenience's sake. I have also developed the recipes such that the greatest number of people can eat them, that is, wheat- and dairy-tolerant, and omnivores.

My kitchen is wheat-free and my husband can't eat dairy, so I don't cook with it either. Therefore, I have learned to make certain dishes, such as enchiladas, without cheese—are you kidding me?!? It can be done, my dears, with you asking for seconds. I use nuts and seeds a lot, and almond butter. (I've found that baking wheat/gluten-free desserts was fairly easy, but finally baking oat bread, real yeasted bread that didn't taste like cardboard or dissolve under a tomato, was a blessed event.

Sorghum, brown rice, oat, and almond meal (plus a starch like corn or tapioca) are commonly used instead of wheat flour. You can't get the same chewy stretch as in a real baguette, but that PBJ on bread that didn't cost over $7.00 a loaf becomes more real.

If you can't eat wheat, adjust the recipes using gluten-free flour, add an extra egg in the baked goodies, and no one will know the difference. If you can't eat cheese, you might be able to use tofu in the cheesecake for instance, or, if you eat it (I do not), you can use fake cheese. If you don't eat meat, you know what to do.

I apologize to anyone who can't eat some of these foods; you are not alone. Creativity is the hallmark of the witch, and we can usually figure out a way to work things out for the best.

Crafty Crafts

Tess Whitehurst

IT'S THE TIME OF the year most associated with witches in the popular imagination, and with good reason. It's that moment when the world of the physical and everyday meets and intermingles with the Otherworld: the world of the spiritual, ethereal, and the great beyond. As such, it's a moment of great power for those of us who prefer to dwell in this place as a matter of course. We don't have to work as hard to get into our magical zone, because—as you're likely to have heard and read a million times—the veil between the worlds is thin.

And there is one symbol that is, arguably, most connected with witches, especially at this time of year: the witch hat! While its historical association with witchcraft is not entirely clear, the witch hat as we know it goes way back. Its earliest known appearance is the third or fourth century BCE, during which three female mummies of Celtic descent (part of a group of hundreds of Celtic mummies that have been mysteriously discovered in China's Tarim region), were believed to have lived. These mummies—known as "The Witches of Subeshi"—wore tall, pointed, cone-shaped, black felt hats with a flat brim.

While these "Witches" may indeed have been some kind of Druidic magical practitioners (it's not clear), these types of hats were not popularly associated with witches in Western culture until the 1700s, which Raymond Buckland suggests happened because conical hats went out of fashion in the courts and cities, so portraying country dwellers practicing the old nature religion as wearing such hats was a way of alluding to their perceived cultural irrelevance.

And then of course, there's the idea that a witch hat is like your own personal cone of power, perhaps funneling divine energy and magic down from above and into the crown of your head.

Whatever its origins, the association of black pointed hats with witchcraft has stuck in such a serious way that it's difficult to believe that there isn't something inherent and archetypal about it. With all of this in mind, how about making your own? I've found this particular pattern to be quite easy, and to turn out a big old floppy witch hat that's equal parts adorable and authentic.

Floppy Witch Hat

Time to complete: 1 to 2 hours (or more if you hand-stitch rather than use a sewing machine)

Cost: $3.00 to $10.00 (or more if you need to purchase basic sewing supplies)

Supplies

1 yard black felt (Please consider recycled felt! It's made out of old bottles.)

Black thread

A roll of old wrapping paper, or a cut-and-taped-together brown paper grocery bag (for the pattern)

Trim for the base of the cone (optional)

Pins

A needle

Sewing scissors

A yardstick and/or tape measure

A protractor

Instructions

1. Make the brim pattern

On the wrapping paper, measure 25 centimeters out in all directions from a central point, making a number of points, perhaps ½ to 1 inch apart to describe a circle. Draw the circle created by the points. Cut out the circle.

Now, also from the central point, describe a smaller circle by measuring about 8¾ centimeters out in all directions. Connect the dots and cut, to make a donut shape.

2. Make the cone pattern

Make a point. Create another point 31 centimeters from that point. Measure a number of additional points the same distance from the first point, to describe a shape a little smaller than a semicircle. Connect the dots and cut. Using a protractor and a ruler, mark and trim the cone pattern so that the central angle is about 114 degrees.

3. Make the hat

Pin the brim and cone patterns to the felt and cut one of each.

After removing the patterns and pins, fold the cone pattern in half, so that the straight edges are meeting, right sides of the fabric together. Pin the edges together and sew them. Turn right side out. If necessary, use something like a chopstick or the handle of a wooden spoon to make the point pointy.

Pin the inside circle of the right side of brim to the outside of the cone, edges aligned, making sure to pin the seam of the cone so that it's pressed out, and sew.

Try the hat on. If it needs any slight adjustments to fit your head, you may need to rip the seams and change the seam allowance slightly, or to cut new pieces in slightly larger or smaller sizes. (You'll have plenty of felt.) If the brim is so floppy that it keeps falling over your face (this might happen if you use a particularly thin felt), enforce the edges of the brim by basting an edge stitch around the outside. This has an added benefit of creating a rustic look.

If you'd like, sew trim of your choice around the base of the cone to make a hatband. You can also add any other flourishes you'd like, such as lace, patches, buttons, appliqués, or naturally shed feathers.

4. Bless and consecrate

When it's just how you like it, if you'd like to consecrate it to give it some added magical oomph, first clean up your sewing supplies. Keeping your hat close by, cast a circle, first placing a representation of each element at each cardinal point: smoking incense in a holder to the east, a lit candle to the south, a chalice or glass of water to the west, and a dish of salt to the north. Next, call on the elements: first Air, then Fire, Water, Earth, and Spirit.

Bathe the hat in the smoking incense as you say,
Air for clarity and insight.

Warm the hat with the candle as you say,
  Fire for energy and passion.

Anoint the hat with the water as you say,
  Water for psychic ability.

Sprinkle a pinch of salt over the hat as you say,
  Earth for power and serenity.

Hold the hat up to the sky as you say,
  I now bless this hat and consecrate it to Spirit. May it be filled with power and magic. May it connect me with my witchy roots and the collective power and magic of the witches of old. May it serve as a reminder of the power and magic that is within me, now and always.
  Thank you, thank you, thank you, and so mote it be.

For Further Reading

Buckland, Raymond. *The Witch Book: Encyclopedia of Witchcraft, Wicca, and NeoPaganism.* Canton, MI: Visible Ink Press, 2001.

Coonan, Clifford. "A Meeting of Civilisations: The Mystery of China's Celtic Mummies." *The Independent.* August 28, 2006. http://www.independent.co.uk.

Waldman, Katy. "Why Do Witches Wear Pointy Hats?" *Slate.* October 17, 2013. http://www.slate.com

All One Family: Secrets for Samhain

Linda Raedisch

"SECRETS ARE SAFE, AND they do much to make you different on the inside, where it counts." This is the advice given by the title character of E. L. Konigsburg's novel *From the Mixed-Up Files of Mrs. Basil E. Frankweiler* to the child protagonists. That was back in 1967, a more innocent time than our own; had Konigsburg been writing in 2015, she probably would have worded Mrs. Frankweiler's message a little differently. But the message itself remains an important one. No, children should never be expected to *keep* secrets, but they might be encouraged to collect them, which is why this year's "All One Family" series of articles is all about secrets.

By secret, I'm don't mean confidences or skeletons in the closet but those forgotten bits of history and hidden knowledge that lie everywhere around us. I like to think of them as the Everyday Arcane. "Everyday" because they touch us on a daily basis; "Arcane" because so few are clued in to these little treasures. Remember how "in the know" you felt when you found out that the old children's song and dance "Ring Around the Rosy" was a mini-reenactment of the Black Plague? And here's a fun one to share at the kids' table at Thanksgiving: in early America, even very young children would have been drinking hard cider along with the grown-ups. In fact, until quite recently, children drank wine, beer, and mead because they were safer than milk, which couldn't be refrigerated, or water, which was often contaminated. (And no, I don't actually *serve* alcohol at the kids' table!)

Why bother with such "trivia," as some would call it? The answer, as your history teacher probably told you, is because the past informs the present: the more you know about the one, the better chance you have of understanding the other. Besides, it's fun. Few of us are born with exceptional artistic or athletic abilities, and even fewer with genuine psychic gifts. How many of you reading this almanac have magic crackling from the tips of your fingers? Not so many, I would guess. The collecting of secrets requires no special abilities, just a sense of curiosity and a determination to dig below the surface, to peek behind the curtain, to challenge that which everyone else takes for granted. Yes, we will be delving into the dark side. Wicca is largely about recognizing and paying tribute to the dead, especially at Samhain, and there's no reason to leave the children behind. Because we want to get the kids involved, I'll be focusing on those secrets embedded in the culture of childhood. But remember: you're never too old to become a collector of secrets.

So what secret have I saved for Samhain? I know what you're thinking: "Now she's going to tell us that jack-o'-lanterns used to be carved from turnips." Don't worry; I have something much better, though a little less cheerful. Here goes: Everybody dies. Oh, so you already knew that? That's because you're a grown-up. If you have children, then you have an especially painful awareness of this truth, but if you're a child, this may be news to you. I am now, for the second time around, the mother of a nine-year-old and I regularly have other nine-year-olds in my car. This is the time when you want to start turning the radio down when you drive so you can hear what's being said in the back seat. I do, and let me tell you, these kids are obsessed with death.

Why? I think it's because, at this age, they're just coming to believe in their own mortality. By now, most of them have experienced the loss of someone close to them, human or animal. Death has become relevant, and yet it is like nothing else in their world. They've learned that pretty much anything that breaks can be replaced, that even broken bones heal, that books can be re-read, movies re-watched, and grades made up the next marking period. But death? Death cannot be undone, and that's something new. We reassure them that we're all going to live long, healthy lives, even though we know there are no guarantees. We do our best to distance our children from Planet Death, but maybe we should respect their curiosity and invite them to take a closer look at the surface, to learn the lay of the land—after all, they'll be going there someday.

I haven't exactly crunched the numbers, but I think it's safe to say that until the twentieth century most of the dead were children. At times in European history, as many as half of all children born died before they reached their teens, with many more expiring before they were even a year old. They don't often show up in the archaeological record because, for one thing, they were so small, their remains swiftly reincorporated into the fabric of Mother Earth. Nor did they have the time to make names for themselves as chieftains, priests, ministers, or queens. They were afforded no monuments. This is not to say they were not loved or were not full-fledged personalities to those who knew them, but they were known to only a small circle of people, people who had little time for grief. During the Christian Era, these children would have been granted their own space in the churchyard while in Pagan times, tiny bodies were often kept close to home, even *in* the home, under the threshold or the stones of the hearth.

Both Mexicans and Mexican-Americans devote one day of the year to the child dead. Though the exact dates and customs vary, child ghosts generally arrive to partake of the treats on the family altar on the night of October 31. These altars to the dead are no solemn affairs but are decked in flowers, fruits, colorful cut-paper decorations, and, of course, candles. Offerings include food, candy, and toys. You don't have to be Mexican to celebrate the Day of the

Dead, and children especially may want take this opportunity to host their age-mates from the other side.

Happily, most of us these days must reach back through a few generations of our family before we come upon a relation who died in extreme youth. If you know of one in your own family, by all means, make an altar for this child. Even if the spirit has already wandered on, the making of the altar can be an educational experience for the living children in the household. Make a copy of any photos you might have of the child. If there are none, you can use history and costume books to come up with a reasonable likeness. A shoebox can be used to make a diorama-style altar with the child's picture or photograph mounted on top. If you're lucky enough to know the name of the child, include it. (I know only that my maternal great-great grandmother had thirteen children, not all of whom survived to adulthood.) Encourage your children to do as much research as they can on their own. If not much personal information is known, they can use the library, Internet, or even an American Girl catalog to find out what sorts of things a child from a particular era and/or culture would enjoy. Silk hair ribbons? A pull toy? Let them exercise their imaginations to guess what things from our world a child from the past would find intriguing. LED lights? Legos? Fruit Roll-Ups?

If you like, you can adopt a ghost from the more distant past. Whenever I go to the Metropolitan Museum of Art in New York City, I like to stop by the case containing the tomb goods of Mayet, a five-year-old "wife" of the pharaoh Mentuhotep II. Mayet, whose name means "kitten," died around 2000 BCE. What fun it would be to make an Egyptian altar for Mayet, to pick out a plush kitten for her and maybe even a Playmobil figure of an ancient Egyptian. What would she make of such things? The fun is in imagining!

Boys might prefer to make an altar for the teenaged Eutyches who also "resides" at the Met and whose likeness we have in the realistic Greek-style portrait that was painted on his sarcophagus. Or, they could propose a name for the anonymous Greek "Girl with Doves" whom we know from her fifth-century BCE grave relief. Her parents would have instructed the sculptor to carve their daughter doing what she liked to do in life, enjoying a quiet moment with her two pet doves.

And then there is my personal favorite, the six-year-old girl, "Disa," whose grave was discovered at the Viking Age trading town of Birka in Sweden. Her face and costume have been reconstructed through the wonders of modern technology, resulting in an adorably moon-faced redhead in a red wool dress. Perhaps red was her favorite color. How dazzled she would be by the wide range of hues available to us now. By the age of six, she would have been familiar with the upright loom on which all cloth was woven, and could perhaps already spin thread. Think how delighted she would be with a Rainbow Loom or friendship bracelet kit!

According to Mexican tradition (and the Mexicans have given plenty of thought to the dead), the spirits of the departed partake only of the essence of the offerings placed upon the altar. After Halloween, your own children can eat the food and candy and donate any toys you bought to a holiday toy drive. After all the work they've lavished on them, they'll probably want to keep the altars.

Samhain Ritual: Laid to Rest

Dallas Jennifer Cobb

EVERY ONE OF US IS wounded, and yet each of us shares in the magic, mystery, and majesty of life. Wounds are visible and invisible: hurt by experiences, injured by accidents, wounded by relationships, bruised by loss, and scarred by life. We carry the marks on and within us. Without awareness, gentleness, and attention to healing, these wounds can fester and become toxic.

The burden of our wounds can become so heavy that we feel crushed: we suffer poor mental, emotional, and physical health. Whole areas of our lives feel numb—as though we are the "walking dead," moving through life injured, limping, and decrepit. We wonder why we are prone to autoimmune diseases, why we sometimes weep inconsolably, what causes that deep-rooted terror that arises in seemingly simple situations, why this widespread depression?

The places within us where we have had to numb feelings, deny emotions, repress fear, forget abuse, and somehow process daily atrocities have become ancient and Crone-like.

Shining the healing light of attention, intention, and community on these wounds can actively transform them from toxic to treasured, from waste to wisdom. Undertaking an internal cleansing at Samhain can allow us to grieve what we have lost, heal our toxic wounds, and transform our attention to the bounty of what we are harvesting. Tonight, by using symbolic means to relieve us of our burdens, we can lighten our load and create space in our lives, welcoming new energy, activity, people, and pursuits.

At Samhain, let us lay the wounds to rest and connect the deep, powerful work of emotional transformation to the transformation of our symbolic lives that takes place at this sabbat. As we invoke death and dying, mourning and loss, we tap into energies that will enable us to excise old pain, resentment, and fear—lay it to rest and free ourselves, readying for the transition into the new year.

This ritual is designed to help you open your own gates of hell, let the demons out, and lay them to rest in preparation for the start of the new year. It's not intended to be undertaken lightly; I urge you to do this ritual alone or with trusted guardians of your well-being. Let the veils between your worlds be thin. Give yourself permission to soften the barriers that contain your shadow self, and welcome those old demons up and out. This ritual will help you to identify difficult and outdated parts of your life, and literally lay them to rest, burying them.

Items Needed

Samhain needs fire, so plan a ritual around a campfire, a chimenea, or candles if you are holding your ritual indoors. You will also need:
Several sheets of newspaper
A lighter or matches
A sprig of sage, and a small bowl of water
And after: a feast, plus offerings of food, sweets, and drink

This ritual can be undertaken alone or in community. If working with other people, it is important to underscore the solemnity of the work and make plans to protect people's vulnerabilities and pain, which may be revealed. Plan who you will invite, consider who might need and want this sort of deep-reaching, personal ritual, and have a wee chat about the nature of the ritual when you invite them, so they are prepared in advance.

Assemble your tools in advance around the fire or candles, and then "sweep" the space, clearing it of physical and psychic debris before anyone arrives.

As people gather, guide them to sit in a circle around the fire source. When working with deep emotions, I like to remind people of the limbic bond shared by humans—how our limbic brains connect, resonate with, and affect one another. From a physiology point of view, we are literally "never alone," and tonight we invite the Crone.

Create Sacred Space

To prepare your ritual area, have everyone gather in a circle to watch as the **group leader** speaks while taking these specific actions.

Inspired with air, (crumple paper and place it under the assembled firewood)

Enlightened with fire (Light matches and ignite the fire)

Cleansed with water (Walk the circle, flicking water with the sage sprig behind everyone present, then return to your place in the circle)

Strengthened with earth (Gather a handful of earth)

Infused with spirit (Make a muddy smudge on your third eye, and then on the third eye of each person in the circle)

Invocation

In the name of the Goddess, the mourning Crone,
and in honor of the God who is gone but not forgotten,
I encircle you with sacred protection and consecrate this altar.
May Goddess and God serve here through wisdom, transformation, and magic.

Tonight, we are bonded and united by fire (or candles). This warmth reminding us of the warm support we enjoy in community, and the light reminding us of the bright burning path of the soul on its eternal journey, the circle enacts our community safety. We are be-

tween the worlds, and what happens between the worlds affects all worlds.

So mote it be.

A Ritual for Release

Gently touching the dark mark on your forehead, say:

This is what I have come to learn.
This is what I must heal.
This is what may die away.
This is what shall be reborn.

Raising and Releasing Energy

Standing, let the circle join hands and start to move the circle clockwise, **everyone** chanting:

I look within to find my pain, I name it and I tame it.

Let the energy build as you circle faster and chant louder.
I look within to find my pain, I name it and I tame it.
I look within to find my pain, I name it and I tame it.

Then stop, loudly stating:

I trust the process and the enduring wisdom of the journey of the soul. I release this _____ *(anger, guilt, grief, pain, suffering… insert whatever you need to release) to be consumed by fire.*

Join with me, saying: I trust the process and the enduring wisdom of the journey of the soul. I release this _____ *to be consumed by fire.*

Now moving the circle counterclockwise, chant:
I trust the magic, I trust myself,
I release my pain, and embrace my health.

Circle faster and chant louder, until finally it culminates in a group scream, and the movement stops.

Arrrggghhhhhh! (Everyone screams together.)

Quiet and still, crouch down to the ground, touching the earth with both hands, urging the others to do so, grounding out the energy, releasing it.

Tonight we let old ways die, release outdated beliefs.
We cast out negative patterns, and in this we find relief.
We beg you Goddess, Mother, Crone,
take our pain and worry.
Heal our hands, our heads and hearts,
and restore us in a hurry.
We have named our pain,
released and confessed,
And we wear your mark
and know we are blessed.

Touch your third-eye smudge.
Later tonight, and as we feast,
let us remember the darkness and what we have released.

Standing, raise your arms wide:
We release the elements to leave this place
but take the darkness upon our face.
Up and out, into the light
we release all toxic emotion tonight.

Leaving the ritual space, be sure to douse the fire for safety's sake, then lead your circle, community, friends, and family to the table to feast. Before you eat, fill a plate, make a space at your table, and welcome the ancestors to join you tonight, and know the darkness is always nearby.

Blessed be.

Notes

Notes

Yule

Yule: Gifts of the Solstice

Natalie Zaman

Word to the Wise

"The Magi, as you know, are three wise men—wonderfully wise men who brought gifts to the babe in the manger. They invented the art of giving Christmas presents."

THE DAY BALTHAZAR LOST his head has become something of a family legend.

Every December 1 without fail, my mother lovingly arranges her plaster crèche somewhere in the house. Wherever she decides to place them, the three Wise Men are always on the opposite end of the table from the other characters until January 6; the Magi didn't arrive at the stable until Epiphany, and it would be unthinkable that their tiny doppelgangers would do things any differently.

The little figures have been an institution for as long as I can remember. The paint is chipped in places, and one of the Magi's heads—Balthazar's—is slightly askew from where it was glued back on. No one's ever owned up to how poor Balty got decapitated, but I recently unearthed photographic evidence of my middle brother dangling him just out of my four-year-old reach—his head still intact. I can't imagine December without the Wise Men. At our house, they, even more than Santa Claus, were responsible for the best part of Christmas—the presents.

Ah, yes, Christmas presents. I remember lying awake at night, clutching my blankets, watching the crack at the bottom of my bedroom door for changes of light in the next room and listening for any sound that would confirm that Christmas had come to our house. I remember not being able to sleep for the excitement over *What was under the tree?!* Large or small, the once-a-year Christmas windfall was—with few exceptions—a guarantee, and nothing was off-limits. You could put anything on a Christmas list and live in hope that you just might get it. Somehow, surprises (even if they weren't *exactly* what you wanted) always managed to happen. And there was an eager magic to it all, the kind that can only be felt through hunger.

It wasn't just the anticipation of Christmas Day, but the entire season that kicked off at Thanksgiving and ended when the decorations were returned to their storage boxes on January 6 that seemed to make everyone glow. Waking up to brisk winter mornings, starry skies at night, mugs of hot chocolate with excessive amounts of marshmallow were treasured treats. There were the special holiday television programs that, if you missed them—a real tragedy, this— you had to endure a grueling 365-day wait until you had the opportunity to see them again. And lastly, and most importantly, there were the people, the ones I only saw at the waning of the year. This was the most magical, the most hallowed part of the holidays.

Like many folks, I came to my path from Christianity, so my Winter Solstice celebrations are still very much steeped in Christmas and the traditions of my childhood. This includes the Magi-inspired gift exchange even though there's nothing particularly Pagan about it.

The Magi's primary accomplice—and rival—for holiday gift giving is St. Nicholas, known eventually as Father Christmas and Santa Claus. The Magi definitely have seniority over the saint. Before he was canonized, the Bishop Nicholas did his good works in the third century, only about a hundred years before the official dates for

Christmas and Epiphany were set into the calendar. While Nicholas did have his own day for veneration (December 6), he didn't begin to transform into Father Christmas-cum-Santa until the sixteenth century. Christmas presents as we know them weren't exchanged on December 25 until Queen Victoria started the tradition by giving a locket with a childhood portrait to her beloved Albert in 1841. Prior to that, gifts were generally given on January 1 (a bit closer to the Magi's arrival at the stable, for what it's worth) as a means of ushering in the New Year on a positive note.

Christianity does not have a monopoly on December gift-giving; the custom spans many traditions and cultures. "Oseibo," gifts of gratitude, are given in Japan in the month of December. Bodhi Day, celebrated around December 8 by various Buddhist sects, honors the day that Buddha achieved enlightenment. While there are no specific gifts given on this occasion, it is customary to celebrate by performing kind acts for others. The Hindu Pancha Ganapati is a modern-day festival purposefully aligned with other winter celebrations that honors the Lord Ganesha with five days of prayer and parties. And, of course, presents are exchanged on each night of Hanukkah and on Imani, the last day of Kwanzaa.

There was at least one Pagan precedent. During the Roman celebration of Saturnalia, gifts of fruit and candles were given in the week leading up to the Winter Solstice. These weren't the line-up-outside-a-shop-on-Thanksgiving-at-midnight-to-get-a-good-deal kind of gifts, but symbolic (not to mention useful) tokens of the return of the sun.

Most solstice celebrations revolved around just that—celebrating. Celebrating the fact that one made it through another cycle of seasons; celebrating that inside, there was fire, food, and fun no matter what was going on outside; celebrating that the days would steadily become longer and longer—all of those aspects of the sun's return that were vital to survival. Gifts, even if they were exchanged, were not a centerpiece. For Pagans, it was—and is—a time to look backward and be grateful, and forward, with hope.

For the past few Yuletides, when I've looked back, it was with a rush to reach out to people with whom I'd promised to keep in touch. And as I looked forward, ready to make the same promises again, I found myself turning to tokens as a replacement of unfulfilled promises.

Throughout my adult life, I've tried to replicate that eager, magical feeling about winter that was so much a part of my childhood. I've succeeded a few times, but rarely has it been the result of something that came wrapped in a package, given or received. A gift is a token of affection, and while an object can't make up for time unspent, it can serve as a reminder of our presence in the lives of others. The magic of the season is captured in the present moment: in a walk down a city street with a favorite cousin, in a shared cup of spiced cider, or in the evergreen ornaments I exchange with the same friend year after year over afternoon tea. I've learned that the best Yule gift is that of time.

♣

I think I will always be reconciling my Pagan present to my Catholic past. I love making connections; the discovery that something I was taught in childhood has older roots is grounding for me. Does the journey of the Magi have a Pagan backstory? The star and Three Wise Men predate Christianity. Three wise men attended the birth of the Egyptian god Horus, and are immortalized as the three stars of Orion's belt—but as in the Christmas story, they play only supporting roles.

Tack a few more letters onto "Magi" and you have the word "magician." In Greek, *Mai'goi* translates to "astrologer," in Persian, the word refers to a scholarly caste who studied astrology and divination. Another translation suggests that the Magi were "men who prayed silently." Depending on which version of the Bible you're reading, they're called the "Magi" or "the Three Wise Men." They've also been called "the Three Kings," though it was more likely that they were advisors to kings rather than kings themselves—they were, after all, wise. Whatever version you choose, they all suggest that the mysterious, star-gazing trio with their camels and coffers of treasure and incense sought knowledge through esoteric means.

Their star, by the way, is also questionable. The Magi followed "a star in the east." Is it the same star that appears at the top of Yule and Christmas evergreens far and wide? The Sun, reborn at the solstice, is, of course, a star—but was the bright object that caught the Magi's eyes and captured their imaginations a star, or something else? It's been theorized that the timing of the story coincides with the appearance of Halley's Comet, believed by many to be a harbinger of great events. Recent scholarship suggests that the star wasn't a star at all, but another astronomical anomaly, perhaps the moon eclipsing the planet Jupiter—this is a theory with symbolic value that begs to be played with. Did the Wise Men see the birth of an important person played out by the moon eclipsing the planet named for the chief of all gods?

It is all conjecture. The Bible, from which the Christian tale is taken, is predictably cryptic. The only reference to the Magi can be found in the book of Matthew—who didn't name names. Documentation of any identifying details came hundreds of years later. Art and the providence of the Western Church have given the Wise Men all sorts of designations, the first being that there were only three. This is a significant number on many levels, but probably determined by the individual gifts that were brought. The Magi were given names, ages, and possible ethnicities: Caspar is seen as an elderly man with a white beard offering a chest of gold. Middle-aged Melchior (often depicted as Arabian) brings a gift from his homeland, frankincense. Balthazar is young. His dark skin and his gift, myrrh, suggest that he could be from Africa. The portrait fits our little crèche set and so many others like it, but is it accurate? Later writers and different branches of the Eastern Church offer different names for the Wise Men. What is correct? The fact is that there are no facts, only many guesses and questionable resources mixed with a large dose of faith—not the best formula for uncovering the truth.

In his story "The Gift of the Magi," it is the wisdom of the Wise Men that the writer, O. Henry, infused into the characters of Della and Jim, a husband and wife who sacrifice their personal treasures to give each other gifts. Beneath the plot of their story is a universal truth, the spirit of the season revealed by a foolish mistake that was ultimately wise:

And here I have lamely related to you the uneventful chronicle of two foolish children in a flat who most unwisely sacrificed for each other the greatest treasures of their house. But in a last word to the wise of these days let it be said that of all who give gifts these two were the wisest. O all who give and receive gifts, such as they are wisest. Everywhere they are wisest. They are the magi.

If indeed the Wise Men invented the art of giving Christmas presents, it's the feeling they inspire at this time of year that transcends their story, real or imagined, and consequently, any material gift: To be selfless is to be wise—the spirit of the season.

⚜

Whatever your beliefs, whatever your path, whatever your family traditions, this December, cherish your loved ones. Surprise people with generosity if it is something you can do. If you cannot, exchange wishes and tokens of good will, and even more importantly, share your time—a commodity that is gone once it has passed.

Bright blessings on your celebrations, and may the light of the Winter Solstice touch you with its gifts, always, and in all ways.

Cosmic Sway

April Elliott Kent

THE WINTER SOLSTICE ARRIVES on December 21, 2015, just before midnight Eastern time (11:48 p.m., to be exact). The Gibbous Moon in evergreen Taurus reminds us that winter—whether in nature's seasons or the seasons of our lives—won't last forever. The Moon's opposition to Venus suggests that getting what we need is more important than getting what we want…a good reminder in the days just before the feast of Christmas!

Mercury will be retrograde during this season (January 5 to 25, 2016). It's a tricky time to initiate New Year's resolutions, as you may be overlooking key details. But it's an excellent opportunity to fine-tune the resolutions you've already drafted, to ensure they are realistic and have the best possible chance of success.

As we celebrate the gradual return of the Sun, the powerful, warming king of the sky, our thoughts turn to the people whom we admire and consider role models. Who are your teachers, your mentors? Besides your parents, are there people whose influence on your character has been profound? Remember them with gifts of love and appreciation; write a letter to someone who changed your life. Even the most successful people appreciate knowing that they've made a difference.

A Living Tree

The Yule log, Christmas tree, and evergreen branches are commonly used to adorn our homes during this season. If a tree is part of your Yuletide celebrations, consider getting a living one grown in a pot that can be transplanted outside your home in the warmer weather. The Moon in Taurus at this solstice favors the symbolism of a live tree growing in your home, festooned with lights, as you imagine it growing taller and stronger toward the Sun's light.

Mars in Scorpio

On January 3, Mars enters Scorpio. After the diplomacy and restraint of Mars in Libra, Mars in Scorpio is like the cork popping out of a bottle—physical energy surges. If you have not resolved your differences with others, now is the time when the gloves come off. Mars in Scorpio reflects intense focus and concentration in all we do, so it's an excellent transit for tackling chores that you've been putting off, delving into projects that are unpleasant or that require painstaking research, and clearing some of the waste and clutter from your life.

Full Moon in Cancer – December 25, 2015

The Christmas Day Full Moon in Cancer is in good aspect to empathetic Neptune, and any family disagreements at the holiday table will be easily defused. Whether it's the wine and turkey or the sheer exhaustion of this hectic season, no one quite has the energy or desire to battle it out.

Jupiter in Virgo suggests more belt-tightening than usual in the gift department. This may be due to a cash flow problem, but it's just as likely that excess just doesn't seem to appeal much to anybody. Consider taking your loved ones outside after dinner to gaze at the Moon, bright and full in the sign of family, home, and hearth. Give thanks for those who are with you today, as well as the ones who are with you only in memory and in spirit.

Mercury Retrograde (Jan. 5 – 25, 2016)

Mercury, planetary ruler of communication, travel, and trade, is retrograde for three weeks, three times each year. During its retrograde periods, Mercury's matters are best treated with reflection rather than initiation. If you are driven by deadlines, schedules, and sales goals, Mercury retrograde will often stymie you with malfunctioning electronics and cars, missed messages, lost objects, and road closures. But Mercury's retrograde periods are beneficial times for catching up; you need only take yourself off your treadmill and take advantage of it. The week before the retrograde begins, back up your computer, make sure your car is in good repair, and gather a handful of projects that have languished and need a little tender loving care to bring them to completion. They will benefit from the introspective quality of Mercury retrograde, and so will you.

New Moon in 19.13 Capricorn – January 9, 2016

The New Moon point is conjoined Pluto and square Uranus, jolting us awake with an explosion of energy. If you enjoy making New Year's resolutions, you are now chomping at the bit to start putting yours into action. But with Mercury retrograde, it's still a better time to review last year's resolutions than to implement new ones. Go ahead and fine-tune your plans for 2016, but hold off until after the 26th to launch them.

We've seen so many cardinal sign lunations in difficult aspect to Uranus and Pluto since 2012 that you'd think we'd be used to them by now. But New and Full Moons in Aries, Cancer, Libra, and Capricorn continue to trigger frustration and impatience—a tough combination with Mercury retrograde's slow, reflective style. Look to Mars's trine to Neptune for an escape hatch; meditation, relaxation, soaking in a hot tub, and ritual are all excellent ways of dealing with the frazzled atmosphere of this New Moon.

Dorothy Morrison's Ritual for Goal Manifestation

This is one of the best New Moons for goal-setting rituals. I've often used this ritual from Dorothy Morrison's book *Everyday Moon Magic* with great results! You'll need:

Paper and pen

Red marking pen

Highlighting pen (any color)

1 yellow candle

Draw a picture of a road that forks in many directions, but leads to the same end. (Don't worry if you're not an artist; this drawing doesn't have to be anything fancy.) Examine the picture and mark the straightest route with the highlighting pen, then write your goal along that route with the red pen.

Light the candle and see yourself traveling directly down the correct path to attaining your goal. Place the map in front of the candle and say something like:

Radiant Mother in the sky
Light my journey from on high
Guide me with your silver glow
So the proper path I'll know
The path of true accomplishment;
The path for which my dreams are meant
And with that guidance, please allow
That I may manifest them now
And bring them to reality
As I will, so mote it be

Leave the map in front of the candle until the wick burns out, then carry the map with you. (*Everyday Moon Magic: Spells and Rituals for Abundant Living,* by Dorothy Morrison, Llewellyn, 2004.)

Full Moon in Leo – January 23, 2016

This Full Moon in dignified Leo makes a square aspect to Mars in Scorpio. Sometimes it can be difficult to decide whether it is more important to be true to yourself or to compromise in order to get along better with others. At this Full Moon, you must follow your own star. You may be amazed at just how positive the results will be.

Mercury finishes its retrograde period on January 25 with a bang, after making a conjunction to Pluto and a square to Uranus. Dig deep into intellectually stimulating projects; your innovation and focus are formidable at this Full Moon. Plenty of knotty problems have been waiting for the ingenious solutions that you now have to offer.

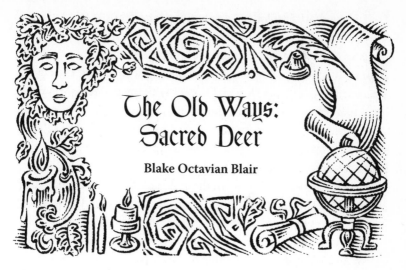

The Old Ways: Sacred Deer

Blake Octavian Blair

DEER OF ALL TYPES are an ever-present symbol included in the lore and celebration of winter holidays around the world. For modern Pagans, the two connections of the deer to come to mind first this sabbat season are likely to be the stag of modern Pagan and Wiccan lore and of course the yearly appearance of Santa's reindeer. However, deer have found a special cross-cultural place in the symbolism of many faiths at Yule time and beyond.

Practitioners of various world traditions celebrate Yule, the Winter Solstice, as the return of the light and the rebirth of the sun. The Stag is itself a solar symbol, representing the divine masculine and the god. The lore of the battle between the Oak King and the Holly King is a seasonal staple for many modern Pagans. Visually, the Oak King is depicted as Lord of the Forest in green leafy finery but he is also commonly antlered—harking back to the stag. However, the associations of these magical and antlered animals with the divine masculine harks back even farther to ancient Celtic and European cultures. Images of what are thought to be the horned god, an antlered human form posed in posture similar to a deer's body, were found in a cave wall in southern France dating back to the Paleolithic period. Similar images have been used to depict the horned god Cernunnos.

To be equated to and used as a manifestation or symbol of a god shows the importance of such an animal to these cultures. European cultures have shamanic elements running deep within them, almost all of which place the deer in a place of significance with the Divine. There are links in Norse lore of the deer with the goddess. Many theorize that Santa's sleigh being depicted as being pulled by reindeer is a carryover from Freya's chariot—pulled by stags. Yule was a celebration of central importance in Norse culture, in fact the term Yule is in actuality an Old Norse term for "wheel." Many Norse considered Yule to be the beginning of the wheel of the year, bringing forth a sense of rebirth and new beginnings, themes carried throughout many cultures and into our modern day Yuletide celebrations.

Druidic traditions place the Stag as a central animal spirit of great power and integrity—a spirit that assists a person in gaining access to the Otherworlds. They too, like many other Pagan traditions, hold the stag as a symbol or manifestation of horned god figures. Additionally, they are considered in Druid lore to be an animal that has been around since the beginning of time and are associated with fertility. This certainly adds to the Stag's power as a fitting symbol for the recurring and central seasonal themes of celebrating birth and rebirth (and thus new beginnings).

It is important to note that while different cultures logically have lore revolving around different species of deer indigenous to their location, there is a great deal of shared lore, symbolism, and characteristics among them. Whether it be whitetail deer, mule deer, elk, caribou, or reindeer, much of their spiritual attributes remain the same even though each also has individual distinctions. A common spiritual characteristic assigned to deer is heightened perception. Looking at the natural behavior of the deer this is not surprising. They appear to have an exceptional perception of the activity going on in their surroundings and the proximity of other beings to themselves—whether this be due to acute hearing, a sixth sense, or a combination thereof. The visual symbol of the antlers are often connected to this characteristic. They visually cue us to the symbolism of antennae. Their being positioned in a way so as they appear to extend from the eyes and upwards toward the sky—perhaps tuning into the signals around them in the physical world and beyond into the ethereal. Interesting to note is that while in the United States we often associate the antlers to male or stag deer, this is not a logical conclusion worldwide. This is because in whitetail deer, the most prevalent deer species in the United States, only males grow antlers. However, in many other species, including caribou and the seasonally iconic reindeer, both sexes exhibit antlers. Due to this, in the United States, Santa's reindeer often experience a case of mistaken identity. We often see his flying reindeer depicted not with images of actual true reindeer but instead with those of whitetail deer.

At this time, it is worth harking back to the art such as that found in south France of the human figure imposed on top of/within that of the reindeer. There is another interpretation of this and similar art that has been found of its kind—shamanic shapeshifting. In this context, the shamanic act of shapeshifting can be described as the merging with or taking of an animal spirit into the body by the shaman, thereby gaining the added power and assistance of the animal spirit. Considering the great importance of reindeer in these cultures, this would not be an uncommon ritual act and therefore stands as a very viable interpretation. Reindeer antlers and furs are often used in the construction of shamanic ceremonial garb among the peoples whom the reindeer is of prime importance to and they are a spirit often called upon in shamanic ceremony.

Reindeer have a long history of importance in Siberia and Mongolia that carries through to modern day—even though Mongolia's climate has changed to the point that reindeer can largely no longer live there. However, its symbolic cultural importance remains. Burial mounds of Mongolian chiefs in the Altai Mountains have included the remains of reindeer bones among other items, such as gold ornaments and ceremonial clothing, showing the level of esteem given to the reindeer. Reindeer were thought to be the perfect animals for riding in the afterlife. In Siberia, reindeer still have both practical and spiritual importance. Reindeer are used to tow sleighs and as transportation and work animals. (With the reindeer's recurring role cross-culturally as a mode of transport, both earthly and Otherworldly, it is no wonder they developed into the steeds that drove Santa's sleigh!) For many peoples the reindeer was and is what the buffalo was to indigenous peoples of the North American plains region—food, clothing, transportation, and spiritual ally. In his classic work, *Shamanism: Archaic Techniques of Ecstasy*, Mircea Eliade speaks of one of the stories from the lore of the Yukagir people of shamans, who when the tribe was threatened with famine would take a shamanic journey to the "Earth-Owner" and plead for the resource of food to sustain his people, and is gifted the soul of a reindeer. After returning from the journey, the shaman goes to a prescribed earthly location, a reindeer appears, and he then shoots and kills the deer with bow and arrow—this was to be interpreted to mean that in the foreseeable future, food would no longer be scarce.

Another story Eliade relays is from the Avam Samoyed people and involves a shaman who during illness experienced a visit to the Otherworlds in which his helping spirits eventually led him to a cave where he witnesses two women giving birth—to reindeer. He was given the gnosis that the reindeer was to be the animal to aid people in all areas of life and serve as a food source. He observes the reindeer leave the cave, each through one of two exits that led north and south respectively, to go into the world and fulfill that prophecy. So many Yuletide themes can be gleaned here all in one story: a sacred birth, the giving of a spiritual gift, the reminder of the importance of helping others selflessly, and even the granting of an animal ally.

The deer and its spirit are so ingrained into magical and spiritual history that it was almost destined to find its way into cultural celebrations clear through to our modern day. The next time a deer appears before you on a holiday card, in a light display, or perhaps live in the flesh before your very eyes—stop and remember the ancient power that is the gift it has brought to you!

Bibliography

Andrews, Ted. *Animal Speak: The Spiritual & Magical Powers of Creatures Great & Small.* St. Paul, MN: Llewellyn Publications, 1993.

Carr-Gomm, Philip and Stephanie. *The Druid Animal Oracle: Working with the Sacred Animals of the Druid Tradition.* New York: Fireside, Simon & Schuster, Inc., 1994.

Eliade, Mircea. *Shamanism: Archaic Techniques of Ecstasy.* Princeton, NJ: Princeton University Press, 1964.

McCoy, Edain. *Sabbats: A Witch's Approach to Living the Old Ways.* St. Paul, MN: Llewellyn Publications, 1994.

Morrison, Dorothy. *Yule: A Celebration of Light and Warmth.* St. Paul, MN: Llewellyn Publications, 2000.

van Reterghem, Tony. *When Santa was a Shaman: The Ancient Origins of Santa Claus & the Christmas Tree.* St. Paul, MN, Llewellyn Publications, 1995.

Vitebsky, Piers. "Excerpt: The Reindeer People." *NPR.* February 11, 2006. http://www.npr.org/templates/story/story.php?storyId=5199713.

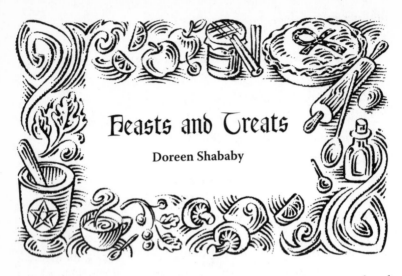

Feasts and Treats

Doreen Shababy

YULE, LITERALLY THE WHEEL, is a time of year which seems to bend in on itself, a sort of trapahedonal rhombatuse of contradiction. We have reached the solstice and from now on the days will be getting longer, but real winter is still to come. It seems appropriate to gather together and bring cheer to each other and to share our bounty, however meager, with others less fortunate. Many Pagan groups run food drives, what about yours?

Stuffed Turkey Breast with Cherry Sauce

A whole, bone-in turkey breast is used for the Yule dinner for ease of preparation, served with a sweet-tart sauce. I use rice stuffing here, made Shababy-style (that is, Lebanese)—with pine nuts and cinnamon. If you cannot abide anything except cornbread or your mama's recipe, please use your favorite. After all, turkey stuffing is a very personal thing.

For the turkey:
> *Prep time:* 20 minutes (plus cooking and cooling the rice)
> *Cook time:* about 1½ hours
> *Serves:* 6, with leftovers

1 6- to 7-pound whole bone-in turkey breast
¼ cup pine nuts
4 cups cooked long-grain white rice, prepared according to package
   directions and cooled
2 tablespoons butter, plus extra for turkey
4 ounces ground lamb or beef, browned and seasoned
1 teaspoon cinnamon
Salt and pepper to taste

Heat oven to 400 degrees F. Rinse and dry the turkey, then season with salt and pepper. Rub some butter on the flesh under the skin and season.

In a skillet over medium-high heat, melt the butter and toast the pine nuts until fragrant—do not burn. Toss the pine nuts with the lamb, rice, cinnamon, and plenty of salt and pepper in a large bowl until mixed. Taste and adjust for seasoning.

In a roasting pan, make a small foil "boat" to contain the stuffing, which will inevitably fall out. Mound the stuffing on the boat (stuff a little in the neck cavity) and place the turkey breast in the pan, positioning over rice. Butter outside of turkey, place in oven and reduce heat to 325 degrees F. Roast, uncovered, for 1 to 1½ hours, basting frequently, until juices run clear and meat thermometer reads 165 degrees F. Remove from oven and let rest 15 minutes before removing stuffing, then slice and serve with cherry sauce.

For the cherry sauce (makes about 2 cups):
   Prep time: 5 minutes
   Cook time: about 20 minutes

1 pound (frozen) pitted tart cherries
4 tablespoons brown sugar, or according to taste
¼ cup water
¼ teaspoon dried basil leaf
⅛ teaspoon ground cardamom
Pinch cinnamon
½ teaspoon cornstarch, dissolved in 1 tablespoon water

Place all ingredients in a medium saucepan and bring to a boil. Turn down to simmer and cook until cherries are soft, about 15 minutes. Add the dissolved cornstarch and stir until fully blended and starch is cooked. Remove cinnamon stick, and keep warm until ready to serve.

Butternut Squash with Orange and Apricot

You will know you have experienced the Winter Solstice when you taste this dish. Bright orange like the sun, it is a reminder of the cyclical turn of the wheel.

Prep time: 15 minutes
Cook time: 45 minutes
Serves: 6

1½ pound butternut squash
¼ cup minced dried apricots
½ cup orange juice
1 tablespoon brown sugar
1 tablespoon butter, plus some for baking dish

Cut squash in half, remove the seeds, and carefully pare away the rind. Cut into 1-inch chunks, place in a mixing bowl with dried apricots, orange juice, and brown sugar, and stir.

Heat oven to 350 degrees F. Grease a lidded casserole dish with butter. Pour the squash mixture into the dish, then dot with butter. Cover and bake for 45 minutes, check for tenderness. Serve hot.

Dessert Gougères

These light, airy little puffs are a variation of *pâte à choux*. The nutty cheese and sweet spices are perfect complements, especially with the wine. And break out the elbow grease; there is much stirring!

Prep time: 15 minutes
Cook time: 5 minutes on the stove, 20 minutes in the oven
Serves: Many: makes about 3 dozen gougères

1 cup water

6 tablespoons butter

1 teaspoon salt

2 tablespoons sugar

¼ teaspoon nutmeg

¼ teaspoon cinnamon

1 cup all-purpose flour

½ cup grated Swiss cheese

4 large eggs, room temperature, plus 1 egg for wash

Heat oven to 450 degrees F. Grease two baking sheets.

In a medium saucepan, bring the water, butter, salt, sugar, and spices to a boil. When the butter melts, remove from heat. Add the flour all at once and beat vigorously until mixture forms a ball and leaves the sides of the pan.

Add cheese and mix well. Next, beat in one egg at a time until thoroughly incorporated.

Using a teaspoon, arrange small spoonfuls of the batter on prepared baking sheets. Mix the remaining egg with 1 teaspoon water and brush on the puffs.

Arrange oven racks to middle and top of oven, reduce heat to 400 degrees F, and bake the gougères for 20 minutes, or until golden and puffed. Remove from oven and serve warm or cold.

A note from Doreen: Do as I say, not as I do. We like to call them "googers." But the correct pronunciation is "goo-SHARE."

Mulled Merlot

You might want to double this recipe because it fits the slow cooker better, plus it keeps. You can also replace the wine with grape juice. This beverage warms one from the inside out and is much appreciated after coming in from the cold.

Prep time: 10 minutes

Cook time: 10 minutes on stove, then kept warm in slow cooker

Serves: 6

1 bottle Merlot wine
2 cups cranberry juice beverage
½ teaspoon allspice berries
4 whole peppercorns
4 whole cloves
1 cinnamon stick, 3 inches long
2 tablespoons honey

Combine all ingredients in a medium saucepan and heat until warm, do not boil. Then pour into a slow cooker and keep on low, uncovered. Serve in sturdy mugs, and enjoy.

Crafty Crafts

Tess Whitehurst

WE MOST OFTEN HEAR about the stocking tradition as it relates to Christmas and Santa Claus. Nevertheless, just as Santa Claus is a contemporary incarnation of a pagan archetype (he has been compared to Lapland shamans, who rode sleighs through the snow pulled by reindeer in their furry red-and-white cloaks), there are other more ancient, pagan roots that link stockings to the Winter Solstice.

As the Norse god Odin made his rounds during the Wild Hunt (during which spirits flew through the skies for the twelve days of Yuletide), children would leave their boots out, filled with food for his eight-legged horse, Sleipnir. As a gesture of gratitude, he'd replace the food with sweet treats that they'd then joyfully discover in the morning. Quite similarly, children in Holland left food in their shoes for the flying horse belonging to their own magical, gift-giving Yuletide figure, Sinterklaas, which he then replaced with trinkets and sweets. Frau Holle (a distinctly witchy figure who accompanied Odin on the Wild Hunt, also known by a number of other names, such as Holda, Perchta, Berchta, and Free) would also offer small gifts such as fruits and nuts to obedient children during these darkest days of winter.

Witchy Yule Stocking

While this stocking is a riff on the mainstream stocking idea, it's quite a bit funkier. In the tradition of the classic witch stocking (a nod to Frau Holle), it's black, white, long, and pointed, but its fuzzy red details give it a cozy Yuletide flair. It'll add a unique and distinctly funky flavor to your wintery décor.

Time to complete: 1.5 to 2.5 hours (or more if you hand stitch)

Cost: $5.00 to $15.00 (more if you need to purchase basic sewing supplies)

Supplies

Paper grocery bag or old wrapping paper (for pattern)

Pen or pencil

Tape measure

Paper scissors

Sewing scissors

Pins

1 yard black felt

⅓ yard white felt

½ yard red trim (I used one with little red pompoms)

6 inches red ribbon

Black thread

White thread

Red thread

Needle (and/or sewing machine)

Green or red spherical pompom for the toe (about the width of a quarter)

Please note: The following pattern-making instructions may seem just a tad confusing, so take them one step at a time. Or, if all else fails, just mimic the shape of the stocking in the picture, or create a shape that you like, leaving room for the ¼-inch seam allowance on all sides. (That's what I did, after all, and it was quite easy.)

Instructions for the Pattern

On the paper, draw a giant "L," 24 inches tall and 15 inches wide. Two inches directly below the bottom right point of the "L," draw another point. Connect this lower point with the bottom left point of the "L," to form a lazy "L." (You can now ignore the first, straight horizontal line.)

Parallel to the first vertical line, draw another vertical line about 6¼ inches to the right.

Outside of the left vertical line, on the top, make a point about ¾ inches to the left. Outside of the right vertical line, on the top, make a point about one inch to the right. Also on the right vertical line, measure 18 inches down from the first point and mark a point.

Now, contour your stocking pattern. Starting at the top of the left side of the stocking, at the outside point, angle a line inward at a diagonal until it meets the original line at about 4 inches down.

Round off the angle at the heel. Arch the line from the heel to the toe slightly to create a slight, natural arch. Round the toe up and around to the point, and then slope the point in, bringing the line in a slightly rounded way up to the next point. From there, go straight up along the original line until you get about halfway up the stocking, and then angle out gradually to the outside point.

Cut your pattern around the outside edges of what you've drawn.

Sew Your Stocking

Fold your black felt in half, right sides together. Pin the pattern to the felt and cut (you will have two pieces).

Unpin. On the right side of the "L" shaped (not the backwards "L" shaped) piece, cut and arrange six white stripes from the white felt. I recommend going for character here rather than perfection, so cut without feeling pressure to make the stripes too straight. Pin the stripes onto the stocking and sew them on with white thread.

Pin right sides of the two stocking pieces together, and sew around the outside edge (except, of course, for the top). Turn right-side out, using the end of a wooden spoon or a chopstick to make sure the pointy toe is pointy.

Sew a pompom to the toe.

Pin and sew the trim around the inside of the top.

To create the hangy thing, fold the ribbon in half, pin to the inside of the back edge of the top of the stocking and sew.

For a variation, substitute the black and white felt for any other colors you desire. For example, in addition to the black and white stocking that I made for myself, I made a red and blue one for my boyfriend. This satisfies his ever-so-slightly more traditional leanings. Not to mention, they look really cute hanging next to each other, and we never get them mixed up.

Yuletide Stocking Magic

No matter what magical deity or gift-giving figure you like to envision and petition this time of year, it's always nice to honor him or her with an offering. So perhaps near your stockings you can place a little image of someone like Sinterklaas, Holda, Santa, or Odin, along with a red votive candle that can be burned safely in a tall jar. The night before Yule (or the night before whenever you like to have your morning celebration), leave out a little plate with some oatmeal cookies, which can be (energetically) enjoyed by the deity/figure, as well as any ravenous horses or reindeer. Light the candle and speak out loud your intention to offer the cookies as a gift. In the morning (if they're still there!), dispose of them in a compost heap or by throwing them in the Yule fire.

And if you'd like to go a more ancient (and eco-friendly) route with your stocking stuffers, choose edibles such as fresh and/or dried fruit, nuts, baked goods, and chocolate.

For Further Reading

Dugan, Ellen. *Seasons of Witchery: Celebrating the Sabbats with the Garden Witch*. Woodbury, MN: Llewellyn, 2012.

Siefker, Phyllis. *Santa Claus, Last of the Wild Men: The Origins and Evolution of Saint Nicholas, Spanning 50,000 Years*. Jefferson, NC: McFarland and Company, 1997.

All One Family: Secrets for Yule

Linda Raedisch

THIS ONE REALLY SHOULDN'T be a secret, but the rampant Disneyfication of our culture has made it one. Here it is: the muted, sad-eyed heroine of "The Little Mermaid" never gets to marry the prince. The author of "The Little Mermaid," Hans Christian Andersen, saves her spirit at the last minute, transforming her into a "daughter of the air," but there's no royal wedding, not for her. Her name isn't "Ariel," either. Andersen's mermaids don't go in for names, or if they do, humans probably wouldn't be able to pronounce them.

While you might not have been familiar with the original ending, I'm sure you have at least heard of "The Little Mermaid." You've no doubt heard of "The Ugly Duckling" and maybe even "The Little Match Girl," "Thumbelina," and "The Snow Queen." But did you know that Andersen actually wrote more than one hundred fifty stories? Some, like "The Bog-king's Daughter" are highly suspenseful while others consist of conversations between kitchen implements. A few, like "The Wild Swans," are based on older folk motifs, and many more were inspired by the deep history and prehistory of the Danish landscape.

As if writing one hundred fifty stories were not enough, old H. C. was also a master of *Scherenschnitte*, the art of snipping lacelike pictures out of single sheets of paper, which he liked to do to illustrate his own stories. Christmas was a season close to Andersen's heart, so I would not be surprised if he could also make all those intricate paper forms that the Danes still make to hang upon the *Juletrae*. In fact, Andersen himself is supposed to have invented the signature Danish Christmas tree ornament—the woven paper heart.

No matter how many woven hearts or paper stars you make, you always need more the next year. To this day, the Danes set aside time on December weekends for the whole family to gather at the dining room table to repair old ornaments and make new ones. While I'm not exactly Danish, this is one of my favorite Yuletide traditions, and I heartily recommend it.

Not everyone is as nimble-fingered as H.C., so you can leave it to the least crafty member of the family to choose and read a tale from Andersen's corpus while the rest of you work. Of course, paper crafts and storytelling are only two of the elements necessary for a magical pre-Yule get-together: the other three are candlelight, coffee, and cookies.

But first, you've got to go up to the attic to get that box of ornaments down and see how many have survived from last year. If a trip to the attic sounds like an uninteresting errand, you can pretend it's actually the attic of some stately brick townhouse in Odense, the kind of fine house to which Andersen himself might have been invited to spend Christmas Eve.

December in the Old Townhouse

As you come to the top of the last narrow flight of stairs, you can hear the risers creaking under your feet while overhead the rafters whisper to one another about happier days spent in the forest hundreds of years ago.

That grouchy red-capped gnome—every old Danish house has one—scuttles into the corner when he hears you coming. He'll make no effort to speak to you, though you might notice his eyes glowing hotly through the cobwebs. Don't let him bother you. He knows you owe him nothing until Christmas Eve when you'll bring him a big bowl of porridge with a pat of butter on top. Not that he'll talk to you then either; if a gnome wants conversation, he'll seek out the cat.

There, under the eaves, is a fresh blossoming of frost ferns on the single, round window pane. If you were to press a hot penny against the glass, you could gaze out over the empty nests of twigs crowning the chimney pots. The storks who wove them in the spring are long gone, having flown off to Egypt to spend the holidays gossiping with the swallows on the banks of the Nile.

If the house is a very tall one, you may be able to make out the ravens clawing at the frozen furrows beyond the city walls or, if you are facing the sea, the wild swans bobbing on the waves. In the opposite direction lies the marsh where the dreaded bog king dwells under a ceiling of frozen peat. A witch, too, lists the bog as her home address, but she is more likely to be found in the meadow, brewing beer for her many children and keeping an eye on the troublesome will-o'-the-wisps.

Now, where is that box of Christmas decorations? You listen for the tinkling sighs of glass ornaments through the cardboard, but there are so many conversations going on up here that it's hard to make out. The old kitchen things are the loudest, but from another box you can hear the more sophisticated exchanges of the porcelain figurines that used to stand proudly in glass-fronted cabinets in the parlor. They complain bitterly of the triumph of Danish Modern and how it has resulted in their exile to the attic. Not to be outdone, an old tin soldier is crying aloud with boredom, having fallen down a crack between the floorboards.

At last you spot the box of ornaments. It's smaller than you remember. You dust off the lid, take the box carefully in your arms and head for the stairs, forgetting the poor tin soldier, the porcelain shepherdess and her chimneysweep, forgetting even to promise the gnome that you'll be back in a few weeks with his porridge. Later on, he'll *complain of this to the cat, but none of that concerns you now. The days before Yule are trickling away, and you have work to do!*

And now back to the twenty-first century. I have one more Yuletide secret to impart. Gather the kids; this is important. It concerns Santa Claus. The truth about Santa is that he doesn't really live at the North Pole; in 1927 it was revealed to a select few via Finnish radio that Santa's workshop is actually located atop Korvatunturi Mountain in Lapland, not far, perhaps, from the Snow Queen's stronghold. I wonder if Hans Christian Andersen knew?

Solstice Ritual: The Yule Ball

Natalie Zaman

THE WORDS "YULE BALL" conjure up delicious images of fancy dress parties in halls bedecked with mistletoe and holly, of wassail and dancing, feasting and merry-making, gifts piled to the rafters, and a Yule log crackling in the hearth. But what if a Yule Ball was an object rather than an experience? What if it was something you could hold in your hand, a present to celebrate the present?

Gift giving has always been a part of my Yuletide celebrations, but more and more the gifts have become simple, symbolic, and consumable. One of my favorite gifts to give at the Winter Solstice is a Yule Ball. The crafting of this seasonal charm is a ritual of generosity and love that extends the warmth of the season beyond the winter.

Small, symbolic, and useful gifts, one to mark each sabbat, are wound up in a ball. As it is unraveled by the recipient over the course of the year, a new item is revealed to help celebrate that turn of the wheel and maintain a connection to the person who gave it to him. It becomes a means of strengthening or forging bonds between friends and family, sharing traditions, and keeping memories alive.

This is a ritual that can be done as a group activity or by a solitary practitioner. Yule Balls can be tailored to an individual recipient or made in multiples for giving and sharing on a larger scale (such as group grab bags and gift exchanges).

Items Needed

One each of the following objects to represent each sabbat and its accompanying message written on a small piece of paper. (Note: Yule Balls can be as large or small as you'd like. The gifts and messages for each sabbat can be altered according to your traditions, needs, and resources; each gift can also be a written message if you chose. The more personal the content, the stronger the magic within.)

Yule – Incense. (Create your own by combining pine needles, a few drops of pine oil, cinnamon, cloves, and a resin such as frankincense and/or myrrh in a mortar and pestle. Freezing the resin before combining it with your other ingredients will prevent it from gumming up as you grind it. The incense can be stored in a small bottle or plastic pouch.)

Sample message:
My crackling scent invokes the sun
And welcomes back the light.
Burn me at the Solstice,
Winter's longest night.

Samhain – A scrying stone. (A small black crystal with a smooth, shiny surface such as obsidian, tourmaline, or jet for meditation and divination.)

Sample message:
Look inside, what do you see?
When you hold this stone, remember me.

Mabon – Fall planting. (A flowering bulb of your choice to plant at the Autumnal Equinox and enjoy at the Spring Equinox.)

Sample message:
A time to reap, a time to sow
As you gather, so you grow.

Plant me now so come the spring,
Life returns with the joy it brings.

Lammas – Bread of life. (A green seed or bean and your favorite recipe for bread or cake. Instruct your recipient to add the bean/seed before baking to symbolically create the traditional green Lammas Loaf.)

Sample message:
Bake bread,
Add a seed,
Know the harvest
Will meet our needs.
What now is green,
Will soon be gold.
I wish you plenty
A hundred fold!

Litha – Shared sun salutation. (Write a note to your recipient with the exact time of the Summer Solstice sunrise for where he lives. Even if you are not together that morning, this serves as a promise to share the moment together by doing the salutation at the same time.)

Sample message:
Rise on Litha morning,
Go out to greet the sun.
Raise your hands above your head,
Feel the season, strong and warm.
I may not be beside you,
But that same sun I'll see.
For I'll rise too,
And stand with you
Together, we will be.

Beltane – Maypole ribbons. (8 lengths of ribbon, 4 white, 4 red, at least 20 feet in length to be tied to the top of a Maypole.)

Sample message:
Inside are ribbons,
You provide the pole.
So on this day of Beltane,
'Round the Maypole you can stroll.

Ostara – Spice dye. (1 to 2 tablespoons of each in separate packets: turmeric, hibiscus flowers or hibiscus powder, chili powder.)

Sample message:
Turmeric for yellow,
Hibiscus for blue.
Chili for red,
Such lovely hues.
A few drops of vinegar, water, and these
Color eggs for Ostara with the greatest of ease.

Imbolc – Stirring seeds. (A packet of seeds to get plants started at Imbolc.)

Sample message:
Into the earth I go,
At Imbolc to stir and grow.

Construction of the Yule Ball

After the messages for each sabbat have been personalized to your satisfaction, the Yule Ball can now be physically constructed. You will only need a few additional items to do so.

Crepe paper in different shades of green (green to represent the life force reborn at the Winter Solstice)
Scissors
Personalized sabbat messages
Tape
Green ribbon

Instructions: Wind a generous length of crepe paper around the first gift, the incense for Yule. (Because the gifts in the Ball go from Imbolc to Yule, the object you'll be starting with—the core of the Ball—will be the gift for NEXT Yule, the incense.). Continue to wrap, shaping it with your hands as you work to make the edges round and smooth. Do not add another gift until the layer is uniform. As you wind the gift for Yule, speak an incantation to bind the giver to the receiver, making the Yule Ball a conduit for maintaining a connection throughout the year:

> *From sabbat to sabbat, with each turn of the wheel,*
> *I wrap, I bind, and our friendship I seal.*
> *From summer to winter, and spring to fall,*
> *Our spirits merge in this Yule Ball.*

Repeat the incantation as you continue to wrap. If you have a specific person in mind for the Ball, speak his name at the beginning of the incantation to deepen the gift's connection to him. As you add each gift, use alternating shades of crepe paper to indicate to your recipient when he should stop unwinding. Add the remaining gifts to the Ball in the following order. (Remember, you're working backwards—the LAST gift you wrap will be the FIRST your recipient will unravel.)

The Scrying Stone for Samhain
The Bulb for Mabon
The Green Seed and Bread Recipe for Lammas
The Sun Salutation Note for Litha
The Maypole Ribbons for Beltane
The Spice Dyes for Ostara
The Seeds for Imbolc

When you have incorporated all of the gifts into the Ball, continue to add layers of crepe paper to smooth it out completely, continuing to speak the incantation. When the Ball is as round as you can make it, secure the last end of crepe paper with a small piece of tape. Finish the Ball by tying a ribbon around it and knotting it three times with the words:

A year of blessings to the bearer be,
And the warmth of the solstice times three!

Tie a bow at the top. For fun, you can also add a tag with a light-hearted sentiment such as, "Do Not Open Till Imbolc!"

Time to Unwind

Give or send the Yule Ball to your recipient at the Winter Solstice, with the following instructions (or write your own):

Warm Solstice Greetings!
You hold in your hand a Yule Ball wound a hundred times with warmth and love. Inside are gifts that will be revealed throughout the year. Unwind the ball until you get to the first gift—then stop! Use what you find to celebrate the season and remember me. Unwind the ball again at the next turn of the wheel.
Be merry!

Visualize the crepe paper as a thread that ties you to your recipient. As the Ball unwinds and the year unfolds, visualize yourselves growing closer, the connection intensifying at each sabbat. That is the true magic of this ritual. All too often, life gets in the way of staying in touch and maintaining the bonds we share with others. Wrap and be merry, and know that the year ahead will be full of love and friendship.

Notes

Imbolc

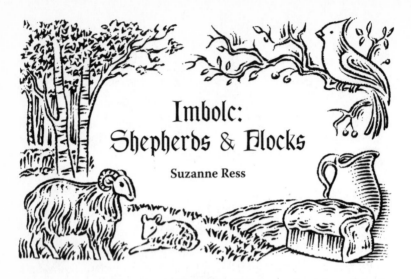

Imbolc: Shepherds & Flocks

Suzanne Ress

IMBOLC, ALSO KNOWN AS Saint Brigid's Day, Ladies' Day, Oimelc, Candlemas, and Groundhog Day, traditionally begins on the evening of February first, and continues through to February second. It falls halfway between Winter Solstice and Spring Equinox, and marks the time when signs of the Earth's first "quickening," or tiny signs of new life after the winter, can be perceived.

Imbolc is a fire festival and is also associated with fertility. Ancient Celtic celebrations involved bonfires, hearth fires, divination (especially weather divination), and visits to holy wells to pray for fertility and bounty. The name, Imbolc, comes from the Old Irish *imbolg*, which means, "in the belly." The alternative Pagan name, "Oimelc" means "Ewe's milk."

Ewes ovulate in the fall of the year, their bodies responding to the diminishing hours of daylight after Mabon, the Autumn Equinox. They remain pregnant for five months, giving birth to new lambs in the early Spring, before Ostara and the Spring Equinox. It is only in the final weeks of pregnancy that a ewe grows round in the belly and begins to show. In olden times shepherds could not be sure which of their ewes were expecting until around early February, or Imbolc— in the belly! This was a time for celebration, for it meant new life in the form of lambs, which would increase the flock or be slaughtered for tender meat to eat with young spring greens, and the ewe's milk was used to make cheese.

Where I live, in the Alpine foothills in Italy, the period around Imbolc coincides with the return of the shepherds and their flocks.

When we first moved here I had no idea there would be traveling shepherds, so I was utterly delighted and surprised when one February day, I found myself inside my car, stopped in the middle of a country road between one village and another, surrounded by over a thousand baaing and milling sheep.

The situation, not to mention the appearance of the shepherds, seemed like something from several centuries earlier. They were all wearing loosely fitting, dark-colored work clothes, wool caps, thick boots, and gloves, and most shepherds had abundant facial hair and rather long, unkempt head hair, and carried staffs. Some of the older ones still wear a thick woolen cloak called a "tabarro" in inclement weather, and some wear gaiters with their boots. All of them looked dirty and wild, as if they've been walking and camping out for months—which, in fact, they had.

Shepherding is an ancient profession, usually passed down from generation to generation for hundreds of years. Where I live, the shepherds have been using the same system of cooperative "alpeggi" and transhumance for over eight centuries. In the Middle Ages, there were thousands of shepherds in these parts. Now there remain only sixty transhumance shepherds in Lombardy. Transhumance means the shepherd travels from one place to another, and back again, seasonally.

The Lombardy shepherds and flocks have their alpeggi, or summer resting places, in the high mountains in the Orobian Alps behind Bergamo, where they stay for a hundred days between June and September. When the nighttime temperatures start to drop, the shepherd, or his collaborator, starts the trek down the mountain with the flock. In recent years, many shepherds have begun using trucks and campers to move from place to place, but there are still some who complete the entire transhumance on foot.

Following woods paths, old mule trails, country roads, and green spaces between small towns and villages, the shepherd moves the flock slowly southward, as far as the lower plains south of Milan, around Pavia, over the course of about three months, arriving in the temperate southern area at the coldest time of year. They may stay there with the flock for a few weeks before starting the circular path northward, heading up toward the Italian lake region. By about Imbolc they reach my area, already headed homeward, to the Alps, as the frozen ground thaws and the first leaf buds start to appear on the trees.

I have seen flocks of thousands of sheep grazing in grassy divisions between highways, although most of my encounters with them have been in the woods and fields around my home, whilst on horseback.

February is usually a delightful time for horse riding in the woods here. Dangerous ground ice has melted away, but there are not yet any insects in the woods to bother the horse. The horses are happy, frisky, and full of energy, sensing the odors of tiny newborn greenstuffs growing, shedding away their heavy winter coats, feeling their own hormone sap rising with the lengthening of daylight. I love the tinkling water sounds of thawed streams and brooks, and the early birds' songs, and the occasional warmer layer of breeze in the air, rustling the new pussy willows and the hazelnut catkins as we trot along, our view through the trees not yet impeded by thick foliage.

Along with all these little heralds of impending springtime, I see bits of white wool fuzz on the lower tree branches, left behind by traveling sheep.

One Sunday in February a few years ago, I was out riding with a friend and fellow horseman, enjoying a canter through the awakening woods as the late-afternoon sun cast long glinting shadows between the tree trunks. We were headed toward home, and slowed to a walk to cross a muddy place on the path. I noticed thousands of little cloven hoofprints in the mud, and then—we both heard it—the plaintive bleating of a newborn lamb.

To our left was a wide flat expanse of chestnut woods, last year's brown leaves and empty hulls making a noisy carpet at the trees' bases. I spotted the lamb first. All alone, tiny, and white as snow, at first I thought she was a plastic bag or other litter. And then she moved, rustling the brown ground cover. She bleated again.

We halted our horses and watched her. Why was she alone? How had this fluffy white preemie been left behind?

"I'm going to try to get her," my friend said.

"We can bring her back to the shepherd. He must have just passed through."

We both dismounted, and I held the horses and watched while he approached the lamb.

She scampered away. He tried again, approaching slowly, speaking softly. As soon as he was within a few feet of her, she ran off on her little spindly legs. After several more failures, my friend, who is neither lithe nor quick, returned for a lead rope he had brought with him. Using it as a sort of lasso, he finally managed to capture the wriggling lamb and carried her back to where I stood with the horses.

I helped him remount with the lamb in his arms, then I mounted my own horse and we left the woods, following in the direction of the sheep's footprints.

We came to an asphalt road and were able to follow the trail of mud and sheep droppings around the corner, onto a second road, and into a large field. The shepherd and flock had been there, but were there no longer. We re-entered the woods, easily following the sheep trail, and continued down the path for a while. In the meantime, the lamb was bleating with ever more desperation, obviously hungry. She was sucking at my friend's little finger but found no satisfaction there.

My friend, who has a small farm, with chickens, rabbits, and a pig, said he'd had experience with lambs before.

"Why don't you take her back to your place and feed her? I'll go on looking for the shepherd."

"Okay. If you find him, tell him to stay put, and I will bring the lamb in my car."

We parted ways, and I went on searching for the shepherd and his flock until it became too dark to see well, and I had to return home without finding him. I telephoned my friend, and he said he had fed the lamb with supermarket goat's milk, and he would keep her overnight and go by car to try to find the shepherd first thing in the morning.

Later the next day he called to tell me he was on his way to work when he saw the flock from a distance in a field. He spoke to the shepherd, who said he hadn't even noticed a ewe giving birth. My friend then rushed back home, got the lamb, and happily brought her back to the shepherd.

Along with the thousand or two of sheep, a shepherd brings five or six donkeys or mules and the same number of working shepherd dogs with him. These animals accompany the flock for the entire transhumance, and each has a job. The donkeys are used to carry newly born lambs, still too weak and young to walk so far alone. The dogs keep the flock cohesive, and are essential when crossing highways, busy streets, and through towns to prevent the sheep from straying, and to keep them moving at a decent clip.

Equines start to really feel their oats as the days lengthen, right around Imbolc. Mares will have their first heat period, and impassioned stallions will not fail to rise to the occasion, in all senses of the phrase. The donkeys that accompany the shepherds' flocks are no exception; they, too, like to have a little fun.

One weekday afternoon I was driving my daughter home from school. We were coming up a hill toward the entrance to a bicycle path bordered on both sides by pastures, when my daughter suddenly squealed in glee.

"Wild donkeys!! Look!"

I slowed, and then stopped the car, as we watched three, then four, then five, six, donkeys of varying sizes run out from the bike path onto the road, and, shaking their heads and snorting, trot merrily up hill. I drove on slowly, wondering where their flock was, but it was nowhere to be seen. I suppose they had lingered behind, enjoying the sunshine and the grass.

The next morning, on horseback, I unexpectedly came upon the shepherd and his flock, and all the donkeys, in a field. There was no way for me to get home but to creep along the edges of the flock, making my way into the woods.

"Hey!" the shepherd yelled at me. "Is that a mare you're riding?"

I turned in the saddle and looked at him.

"No, he's a gelding!" I called out.

"Good. Because I have a donkey stallion here."

He gestured toward a tall, dark, good-looking donkey, one leg hobbled to his neck with a ragged cord.

I waved and departed into the shadows of the woods.

The following day I took my mare for a ride, trying to avoid the areas where the flock had been or might be.

It was early afternoon, and the sun's warmth and light on the tree trunks was lovely. I stopped a minute, dismounted, and put my ear to a wild cherry tree's trunk, to hear the glug-glug-glug of its rising sap, like a heartbeat.

Once remounted, I noticed that my mare's ears were pricked, and she was frozen, staring. I looked where she was looking, and, to my horror, saw the tall, dark donkey stallion running, with a limp, toward us. The hobble rope didn't slow him down much. My mare's body tensed and then she sprung into a canter, and, as the donkey chased her, a gallop. I had a terrible vision of being mounted while still mounted, and I did not really want a baby mule.

Suddenly I had an idea. I pulled my mare to a halt, turned her to face the donkey, and yelled at him, "Go away!"

Understanding my alarm, my horse pinned her ears back, kicked up one front leg threateningly, and let out a mean sound to let the donkey know she wasn't interested. Rejected, the donkey turned and trotted away, back to his flock.

Although the first faint signs of nature's awakening may not always be easy to detect at Imbolc, they are there. Sometimes all one needs to do is go for a long walk in the woods, or a city park. Even if you do not run into a flock of sheep, there are many other little signs of impending spring that will reveal themselves to you.

Cosmic Sway

April Elliott Kent

THE IMBOLC SEASON OF purification, fertility, and light begins on a Last Quarter Moon in Scorpio, with the Sun square Mars in Scorpio and Venus conjoined Pluto. We are emerging from winter's darkness to give birth to a new spirit within ourselves, and these are the final stages of labor.

The first of this year's eclipse seasons gets underway with a Solar Eclipse in Pisces on March 8. Eclipses are astrological symbols of dramatic change; falling this year in Virgo and Pisces, they mean many of us are experiencing critical transitions related to our work, health, spirituality, and the way we handle the practical affairs of our daily lives.

It's particularly important, then, to strengthen and purify in order to reap the greatest benefit and renewed energy from this season of change. Here is a ritual to purify your home and spirit and to celebrate the return of energy and light.

Ritual for Purification and the Return of Light

What better or more practical rite of purification than to give your home a good scrubbing? Wash all the bedding and clean every floor.

Make a game of decluttering your closets and pantry. Sweep out the fireplace and prepare for a ritual fire.

Then, at sunset before Imbolc, gather seven red and white candles. As darkness falls, turn on every light and lamp in your house, light every candle, and kindle the fire in your stove or fireplace, saying something like, "With this healing fire, I purify my space and heart, and ready myself for the birth of new spirit."

Mars in Sagittarius

Mars enters the sign of the Archer on March 5. Since it turns retrograde in this sign on April 17, Mars will spend more time than usual in Sagittarius this year. Apart from a regression into Scorpio between May 27 and August 2, Mars will be in Sagittarius through September 26.

Mars in any sign symbolizes the quality of our physical drive, competition, and conflict. In Sagittarius, Mars wants to run free and do exactly as it pleases. Most serious conflicts during this transit are related to beliefs and opinions, particularly when one person is trying to change another's mind.

While Mars is in Sagittarius, adventure calls; travel looks tempting; even returning to school seems alluring. Sagittarius is a mutable sign, however, and the archer's arrow does not always move in a straight line nor reach its intended target. No matter; simply imagining a bigger life for yourself, and trying something new, can move you in an exciting direction.

Here is a guide to Mars's influence in each house of the horoscope. Find the houses of your chart with Sagittarius on the cusp(s) to identify where the archer will release his arrow:

1st house: Self-defense, physical exercise, emergencies
2nd house: Resources, earnings, possessions
3rd house: Communication, siblings, neighbors, learning
4th house: Home, family
5th house: Hobbies, creative and recreational activities, lovers, children

6th house: Work, health, habits and routines, diet

7th house: Close relationships, partners, enemies, collaborators

8th house: Shared resources, intimate relationships

9th house: Religion, politics, beliefs, travel, philosophy, higher education

10th house: Career, authority figures, ambition, goals

11th house: Groups, friends, networks, organizations, friendships

12th house: Rest, retreat, meditation, hidden matters

New Moon in Aquarius – Feb. 8, 2016

This a fresh, invigorating New Moon, with the Sun and Moon in exciting Aquarius in a bracing square to Mars. You're ready to get things moving, even if it means stepping on a few toes along the way! At the Capricorn New Moon, you made your resolutions for the new year; at the Aquarius New Moon, expand your vision to include your long-term goals and the legacy you hope to leave to the future. Sometimes we need to unite with other like-minded people to achieve the greatest possible good, and this is the New Moon to call those people to you. And since Aquarius is the sign of friendship, it would be nice to include wishes for your friends in your New Moon observances.

Full Moon in Virgo – Feb. 22, 2016

This Full Moon in Virgo, with the Pisces Sun conjoined Neptune, demands we find a better balance between the intuitive, relaxed energy of Pisces and the organized, rational consciousness of Virgo. This is a relatively quiet lunation, the calm before the highly charged eclipse season that begins at the next New Moon. The Sun is building to a square aspect to Saturn, and this makes energy measured, even a bit low. This is a period where perseverance is required, especially when it feels as though you're not getting anywhere. After the square is exact on March 5, a tremendous amount of energy will be released, leading into the New Moon Solar Eclipse.

New Moon/Solar Eclipse in Pisces – March 8, 2016

The New Moon Solar Eclipse at 18.55 Pisces is exactly opposed Jupiter and square Saturn. There is tremendous conflict between the desire to take a chance and do more with your life, and the practical considerations that have to be addressed in order to make that happen.

Eclipses carry messages throughout your life, crossing over the same points in your birth chart every nineteen years and opposing them every nine and a half years. Previous eclipses at the same degree as this Solar Eclipse occurred on March 9, 1997; September 7, 2006; September 11, 2007; and September 13, 2015. If significant events happened in your life then, you now have another opportunity to complete any unfinished business related to those matters.

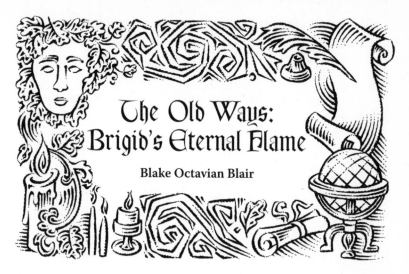

The Old Ways: Brigid's Eternal Flame

Blake Octavian Blair

THE SABBAT OF IMBOLC is inexorably linked to fire. One might argue that among modern Pagans of a wide variety of paths, the holiday is also synonymous with the stories and magick of the Celtic goddess Brigid, who is almost inexorably linked with this season and with fire. Fire, Imbolc, and Brigid are a seasonal trifecta. While being a goddess of healing, poetry, music, smithcraft, and motherhood, Brigid is likely most universally noted as a goddess of fire. So much so that the practice of tending her eternal flame carries through to modern day, bringing people together from diverse spiritual lineages and points of view in shared practice.

Brigid has dedicated followers from both the Pagan and Christian ends of the spectrum. It is well known that the Goddess Brigid was transformed into or incorporated as a saint into the Christian milieu. It is the opinion of many that Brigid's foothold on the culture of the Celts was so strong and ingrained that the Catholic Church realized that it would be impossible to purge her from the culture's spiritual practices. Therefore, she was lightly cloaked and framed as St. Brigit of Kildare. A great number of her modern-day devotees even admit that St. Brigit and the goddess Brigid are essentially one and the same—differing in semantics alone.

Whether framed as a goddess or a saint, Brigid's actions were magickal through and through. Her main shrine is considered to be in Kildare, Ireland, although exactly which Brigid shrine is the main one, and which was the original site of the eternal flame, is debatable and varies from source to source. Many claim the main square in Kildare as the site; others claim the fire pit at St. Brigid's Cathedral in Kildare. The flame was tended for literally centuries, first by pre-Christian priestesses and later on, after Christianity's spread, by Brigidine nuns as well. Brigid was associated with miracles that affected things within the daily lives of the people. A typical account of such a miracle involves a young child who gives away his family's entire supply of butter or other food and their supply is magickally restocked by a blessing from Brigid. It is said by many that flowers bloomed in the footsteps of Brigid, that livestock never starved, miraculous healings occurred, and as mentioned, depleted foodstocks were replenished. Brigid was admittedly (even by those newer followers of the Christian variety) overtly more magickal in nature than many garden-variety saints... almost goddesslike!

Because Brigid touched so many areas of so many people's lives through her magickal miracles the tending of her eternal flame was and we will learn it still is an act of devotion in honor of all she did for the people.

The concept of tending the hearth flame and its spirit reaches across cultures. The similarities of the practices are often readily visible despite the varying theological details and ritual practices from culture to culture—from the tending in Greco-Roman traditions of the hearth fire of Vesta and Hestia to the tending of sacred fires in shamanic cultures the world over. However, the tending of Brigid's eternal flame has some traditions, practices, and details specific and special unto itself. For example, the traditional cycle of tending to Brigid's flame consists of a cycle of twenty days. For nineteen days, individuals are assigned a shift of a full day to tend the flame. The day's shift runs from sundown to sundown, as the traditional Celtic day does. The twentieth day, Brigid traditionally tends to herself.

While many people throughout time have honored Brigid as a goddess of hearth and home, historical accounts often attribute the official tending of her flame to priestesses and nuns (at least as far as "official" records are concerned). However, I think it'd be pretty safe to say that the eternal flame was tended to and honored in more places by more people than we know. Today, there are a few different organizations dedicated to keeping the practice of tending to the eternal flame alive. Those persons that tend to her flame are often referred to as "flamekeepers." The Ord Brighideach International is one such organization dedicated to organizing and coordinating modern day flamekeepers.

Modern-day flamekeepers may well indeed include nuns and priestesses, however, they include people from a wide variety of other backgrounds, roles, and vocations. Most modern organizations, including Ord Brighideach International, encourage persons of all backgrounds who are dedicated to their devotion of Brigid and carrying out her work in any of its myriad of forms to consider tending her eternal flame. Some organizations, like Ord Brighideach, welcome flamekeepers regardless of gender while others restrict membership to women, such as Daughters of the Flame. Like all practices and traditions, while many things stay the same, other parts evolve over time. No longer is Brigid's eternal flame one specific physical flame but many. Modern flamekeepers can choose to light a flame that they dedicate and tend as the eternal flame for their twenty-four hour shift. It can be a candle, an oil lamp, their fireplace, etc. Others actually use the Kildare flame, which has been passed from candle to candle to them directly. Some flamekeepers are solo independent agents and choose a day each month on their own. Other flamekeepers choose to join an order or organization that coordinates "cells" or groups of flamekeepers in the traditional twenty-day cycles. As is the case with much of modern spirituality, flamekeeping practitioners are afforded great autonomy and a number of choices in how to carry out their devotions.

᭟

Fire is magickal, of that there is no doubt. It is used for banishment, manifestation, cleansing, transformation, creation, destruction, inspiration, and divination. Many of its uses blur and blend the lines between the mundane and the magickal. Its purpose can be shifted with intent and not surprisingly, Brigid—goddess of fire—is also known as a shapeshifter. Philosophically we can all relate to the plurality of Brigid's specialties and the uses of fire. We all wear many hats in life, and whether we are expressing our self through poetry or perhaps musically, parenting children, cooking dinner on our hearth, creating or smithing with our hands, or scrying in the flickering flame of a candle, we too have a place in the honoring of Brigid's Eternal Flame.

Bibliography

"Daughters of the Flame." *Obsidian Magazine.* Accessed September 4, 2014 http://www.obsidianmagazine.com/DaughtersoftheFlame/.

Ord Brighideach International. Accessed June 11, 2014. http://www.ordbrighideach.org/.

Illes, Judika. *The Element Encyclopedia of Witchcraft: The Complete A-Z for the Entire Magical World.* Hammersmith, London: Harper Element, 2005.

Illes, Judika. *Encyclopedia of Spirits: The Ultimate Guide to the Magic of Fairies, Genies, Demons, Ghosts, Gods & Goddesses.* New York: Harper One, 2009.

K, Amber, and Azreal, Arynn K. *Candlemas: Feast of Flames.* St. Paul, MN: Llewellyn Publications, 2001.

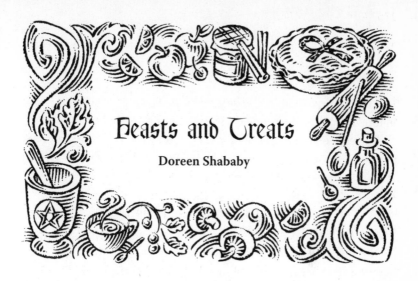

Feasts and Treats

Doreen Shababy

IMBOLC BRINGS TO MIND sparse landscapes waiting on the edge of potential. We can smell it in the air, hear it in the wind. We see it in the lengthening daylight hours, and it welcomes us home to simple foods that satisfy something at the root of change, something to keep our inner flame burning. This menu reflects the unpretentious mood of late winter and is easy to prepare—even the cheesecake.

Slow Cooker Italian Beef

A hearty pot roast to nourish and sustain. As a hedgewitch, I like to think of my clean sweep in terms of an early spring cleaning, so I need food waiting for me when I am finished working... in case I get lost in my work and forget to cook!

Prep time: 10 minutes
Cook time: 8–10 hours in a slow cooker
Serves: 6 (with leftovers!)

4-pound beef rump roast
Seasoned flour for dredging (use plenty of black pepper)
1 small onion, peeled and quartered
2 cloves garlic, peeled
1 celery rib, cut into pieces

2 ounces salt pork (or pancetta), cubed
1 onion, sliced
Soy sauce

Lightly flour roast. Place the quartered onion, garlic, celery, and pork in food processor or blender and grind until smooth. Rub onto roast.

Place sliced onion in slow cooker, and shake a little soy sauce over to season. Place roast on top of onion. Cover and cook on low for 8 to 10 hours. Slice thinly to serve.

Baked Polenta with Pesto

I won't be instructing you on how to make polenta from scratch, not because it's difficult, but because it's somewhat time-consuming with the stirring and chilling, and then the slicing and baking. Sometimes convenience food is in order! What we're after here are the crispy, golden slices of earthy simplicity garnished with a slather of pesto. It's way more than fried mush, and a great side to any type of roasted meat.

Prep time: 5 minutes
Cook time: 20–30 minutes
Serves: 4

1 roll (tube) ready-made polenta, organic if possible
Olive oil pan spray
1 carton prepared basil pesto

Spray a large baking sheet with olive oil. Preheat oven to 425 degrees F. Remove polenta from sleeve and slice about ¾-inch thick (too thin will dry out, too thick will not crisp up as nicely). Place slices on prepared baking sheet and lightly spray with oil. Place in hot oven for about 20 minutes or till edges start to brown, then flip the slices over. Turn oven down to 350 degrees F, and when browned to your liking (or according to package directions) remove from oven. Serve with pesto.

Ricotta Cheesecake

This fabulous full moon of a cake (which needs to be prepared several hours or the day before serving) is not dense like New York–style, but tall and rustic-looking and just sweet enough. Perfect for watching baby lambs frolic in a clover-studded meadow.

Prep time: 10 minutes
Cook time: 70–80 minutes (and chill overnight)
Serves: 8–10

2 15-ounce containers whole milk ricotta
1 tablespoon soft butter
¼ cup plain dry breadcrumbs
1 tablespoon sugar
2 8-ounce packages cream cheese, room temperature
2 eggs
¾ cup sugar
2 tablespoons cookie crumbs (plain ones such as shortbread)
1 tablespoon fresh lemon juice
Zest of 1 lemon
2 teaspoons vanilla extract
Pinch salt
Powdered sugar for dusting

Set ricotta in a mesh sieve over a bowl and drain for 30 minutes.

Arrange to bake on lower rack in oven and set at 350 degrees F. Grease an 8-inch springform pan with butter. Mix breadcrumbs and sugar, and sprinkle over the buttered pan to cover.

Place drained ricotta in a food processor or large bowl of a mixer. Purée for several seconds, then scrape down the sides. Add cream cheese, purée, and scrape down sides. Add remaining ingredients except powdered sugar, then purée until smooth, about 30 seconds. Pour into prepared pan.

Bake until golden brown and just beginning to set, 70 to 80 minutes. Remove pan to a rack and let cake cool; it will fall slightly. Refrigerate uncovered for 3 hours, then cover and chill overnight.

When ready to dish, carefully run a warm knife around edges and open the sides of the pan. Dust with powdered sugar, then cut into wedges to serve.

Anisette Hot Coffee

This drink—with its intriguing, bitter flavor—goes nicely with the cheesecake. Coffee is not the bad guy it was once considered, in moderation that is, and I am amazed at the people who can drink it in the evening and still go right to sleep. That wouldn't be me, and that's why they make decaf.

Prep time: 5 minutes
Cook time: 10 minutes or so, depending on coffeemaker
Serves: 6–8 (depending on your coffeepot)

1 pot of hot coffee, brewed in your usual way
1 ounce anisette liqueur for each imbiber

Pour coffee into appropriate mugs (be sure your demitasse can hold both the liquor *and* the coffee!). Add anisette and drink black, no cream.

If you wish to leave out the liquor, simply add a level teaspoon bruised aniseed to your ground coffee and brew, sweetening at the table. Very nice!

Crafty Crafts

Tess Whitehurst

THE HUSTLE AND BUSTLE of the holiday season has slowed to a halt, yet the fresh warmth and expansion of spring has not yet arrived. In the words of the illustrious author and Garden witch Ellen Dugan, "At the coldest time of the year, when connecting outdoors with nature would be uncomfortable or risky due to extreme cold for many of us, your best option [at Imbolc] is to bunker inside your warm, comfortable home." Indeed, just as the earth rests and renews in preparation for its young fresh greenery to burst forth in all its splendor, now is the time to get the most out of these final days of winter: to relax, sleep deep, and shore up your energy for the promise of the scintillating springtime that's just around the bend.

Sleep and relaxation, after all, are magical things, and important prerequisites to living our beauty, as well as to sustaining the vital health that nourishes our intentions, happiness, and spiritual power. What's more, our dreams hold important keys to our mental health and emotional well-being. When we honor them and work with them consciously, they can help us heal from the past, enjoy the present, and make the most of our future. (All of this is very much in alignment with that which the Goddess Brighid, who is honored at Imbolc, holds dear: intuition, inner illumination, and holistic vitality.)

109

Herbal Dream Pillow

This magical, herbal dream pillow will help you soothe stress, rest well, sleep deeply, restore your strength, and remember your dreams, all while healing your mind, body, spirit, and emotions during your nightly adventures.

The following is a summary of the relevant magical properties of each herb it contains:

Lavender is the quintessence of relaxation, inner equilibrium, joy, and holistic well-being. It relieves stress, balances the emotions, alleviates headaches, and supports restful sleep.

Mugwort is the go-to dream herb for many magical practitioners. It promotes vivid, lucid healing and/or prophetic dreams while

opening up the third eye (the chakra and psychic portal at the center of the forehead) and enhancing intuition.

Patchouli is sensual and grounding. It helps you get out of your head so that you can connect with the cozy comfort of being curled up in a warm bed. With a scent and vibration that's very in alignment with the earthly soil (the cornerstone of magical power), it also helps recharge your magical batteries. This, of course, can be especially helpful after being cooped up indoors for the winter.

Linden and **passionflower** are extremely soothing. They soften hard edges and help one drift peacefully into a deep and restful sleep.

Time to complete: 1 hour or less (not counting prewash time)
Cost: $8.00 to $10.00 (or more if you don't already have basic sewing supplies)

Supplies

One piece of paper or tissue paper
Paper scissors
Fabric scissors
Pins
¼ yard flannel in a print and/or color that feels very soothing and restful to you (Optional: ¼ yard of another color print of flannel)
Needle and thread
1 cup dried lavender blossoms
½ cup dried mugwort
2 tablespoons dried linden flowers
1 tablespoon dried patchouli
1 tablespoon dried passionflower
(Note: Instead of the above combination, just use 1¾ cup lavender if you prefer simpler or less earthy scents)
A large bowl
An iron

Instructions: First, wash and dry the flannel. Using the paper, create the pattern by cutting a 10 by 4 ½-inch rectangle.

Fold the flannel so that right sides are together (or, if you're using two pieces of fabric, place the right sides together).

Pin the fabric to the pattern and cut.

Remove pattern and pins, and leaving the fabric pieces with right sides together, pin them to each other.

Sew the long edges of the rectangle, leaving a ¼-inch seam allowance. Remove pins and turn right-side out.

Fold one of the open ends of the pillow about ¼ inch inward, hiding the rough edges. Using the iron, press them this way, then pin them together and sew. After sewing, remove the pins.

Mix all the herbs together in the bowl. If there's sunlight outside, take them outside or hold them by a sunny window and bathe them in the light to bless and activate them. (Otherwise, just visualize them being filled and surrounded by very bright white light.) Ask the Goddess Brighid to bless them and to empower them with the purpose of restful sleep, intuitive activation, and dreams that are both healing and illuminating.

Using a spoon, or whatever way is easiest for you, stuff the pillow with the herbs. (It shouldn't be too full; it should be able to rest on your eyes comfortably.) Then press the open edge closed as you did on the other side. Pin together and sew. Remove the pins.

Bless and Consecrate Your Dream Pillow

Create a simple altar to Brighid, perhaps with an image of her and a candle. You might also add items that represent or hold the energy of restful sleep, such as an amethyst crystal, some chamomile tea, or an image of the moon and stars. Light the candle. Hold the dream pillow in both hands and say:

> *Goddess of illumination, Lady of light,*
> *Please bless me with relaxation, prophetic dreams, and psychic insight.*
> *Help me shore up my strength and magical might,*
> *By sleeping soundly and deeply throughout the night.*
> *With honor and thanks a plenty for thee,*

I consecrate this dream pillow,
And so mote it be.

Hold the dream pillow a little distance over the candle, letting it be lightly warmed (but not burned!). Then, hold it to your brow, your heart, and your belly, setting the intention to nourish yourself with clean and comfortable bedding, a peaceful and clutter-free sleep environment, and plenty of time for a good night's sleep.

How to Use Your Dream Pillow

If you sleep on your back, you can rest the pillow over your eyes. This will help block out light while supporting relaxation with aromatherapy and magical energy. Otherwise, you can just sleep with in near your head so that you can still inhale its peaceful scent and benefit from its vibes. Additionally, you might consider using it while meditating on your back or taking a small nap break any time during the day. I've also found that resting with it over the eyes can help alleviate headaches.

For Further Reading

Dugan, Ellen. *Seasons of Witchery: Celebrating the Sabbats with the Garden Witch.* Woodbury, MN: Llewellyn, 2012.

Budapest, Z. *The Goddess in the Office: A Personal Energy Guide for the Spiritual Warrior of Work.* San Francisco, CA: HarperSanFrancisco, 1993.

All One Family: Secrets for Imbolc

Linda Raedisch

WHEN MY DAUGHTER MIKA was little, I found it appropriate to read English translations of Chinese and Japanese nursery rhymes and to sing the handful of German children's songs I remembered from my childhood. This seemed appropriate for a Chinese-German-American child with a Japanese name—the name having been her teenaged, manga-loving sister's idea. I also made a point of reading and reciting the Mother Goose rhymes to her. I can't say I ever *loved* Mother Goose—not the way I loved *Bambi* or *Monika Beissner's Fantastic Toys*—but, like the Bible, alcohol, and dairy products, Mother Goose is one of the cornerstones of Western Civilization, and if we stop reciting them to our children, they're going to fade away.

A few years ago, I was one of the few non-Asian guests at a baby shower. Our hostess had never attended an American baby shower but threw herself into the preparations nevertheless, printing out a list of party game suggestions, including, "Guess that Mother Goose Rhyme." The results were mixed, to say the least. While I, I'm happy to say, nailed every question, the other guests were baffled by the rhymes, even though they were fluent in English, several even having attended English-language boarding schools. They knew the lullabies of their own home countries, of course, but they did not know Mother Goose.

Nursery rhymes are not part of the school curriculum; they're fragments of folk history that must be passed on to the very young if they are to be passed on at all. They hold our interest for a very brief spell, after which we dismiss them as nonsense. But Mother Goose, as it turns out, is not just a spinner of silly rhymes; she is also an inveterate keeper of secrets.

Now a staple of American childhood, many of our Mother Goose rhymes originated in England, which is why there are so many rhymes about sheep. In honor of Imbolc, aka *Ewemeolc*, "ewe's milk" in Old English, I thought I'd interview the old girl herself.

Tea with Mother Goose

She arrives, as expected, on the back of an overlarge goose, which she insists on bringing inside despite my suggestion that she hitch it to the lamppost in the front yard. She's an imposing woman of a certain age, dressed in a black, high-crowned hat, white ruff, shawl and sweeping skirt. Her goose, a gander if I'm not mistaken, proceeds to explore the house, tugging at the down pillows and engaging in hissing matches with my cat. It's not until I have the idea of filling up the bathtub for him to paddle around in that Mother Goose and I are able to sit down to a quiet cup of tea.

"So," I begin, "what's the story behind 'Baa Baa Black Sheep'?"

"It's about taxation."

"Well, that's not very exciting."

Mother Goose shrugs, spooning sugar into her tea.

"What about 'All the Pretty Horses'? In America we have just the first verse, but in England, there's a second verse about a little lamb getting its eyes pecked out. That's a horrible thing to sing to a baby, don't you think?"

"Life wasn't always pretty in those days."

"I see." *I can hear the goose down the hall, splashing furiously and knocking all the shampoo bottles into the tub.* "What about 'Ring *around the Rosy'? Can you settle the question once and for all if it's really about the Black Death?"*

"That's a song and dance, not a rhyme. Not my area of expertise. These are very strange biscuits."

"They're Oreos. Okay then, what about 'London Bridge'? Is it true it's an echo of a ritual in which a child was chosen to be sacrificed and buried at the foot of a bridge? Because, you know, human bones have been found—"

"Again: a song and dance. I thought you wanted to talk about sheep."

"Yes, but this is for the Sabbats Almanac, *so I'm trying to hit on subjects that might be of interest to witches."*

"You a witch? Don't make me laugh!"

"How do you know I'm not a witch?"

"Where's your pointy hat? Where's your broomstick? All you've got is that nasty little cat. If you're a witch, then I'm the Queen of Sheba." She snorts and dumps more sugar in her tea.

"Actually, it's been suggested that there might be some relationship between you and the Queen of Sheba. She liked to keep her feet hidden under her skirts, just like you're doing now. I've also heard that the reason you're called Mother Goose is not because you ride a goose but because you have a goose's foot. And if you ask me, you look plenty witchy yourself."

"Who were you expecting: Little Bo Peep?"

"How about Little Bo Peep? Does she ever find her sheep?"

"Yes, but they've had their tails cut off and hung up to dry."

"Wow. Could they have been Mongolian fat-tail sheep? You know, the ones with the really fatty tails that you could cut pieces from if you were really starving?"

"In England?" Mother Goose shoots me a disparaging look from under the broad brim of her hat. She takes a last, noisy slurp of her tea.

"Another Oreo?" I say weakly.

She wrinkles her nose. "Rather have another cup of tea."

"The pot's empty."

"Did you tickle it?"

"Yes, I did. And I'm afraid that's all we have time for anyway. Thank you so much for coming. Please don't forget the goose on your way out."

To brush up on your Mother Goose rhymes, just head to the 398.8 shelf in the children's room of your local library. There are plenty of editions to choose from. To plumb the depths of these deceptively innocent little verses, I recommend Chris Roberts' book, *Heavy Words Lightly Thrown: The Reason Behind the Rhyme.* If you want to sample a little something from the East Asian nursery, my favorites are *The Prancing Pony: Nursery Rhymes from Japan* by Charlotte B. DeForest and Keiko Hida, and *Dragon Kites and Dragonflies: A Collection of Chinese Nursery Rhymes* by Demi. Be warned: these Asian rhymes are not all sweetness either. Take this one from *Chinese Mother Goose Rhymes* selected and edited by Robert Wyndham:

> *We keep a dog to guard the house;*
> *A pig will make a feast or two;*
> *We keep a cat to catch a mouse;*
> *But what is the use of a girl like you?*

In the long run, the success of a nursery rhyme depends not on which are prettiest or which ones the mother likes best but which rhymes the small child calls for again and again. During infancy, it's all about cadence, but when the children get a little older, they begin to appreciate that little shiver of horror that comes from hearing about cut-off tails, broken crowns, and young women imprisoned in pumpkins. Long live Mother Goose!

Imbolc Ritual: Crone to Maiden

Suzanne Ress

THIS TIME OF YEAR is amongst my favorites because, although it may still be cold and look barren outside, I can begin to sense the beginnings of new life in subtle ways, even in the scent of the air. The following Imbolc ritual mirrors the changes going on in nature through the use of symbols of rebirth, and growth, which also represent the transformation of the Crone back to the Maiden.

Around midday on February 1, one or two female coven members should go together to a riverbank or to a place where a hidden spring or stream lies underground and willow trees grow. Bring with you a strong trowel or shovel, and a small bucket or empty flowerpot, and a pair of gardening clippers.

Near the base of a great willow tree, where the earth is warmer, use your shovel or trowel to dig up just enough dirt to fill your bucket or pot about three quarters of the way.

Using your clippers, cut off some slender willow branches; one for each member of your coven, each about 12-inches long. Make sure these branches have catkins on them.

That evening, coven members should meet in a chosen location. Weather permitting, this could be outdoors under an open sky; otherwise, indoors. In any case, you should be able to safely build a small fire, so your chosen place must have a fireplace, outdoor grill or pit, or a wood-burning stove.

All participants take care to dress for the ritual in colorful, patterned clothing covered completely with a brown garment such as an overcoat, work smock, poncho, or blanket. Special jewelry may also be worn.

Items Needed
For the ritual:

5 white tealights

Willow wands, 12-inches long, fresh cut with catkins on them (one per participant)

Pitcher of fresh water

A small container holding the cooled ash from a bit of dried greenery, if possible left over from Yule (such as a sprig of evergreen from a wreath or tree, dried mistletoe, or holly). Lacking this, you may use the ash from a few sprigs of dried rosemary or several dried bay leaves.

Bucket or pot of earth

Paperwhite bulbs (*Narcissus papyraceus*)

Milk, a small amount

Athame (optional)

Drum to raise energy (optional)

Tarot deck for divination (optional)

Refreshments:

Golden ale

Seeded bread or cake

Wedge of sheep's milk cheese (pecorino, feta, or Roquefort)

Preparation

Bring the bucket or pot of earth and the willow wands in a pitcher of fresh water. Bring an odd number of paperwhite bulbs (*Narcissus papyraceus*), a little bit of milk in a tiny container, and, for refreshments, some golden ale, some seeded bread or cake, and a wedge of sheep's milk cheese such as pecorino, feta, or Roquefort. You might also bring an athame if you normally use one, a drum for raising energy, and a deck of tarot cards for divination.

Light a small wood fire and place the bucket or pot of earth safely near it to warm while you set up your altar. This fire, and any additional candle lantern lights set safely outside the circle, will be your only lighting.

Place the paperwhite bulbs, the white tealights, the container of milk, the container of ash, and the willow branches in their pitcher of water on your altar in a circular formation. Finally, place the pot of earth on the altar, in the center of the circle.

The Ritual

Begin the ritual by raising a protective shield of light around all participants, standing in a circle around the altar. Drumming and dancing or simple circling around holding hands may be used to raise energy and form the shield.

The leader, or selected participant, should form a pentagram over the pot of dirt using the athame, or an index finger in the air, and call out the quarters as they are pointed to.

When everyone is ready, the leader shall say:

Now the daylight hours increase, the sun warms tiny roots below ground back to life and growth. Now the old Crone dies and the young maiden is arising from the ash.

The ash of the dried greenery is sprinkled upon the warmed soil. The leader holds up one flower bulb in her hand, toward the east.

Into the open grave of the Crone we plant this bulb, which holds the secret of new life, and, like the phoenix, will rise from the ashes of the old.

The paperwhite bulbs are each pushed, pointed side up, into the soil. (Don't worry if they are close together; they should be fine.)

Sprinkle a few drops of milk onto the soil, and say:

We nourish you with white milk, you who are just beginning to be born—

Take the willow wands from the pitcher of water and lay them temporarily aside. Water the soil in the flowerpot well and say:

We quench your thirst with water from the magical well of Bride—

Put the wands back into the pitcher.

Now place the five tealight candles on the surface of the soil and light them.

At this point say:

We, too, are transforming, with each new season we are renewed, now changing from the old crone of winter to the fresh young maiden of Imbolc.

Everyone should now remove their outer brown layer of clothing, throwing it outside the circle, to reveal their brightly colored clothes beneath.

Let our spirits be renewed, our spirits are the life force itself— ever-enduring. Our past is dead, turned to ash, and our future lies ahead, unfurling before us like a new green bud into leaf. Like the snake, we crawl from our old skins, splendid in our new ones.

Whoever wishes may now request that a special item of jewelry be magically charged, by removing it and placing it at the center of the altar, near the tealights on the pot, and calling Brigid, goddess of metalsmiths, to bless it.

Likewise, Brigid's presence may be called upon for raising healing energies to be sent the way of those in need.

Those desiring so may request a tarot card reading from a fellow coven member, to divine the next few months' future, or the outcome of a spiritual or fertility-related question.

The protective shield of light may then be lowered, and partici-pants can enjoy a tankard of golden ale, some seedy bread or cake, and a bit of sheep's milk cheese, whilst conversing freely.

Before parting, each member of the coven shall be given a willow wand to take home. These should be put into a glass of water until its catkins open and it forms roots, at which point the green wood can be planted somewhere damp, for magical growth. The potted paperwhite bulbs will be taken home and cared for in a sunny place indoors by one of the coven members. These are to be brought to the next meeting, at Ostara, when they should be in full bloom.

Notes

Notes

Ostara

Ostara: The Blossoming Time

Elizabeth Barrette

As THE WEATHER BEGINS to warm, plants awaken from dormancy and the first blossoms open—snowdrops, witch hazel, snow crocus, and so forth. These give way to tulips, daffodils, and hyacinths in mid-spring. Later come lilacs and most of the fruit trees, although apricots are very precocious bloomers. These spring flowers appear as vivid spots of color in a landscape that is still largely drab and brown, with few green leaves to hide them. The blossoms represent the return of life and growth, so they are closely associated with Ostara and other spring holidays.

Many Ostara traditions revolve around flowers, and they play a significant role in most Ostara rituals. This holiday celebrates the awakening of the land after winter. Flowers are associated with feminine energy in general, few of them having masculine tone, and with vernal goddesses such as Kore and Eostre. Look closer and you'll see that spring flowers often correlate to Water, the element of intuition and cycles. Let's explore some of the favorites.

Ostara Flowers

The flowers most closely associated with Ostara tend to be ones that bloom in spring. Because "spring" arrives at different times based on your location, and some plants have a very wide blooming season, this set spans flowers that open from early to late spring. Tulips and apples, for instance, have a period over a month! A typical bloom order for fruit trees, based on the earliest variety of each, is: apricot, sweet cherry, peach, European plum, tart cherry, pear, apple. Ideally, for your Ostara ritual, you should use whatever is blooming in your area at that time. Choose colors or correspondences to match your ceremonial theme.

Apple blossoms—*White to pink.* Used for healing. They correspond to the element of Water. Sacred to the Goddess; used by the Bandraoi or woman-druids.

Carnation—*White to red.* Carnations are also exceptional for dyeing. Cut white carnations on long stems, put them in water with some food coloring, and the tint will show up in the petal veins; so they can be any color. They convey strength, protection, and healing. These are masculine, Fire flowers.

Cherry blossoms—*White to pink.* Use for love or divination. They correspond to the element of Water. They symbolize feminine energy and the beauty of ephemeral things.

Clover—*White to dark pink, also yellow.* Correspondences include good luck, love, protection, and success. Clover relates to the element of Air and masculine energy.

Crocus—*White to purple, also yellow.* Saffron from crocus is an ideal spice for Ostara.

Daffodils—*White to yellow.* Daffodils apply to fertility and good luck. The narcissus type is associated with self-love. They have masculine energy and a Water correspondence.

Dogwood—*White to deep pink.* A symbol of sacrifice, also associated with dogs. Good for wish magic.

Eastern redbud—*Pink.* The small tree bears masses of tiny flowers and heart-shaped leaves. The flowers represent the blood of betrayal, and the leaves a forgiving heart. Excellent for working through shame or guilt.

Forsythia—*Yellow*. The shrub bears long thin branches festooned with yellow flowers, which may be cut to make wreaths. It symbolizes anticipation.

Hyacinth—*Many colors*. A symbol of homosexual love in Greek tradition, also associated with happiness.

Iris—*All colors*. Good for purification and wisdom. Corresponds to Water and feminine energy. Sacred to Iris, the Greek goddess of rainbows.

Lilacs—*White to purple, also pale yellow*. Useful for protection. Corresponds to Water and feminine energy.

Lily of the Valley—*White*. Sacred to the Goddess, and a symbol of motherhood.

Pansies—*All colors*. They represent thoughtfulness and love. Feminine energy.

Peonies—*White to deep pink*. They stand for prosperity, honor, romance, good fortune, and beauty.

Pussy willow—*Silver to pale yellow*. Small fuzzy buds open into fluffy flowers. The stems are usually cut at the bud stage and put in a vase for display. They represent feline magic as well as spring, and willows connect to Water.

Tulips—*Many colors*. They manifest prosperity. They relate to the element of Earth and feminine energy.

Violas—*Many colors; the famous Johnny jump-ups are purple-and-yellow*. Ironically they correspond both to sex and love (flowers), and to modesty (leaves)! They relate to feminine energy and the Triple Goddess.

Violets—*White to purple, also yellow*. They bring good luck, healing, love, peace, protection, and wishes. They represent Water and feminine energy.

Witch hazel—*Yellow or red*. Threadlike flowers appear on bare branches in earliest spring. Associated with witches, with a strong magical connotation.

Making Flower Baskets

Flower baskets appear both in Ostara and Beltane celebrations. The Ostara baskets are customarily lined with grass or tissue, then filled with eggs or candy. Baskets, like other hollow objects, represent feminine power. This is especially true if they are filled with eggs or flowers, which are fertility symbols. You often see Goddess icons holding a basket of flowers for this reason. Several different types of flower baskets may be used, although some are easier to make than others.

One of the simple versions is to take any craft basket and decorate the outside with fresh, dried, or silk flowers. First remove the flower heads. Then put glue on the outside of the basket. A hot glue gun is ideal for this project because its glue sets quickly, but you do have to be careful of the hot tip. Craft glue also works. Press the flowers into the glue, working your way around the basket. After all the glue dries, the basket may be filled. Fresh flowers will only last about a day, but dried or silk ones may be reused year after year.

To make a basket for displaying fresh cut flowers, first line a sturdy basket with plastic so it can't leak. Trim a piece of florist's foam to fit inside the basket. Soak the foam in water. Put it into the basket. Trim your flower stems to the desired length. Carefully push them into the foam to make your arrangement. Pack the flowers as densely as you can so the foam doesn't show through. If necessary, you can fill a few gaps with fern leaves or florist's moss. This should keep about as long as flowers in a vase.

More ambitious is weaving your own basket, although it's still pretty easy if you are at all good with crafts. This option allows you to use either flowers with long tough stems (such as carnations or daisies) or any of the twig flowers (apple, dogwood, forsythia, pussy willow, witch hazel, etc.). Cut three long twigs and cross them to make a star shape. Tie them together in the center. Tie another twig across them and carefully begin weaving it over and under the others to make a woven circle. When your current twig gets short, add a new one alongside it and keep weaving. Once the base is as big as you want, bend the six main twig ends upward to begin making the sides of the basket. When it's as tall as you want, bend down four of the main twig ends and weave them around the rim, so that there are two opposite ends of the same twig left. Bend those toward each other and twist them together to make the handles. You can tie the loose end of each to the opposite base if necessary, or push it between the other twigs, to secure it. If there are fresh flowers on the twigs, they'll last about a day, but the twigs should dry and keep indefinitely.

Making Candied Flowers

Candied flowers are an Ostara tradition that goes back to the days when greenhouses didn't exist. With very few plants in bloom, flowers were often made of sugar frosting or tinted white chocolate in lieu of adding a candy coating to candy real flower petals. Today, there are many edible flowers spanning the rainbow, which include apple blossoms (white to pink), calendula (yellow to orange), carnations (white to red), chives (pink to lavender), clover (white to dark pink), garden peas (white to pastels), lilacs (white to purple), roses (many colors), peonies (white to red), scarlet runner beans (red), tulips (many colors), violas and pansies (any color), and violets (white to purple, or yellow). You can use the different shades for color magic, elemental correspondences, or other magical purposes.

Flowers or their petals may be candied in multiple ways. The old-fashioned method is to brush them with egg white and then sprinkle with sugar; no heat is required but you have to deal with the raw egg whites. It's also possible to make a sugar syrup, which avoids the egg whites, but then you've got the hot sugar to handle.

First pick clean, perfect flowers. Rinse them and let them air-dry. Mix together 1½ cups water and 1 cup white sugar. If you're using unflavored sugar for the sprinkling later, add ¼ teaspoon to 1 teaspoon of flavoring to the syrup (vanilla, mint extract, rosewater, etc.) at the cooking stage. Heat the sugar and water until all the sugar dissolves. Dip each flower into the liquid sugar, then set it on wax paper. Sprinkle with fine sugar until fully coated, and allow to dry. This is where you can use a flavored sugar such as cinnamon sugar or vanilla sugar for the coating.

Flower Divination

The art of divination with blossoms is called floromancy, a popular form of magic in spring celebrations such as Ostara. The type of flower found sends a message about what is relevant to you now or what may happen in the future. When working in a group, it helps to have a list of correspondences so that people can look up the meaning of their flower(s). There are various methods for practicing floromancy.

One method is walking, and it relies on potent timing as well as chance encounters. Either you count the first flower you see in spring, or you go out on Ostara morning and look for the first flower. If you're heading home and see a new flower you didn't spot on the way out, then that one counts as a second omen, which may enhance or ameliorate the first.

A very pretty method that requires some preparation involves flowers and water. Fill a large basin or a wading pool with water. Choose some flowers that float well; flat or cup-shaped ones work best, although you can float other shapes on cork if necessary. For any method that involves selecting a set of divinatory flowers, make sure to include a variety of positive and negative ones along with diverse messages. Carefully cut the stems off the blossoms. Float the flower heads on the water at one edge of the bowl. A light breeze will set them drifting. If you are indoors, you may need to use a fan to move them. The flower that reaches the far edge first is the answer; if two arrive together, their meanings are related. You can ask a question this way, or just look for general omens.

Flowers may also be drawn like any other divinatory item. You'll need to cut the stems off and put the blossoms into a large bag, basket, or other container. You may wish to enclose each flower head in a little box, twist of paper or cloth, etc., so they'll all feel the same. Then have people draw out a flower one at a time.

Here are some flowers and their divinatory meanings:

Apricot blossom—long life, durability, the body

Carnation—strength, protection, masculine energy, the God

Cherry blossom—mortality, loss, fleeting joys, "no"

Clover—happy marriage, prosperity

Daffodil—sincerity, masculine energy, the God

Daisy—happiness, the Sun

Heather—good luck, magic, "yes"

Lily—strength, innocence, memory, feminine energy, the Moon

Pansy—thoughts, intellect

Pear blossom—good fortune, "yes"

Plum blossom—sickness, take extra care with health, "no"

Primrose—new love blossoming, courage in adversity

Rose—love, healing, feminine energy, the Goddess

Snowdrop—purity, new beginnings

Violet—kindness, faith, advancement

Making flower baskets, candying flower petals, and floromancy are just a few of the activities you can do with spring blossoms. You'll see these later, incorporated into the Ostara ritual at the end of this chapter. You can also mix and match them to design your own celebrations, or use the information about the flowers to think up whole new projects. Use your imagination!

Cosmic Sway

April Elliott Kent

THE VERNAL EQUINOX ARRIVES just after midnight on March 20 (12:30 am EDT to be exact), and Ostara bursts open like a brightly colored egg. Spring is here at last, and we can barely wait to run outside and frolic like bunnies in the tall, tender grass. But the Leo Gibbous Moon whispers, "Not just yet!" The Full Moon in Libra, just a few days from now, will reveal why you have been waiting—and why this spring may require more restraint and introspection than dancing amidst the heather.

Many planets turn retrograde during this Ostara season. Retrograde periods, when planets appear to be moving backward in their orbits, are common, but it is a little unusual to have quite so many turning retrograde within one month! It suggests that a little caution is in order, since we can't see everything that's waiting just around the corner.

Retrograde periods have a bad reputation, but each planet's retrogrades are actually well-suited to certain things. When Saturn is retrograde (March 25 to August 13), switch your focus from outward achievement to inward, more heartfelt goal-setting. Mars's retrograde periods (April 17 to June 29) can be frustrating if we try to move too fast, but they also teach us about conserving our energy to tackle life's marathons as well as its sprints. Pluto retrograde (April 18 to September 26) encourages us to look within for the source of empowerment and to exercise the one real area of control available to us: control over the way we choose to look at things. And Mercury retrograde (April 28 to May 22) is an effective time to sit and download your thoughts into a journal or book, catch up on correspondence, or just sit quietly with your own thoughts.

Full Moon/Lunar Eclipse in Libra – March 23, 2016

This Full Moon at 3.17 Libra marks the last eclipse in the signs of Aries and Libra until 2023. It's the end of a year and a half cycle of adjusting to new realities in our closest relationships. When transiting Jupiter moves into Libra in September of this year, we begin to see the reward that comes from letting go of what isn't working and moving in the direction of more balanced relationships.

This Full Moon chart features a conjunction of Venus and Neptune, opposed Jupiter and square Saturn. Relationships that begin under the influence of Venus and Neptune can too often dissolve when they meet with practical reality. The ones that begin now, however, benefit not only from the idealism and optimism of Venus, Jupiter, and Neptune, but (perhaps most importantly) the practical, sensible influence of Saturn as well. These are relationships that could very likely go the distance, because they balance faith and optimism with realistic expectations.

New Moon in Aries – April 7, 2016

This powerful New Moon at 18.04 Aries is conjoined Uranus and square Pluto, planets of revolutionary change. If you have been sleepwalking through your life, this New Moon will wake you up! The Sabian symbol for the New Moon degree echoes this exhilaration: "*A magic carpet hovers over the depressing reality of everyday life in an industrial area.*" Where is your magic carpet? Look for the house in your chart where 19 degrees of Aries falls!

The romantic spirit of the last Full Moon continues, with affectionate Venus in idealistic Aries trine passionate Mars in Sagittarius. When Mars turns retrograde on April 17, though, forward movement is delayed to some extent until after June 29. If your relationship is meant to be, you will both be content to wait it out and enjoy it all the more when everything is resolved.

The Energetic New Year

The calendar tells us that the New Year begins on January 1; but our experience of the natural world tells us that the Vernal Equinox, and the Aries New Moon, are when the energy of the New Year really kicks in.

Infuse your rituals and affirmations with passion and care at this New Moon—you're planting seeds for an entire cycle of growth. Affirmations related to the Aries New Moon are deeply personal, but should generally include wishes related to:

Identity
Independence
Strength, bravery, and self defense
Ability to handle emergencies
Initiative and motivation

Putting Aries energy into the world can sometimes feel "selfish" to us. But unless we honor our own wishes and needs, we will not have a strong enough sense of self to enter into happy and rewarding collaborations with others.

Full Moon in Scorpio – April 21, 2016

After the sturm und drang of the thrilling Aries New Moon, the chart for the Full Moon in Scorpio looks relatively peaceful … other than Venus in a conjunction with Uranus and square Pluto. If you are in a relationship that has faltered, this could be a likely time to part. Venus and Uranus in combination demand absolute freedom and autonomy for each partner; the relationships that flourish under this influence are the ones that feel equal and balanced. This could also be an unstable time for finances, with sudden loss or a change in income or expenses. But it is also a good time to free ourselves from debt, unnecessary possessions, and the cycle of earning more just so we can spend more.

Rope Magic for Releasing Unhealthy Situations

If you are emotionally connected to someone, something, or a situation that is not healthy for you, the Scorpio Full Moon is the perfect time to set yourself free. At sunset before the Scorpio Full Moon, build a roaring fire. Get a thick piece of rope and tie it in the tightest possible knot. As you pull the rope tighter and tighter, visualize all of the emotions and memories that bind you to this person or situation. Envision every happy memory as well as the painful ones, in the most vivid possible detail. When you feel ready, throw the rope into the fire and watch as it burns, and address the person or situation directly, saying something like, "I release the love, pain, hate, fear, and all sentiments that bind me to you."

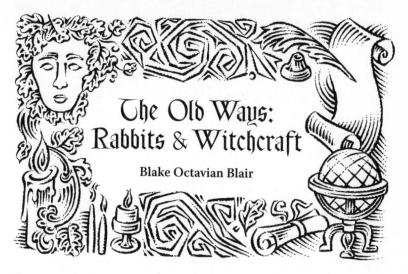

The Old Ways: Rabbits & Witchcraft

Blake Octavian Blair

OSTARA MARKS THE JOYOUS heralding of spring! The green of the land is returning and in some places, even at this somewhat early date, flowers are blooming in a fanfare of color. The Vernal Equinox is upon us! As nature begins to stir and growth and fertility is apparent all around us we are likely to notice during our increased time spent outdoors the living physical manifestation of one of the most iconic symbols of Ostara—the rabbit! The rabbit's association with Ostara is so ingrained that it is one of the symbols carried over into even the more mainstream celebrations of this holiday. Subsequently, the rabbits of Ostara have found themselves celebrated in Christianity in addition to Paganism, manifesting as the much beloved Easter Bunny. However, the rabbit simply cannot be separated from its mystical associations; it is a creature of magick through and through.

The time in which many animals are giving birth usually coincides with the arrival of the Ostara season. The rabbit itself has a longstanding association with fertility, which makes its marriage as one of the quintessential symbols of spring, a time of celebrating the earth's fertility, a perfect match. Rabbits and hares are closely tied to the Germanic goddess Eostre. Her festival coincides with the Spring

Equinox and as the tale goes, a hare was among her followers. The hare desired to give a gift to the goddess to show both his appreciation and devotion. He settled upon gifting Eostre with an egg he had come into possession of, as the egg held great value in that it varied greatly from the normal diet for hares, which consisted merely of whatever vegetation they could graze upon. However, needing a way to make the gift a unique one, he painted and decorated the egg into an elegant masterpiece. As the tale goes, the gift was so well received that both the eggs and the legendary rabbits that allegedly deliver them at her festival time each year now bear her namesake as Eostre eggs and Eostre rabbits or bunnies. In what has become a pattern with many of the sabbats, Christianity began to integrate some of the Pagan practices of seasonal celebrations into its own religious traditions; both the rabbits and the ornamental eggs were inducted into the milieu of Easter customs.

The rabbit, however, is seen to not have simply a season of power but to hold magick for the whole year long. In fact, rabbits can often give birth to up to five litters per year! Chinese lore associates the rabbit with the power of the moon, and it is one of the twelve animals of the Chinese Zodiac. People of the Rabbit or Hare sign are seen to be perceptive, energy sensitive, emotional, and artistically talented. They are said to make wonderful friends, but are also extremely cautious—mirroring the traits of their animal counterpart. The association of rabbits with the moon in Chinese astrology is syncretic with the rabbit's ties to the divine feminine as in the tale of Eostre and the hare—further affirming the associations of the rabbit with the qualities of intuition, sensitivity, and creativity. Furthermore, the Chinese also view the rabbit as an animal associated with witchcraft and alchemy and as the creator of an alleged elixir of immortality!

The "Charmed" Rabbit's Foot?

However, not all rabbit magick is so pleasant for the rabbit—even if it has found its way into mainstream popular culture. One example is the lucky charm of the rabbit's foot. Its actual history and origins are a bit murky. There are various (and often contradictory) accounts of what its original intent and use was, as well as what culture was its original creator. One popular origin story is that its genesis was as a protection against witchcraft in Britain. Ironically, it has become synonymous as a magickal charm; its use was widely adopted by African American conjure workers, and it remains a staple of modern conjure workers of diverse backgrounds through to the present. Who definitively had the concept in use first is up for debate. Some say the charm originated within the conjure traditions. However, we do know that it is used for myriad magickal goals, with the most common being general good luck, money, and success, and as a gambler's charm. It has also been put to use—perhaps logically so given the rabbit's ability for rapid proliferation—as a fertility charm.

Most of the modern rabbit's foot charms available are mounted on a ring so that it can be used as a keychain or attached to a coat, purse, or perhaps a mojo bag. The majority of mass-produced rabbit's foot charms today are made from the feet of rabbits bred en masse for the meat and fur industries. Also, if you choose to buy one, know that many are also made from completely synthetic materials. Some of them appear so similar to an actual foot that it is hard to decipher their synthetic or natural status while others are quite obvious. However, you will rarely find a label declaring which it is. For many individuals, the ethics revolving around buying the authentic severed foot of a deceased rabbit from such origins are questionable; many also feel there is little magickal value to the synthetic foot and opt for alternative charms.

One of the darker bits of lore associated with the rabbit's foot charm draws upon the rabbit's associations with witchcraft. Rabbits have long been held in magickal lore as one of the classic animals a witch could shapeshift into. This led to the theory that cutting off the foot of a rabbit could prevent it from shapeshifting back into a witch, effectively killing the alleged witch along with the rabbit. The charm served then not only as a protective talisman but additionally as a sort of trophy for murdering the alleged witch.

Luckily for both us and the rabbits, there are many other traditional ways to integrate a little rabbit magick into our lives. In keeping with the lore of a rabbit's food being lucky, it also brings good luck to stroke and pet the foot of a live rabbit or hare as well! The hair of rabbits is considered to be a powerful magickal object. A rabbit hair added to a spell bag, bottle, or other magickal mixture is said to increase one's ability for travel on the astral planes and to sharpen divination skills. It is also said in lore that to see live rabbits upon your land is a blessing from one of the various goddesses that rabbits are associated with, for abundance, fertility, or even protection. While you may feel at odds with the rabbits helping themselves to plants in your garden, with the insight of their blessings, perhaps it is best to find a nonviolent way to address that problem so that things end well for both you and your furry friends.

As you are enjoying the arrival of Ostara and all the beauty and magick that spring has to offer, don't forget to add a little rabbit magick to your celebrations! After all, utilizing the energy of this classic creature could put your spellworking ahead by a hare!

Bibliography

Andrews, Ted. *Animal Speak: The Spiritual & Magical Powers of Creatures Great & Small.* St. Paul, MN: Llewellyn Publications, 1993.

Illes, Judika. *The Element Encyclopedia of Witchcraft: The Complete A-Z for the Entire Magical World.* Hammersmith, London: Harper Element, 2005.

McCoy, Edain. Ostara: *Customs, Spells & Rituals for the Rites of Spring.* St. Paul, MN: Llewellyn Publications, 2003.

New World Encyclopedia. "Rabbit's Foot," accessed June 14, 2014, http://www.newworldencyclopedia.org/entry/Rabbit's_foot.

Wu, Shelly. *Chinese Astrology: Exploring the Eastern Zodiac.* Franklin Lakes, NJ: New Page Books, 2005.

Yronwode, Catherine. *HooDoo Herb and Root Magic: A Materia Magica of African-American Conjure.* Forestville, CA: Lucky Mojo Curio Company, 2002.

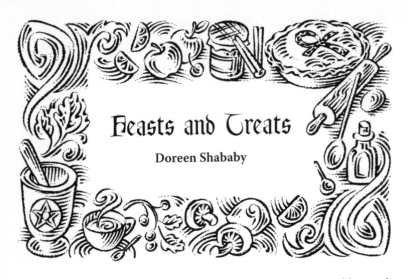

Feasts and Treats

Doreen Shababy

OSTARA MAKES ME FEEL young and enthusiastic—in an older, mellower sort of way. It makes me aware of the burgeoning life force that is so apparent everywhere I look. Daffodils and hyacinths emerge with vigor. The first tiny leaves of wild edibles present themselves, a prelude to their cultivated cousins. It is a time of gathering together after winter's seclusion, a time to breathe in the sweet air of spring, and revel in friendships new and perennial.

Hashbrown Casserole
with Sausage and Three Cheeses

You can trade out any number of ingredients in this casserole for variety, such as adding bell pepper or a different type of sausage or using frozen potatoes or even different cheeses. This recipe works well because it feeds a crowd without anchoring you to the stove schlepping out individual omelets. I love breakfast food no matter what time of day, but for the Spring Equinox celebration, this seems perfect to me. Just so you know, this is not a low-calorie dish.

Prep time: 20 minutes
Cook time: 45 minutes
Serves: 8

4 cups shredded cooked potatoes (Note: Cook and shred the potatoes the day before and refrigerate overnight.)

1 medium onion, chopped

1 tablespoon butter, plus extra for pan

2 cups milk

10 eggs

Dash nutmeg

1 teaspoon salt

1 teaspoon black pepper

2 tablespoons prepared Dijon mustard

1 pound breakfast sausage, well-browned and drained

8 slices French bread, torn roughly into 1-inch pieces

1 cup shredded cheddar cheese (about 4 ounces)

1 cup shredded Parmesan cheese

2 cups shredded Monterey jack cheese

Butter a 9 × 13-inch pan with butter and set aside. Preheat oven to 350 degrees F. In a small skillet, sauté onion in butter until translucent, and toss with shredded potatoes.

In a large mixing bowl, beat milk and eggs together with seasonings and mustard.

To assemble in prepared pan, first layer potatoes and onions, next the bread, the browned sausage, the milk-egg mixture, then most of the cheese. Bake for about 40 minutes or until mostly set, then sprinkle with remaining cheese just long enough to melt. Serve hot from the oven.

Asparagus and Black Bean Salad

While I wouldn't usually consider combining asparagus with any type of cooked dry bean, this beautiful and unique salad certainly turned my head when circle sister Jan served it for the feasting. I have wanted to share it with others ever since.

Prep time: 15 minutes working time, plus 4 hours chill time
Cook time: About 10 minutes for the asparagus
Serves: 6

1 pound fresh asparagus, trimmed and cut into 1-inch pieces
¼ cup olive oil
2 tablespoons apple cider vinegar
½ teaspoon cumin seed, crushed
½ teaspoon salt, or to taste
Black pepper to taste
1 16-ounce can black beans, drained and well rinsed
1 red bell pepper, cut small
1 tablespoon minced sweet onion
1 tablespoon chopped fresh cilantro

Steam asparagus until just done, drain, and set aside. In another bowl, combine olive oil, vinegar, cumin, salt, and pepper, whisking to blend. Stir in the beans. Gently mix in the asparagus along with the pepper and onion, and then finally the cilantro. Refrigerate for at least 4 hours before serving.

Lemon Dessert Bread

I have a whole stack of lemony dessert recipes, so making me pick one for the Ostara feast is like asking me what kind of chocolate I like—I really love lemons. And they always make me feel "sunshiny." I think this sweet lemon bread will make you feel that way too.

Prep time: 15 minutes, plus 2 hours for cooling
Cook time: 1 hour
Serves: 6–8

1½ cups all-purpose flour
½ cup almond meal (pre-ground or grind your own)
1 teaspoon baking powder
½ teaspoon salt
½ cup butter, room temperature
¾ cup natural sugar
2 eggs
½ cup milk
1 teaspoon lemon flavoring

For the syrup:

¼ cup sugar

3 tablespoons fresh lemon juice

1 teaspoon lemon zest

Grease and flour a loaf pan and preheat oven to 350 degrees F. Mix the flour, almond meal, baking powder, and salt in a bowl; set aside.

In a large bowl, beat the butter and sugar until soft. Blend in the eggs one at a time, then stir in the milk and flavoring. Add the dry ingredients to the moist ingredients, blending well. Spread evenly in a prepared pan. Bake about 1 hour or until done.

While bread is baking, make the syrup, making sure the sugar is well dissolved in the lemon juice. (I would say to use powdered sugar, but most of it has cornstarch added, which we don't want here.)

When bread is done remove from oven and, using a skewer, poke holes all over the loaf while still in the pan, then pour the syrup over all, sprinkling with lemon zest. Cool in pan 15 minutes, then remove to wire rack to cool completely before serving.

Fruity Citrus Floats

All the kids will like this fruity delight, and why not let them dish it up? It's their celebration too.

Prep time: 10 minutes

Serves: 6

4 cups orange juice

1 cup grapefruit juice

1 cup pineapple juice

1 tray ice cubes

1 pint raspberry sorbet

Mix all the juices in a large pitcher and stir in a tray of ice cubes. To serve, pour some juice into a tall glass then top with a scoop of sorbet, remembering to hand everyone a straw and a long-handled spoon. Let the games begin!

Crafty Crafts

Tess Whitehurst

FOR MAGICAL FOLK EVERYWHERE, springtime isn't just associated with cleaning the physical home, but also with clearing the space energetically: moving old, stuck energy out and calling fresh, sparkling energy in. Of course, springtime is also associated with faeries! As a fun fusion of both these associations, it feels so right this time of year to clear the space with a small, homemade, faerie-like broom tied with fresh flowers and herbs and tinkling with tiny bells.

Spring Cleaning Faerie Broom

Indeed, according to author Deborah Blake in *The Witch's Broom*, "Early Celtic pagans connected brooms with faeries." Feel this connection come alive, first as you construct the broom, and then again when you use it in a ritual.

Time to complete: One hour or less

Cost: $10.00 to 15.00

Supplies

A ting ting bunch (a type of dried, curly, reedlike grass available at floral supply and craft stores)

Twig branches (from outside or a craft store)

A bundle of jute twine

A string of tiny bells (available at Asian import stores, or make your own with bells from a craft store)

Ribbons, lace, and/or trim (this is a good opportunity to use up odds and ends)

Optional: other decorative items such as strings of crystals and beads

A few fresh flowers and sprigs of herbs (fresh picked or store bought)

Optional: a hot glue gun and hot glue

If it's sunny outside, cleanse and bless the ting ting and twigs by holding them in sunlight and saying a quick prayer or invocation, such as:

Lugh, Celtic God of light, healing, and the sun, please cleanse and bless these ingredients with your bright positivity and power. Thank you.

Arrange the twigs among the ting ting bunch so that they help fill it out, and, with a piece of jute twine, tie it all together tightly at the place near the middle where the narrow end of the bunch begins to branch outward.

Starting at the place where you just tied the twine and moving down along the narrow half of the bunch to the end, wind more jute twine around what will now become the handle of the broom, covering the entire thing neatly and binding it together. Affix it by tying tightly at the end. (If you want, you can use the hot glue gun for this purpose.)

Also tie a bit of jute in a loop onto the end in case you want to hang your broom as a decoration.

Close to the area where you first tied the jute twine (where the full part of the bunch begins to branch out), tie the string of bells around the broom.

Embellish the broom handle by tying the ribbons (and/or lace, trim, etc.) as desired over the jute. (Again, you can use a hot glue gun, although I found that tying alone worked just fine.)

Snugly, but not so tight that you bind the ting ting and twigs more closely together, somewhat randomly wind and weave another little bit of jute through the base of the broom bristles and tie with a knot. Use this to arrange the blossoms and herbs into the broom for the purpose of springtime space clearing.

You can remove the flowers and herbs when they wilt or dry out, and refresh them as desired. Still, even without the fresh flowers and herbs, your broom can clear the space quickly and effectively, particularly if you set the clear intention and perform the blessing ritual below.

Faerie Broom Blessing Ritual

First, a caveat: are you sure you want to call on the faeries to bless your broom? Of course it *is* a faerie broom, but once you call on them they might just want to stay, and you should still be advised that some people find living with faeries a bit, well…challenging. Faeries love laughter and mischief, so they might attempt to thwart your orderly existence if they decide that you're overly serious or goal-oriented. (For example, they are notorious for hiding car keys.) On the other hand, if you're ready to go with the flow, giggle helplessly at the discord of life, and surrender your need to control and micromanage every detail, faeries can provide a generous scoop of sparkle, color, and fun. So—while I personally adore living and working with faeries—of course, the choice is yours. (Just don't say I didn't warn you!)

Just before sunrise on Ostara, take your broom outside. (It's okay if you do this with the fresh flowers and herbs tucked in, but it's also just fine if you do it without.) Face east and arrange a small offering of chocolate chips and/or berries (or crystals if you're worried about ants), along with a few walnut shells filled with beer, wine, ale, or mead.

As the sun peeks above the horizon, hold your broom toward the rising sun as you say:

Faeries now I call on you
To help clear out the old and summon the new.
At this portal betwixt the worlds,
I beckon that magic which twirls and unfurls.
May this broom be blessed, and consecrated too,
Bringing sparkling enchantment to all that I do.

(Be sure that you don't say thank you, as faeries don't understand and are unsettled by the concept of spoken words of thanks. Instead, let the offering be your gesture of appreciation.)

Bring the broom to touch your heart to align yourself with its energy. Then sweep the air around yourself powerfully. First, move in a counterclockwise circle to clear yourself, and then a clockwise circle to call in positivity and seal in positive energy and magic. In addition to providing a powerful personal clearing and blessing, this will activate the broom and further align you with its energy, while creating an additional offering to the faeries in the form of the tinkling sound of the bells.

How to Use Your Broom

As you've probably gleaned, this is not a broom for physical sweeping. Rather, like a bundle of dried sage or a mister of water and essential oils, it's a space-clearing tool. To use it, simply make powerful sweeping motions in the air while moving in a counterclockwise direction through each room and area that you'd like to clear. Pay special attention to corners and any area where you might imagine that the energy could get stuck. You can sweep a foot off of the ground, along the walls, and even up high, a foot or so away from the ceiling.

I also like to use it to quickly cleanse my ritual space before meditations, spells, and any spiritual work.

To keep your broom's energy fresh and vibrant, clear it periodically by bathing it in bright sunlight and/or smudging it with sage or incense. You can also refresh the consecration ritual by performing it again next Ostara.

For Further Reading

Blake, Deborah. *The Witch's Broom: The Craft, Lore, and Magick of Broomsticks.* Woodbury, MN: Llewellyn, 2014.

Geddess, Neil, and Alicen Geddess-Ward. *Faeriecraft: Treading the Path of Faerie Magic.* Carlsbad, CA: Hay House, 2005.

Whitehurst, Tess. *Magical Housekeeping: Simple Charms and Practical Tips for Creating a Harmonious Home.* Woodbury, MN: Llewellyn, 2010.

All One Family: Secrets for Ostara

Linda Raedisch

OSTARA IS THE TIME we start to think about spring cleaning. What, not you? In that case, I have a secret for you: cleaning is fun, and I speak as someone who has done it for a living. If you've lost the joy of cleaning, get the kids to help you. Kids love to clean. No, I don't mean "picking up;" *no one* likes to pick up. I mean real cleaning: sweeping, scrubbing, dusting, washing, mopping, and polishing.

In our school district, the third graders take a yearly field trip to the working farm of Foster Fields in Morristown, New Jersey. Their favorite activity there is doing the laundry: working the laundry stick up and down in the tub, scrubbing the little blue rags on a glass washboard, then running them all through the wringer and clipping them to the clothesline to dry. A few generations ago, you could buy toy cleaning sets for children—not the toy vacuum cleaners that don't really vacuum, but scaled-down brooms, brushes, buckets, and washboards. They were small, but they could still get the job done.

As practical as it sounds, spring cleaning is as much a ritual as hiding Easter eggs or serving up a Seder. In China and Japan, houses are swept out and scrubbed at the New Year, when it's not yet even beginning to get warm outside, but in Europe and North America, the big clean happens in spring. Why? In the old days, the maids had to wait for fair weather before they could give the house a thorough "going over," which involved carting all the furniture outdoors and taking up the carpets (which were tacked to the floor), rolling them up, hanging them on a line, and beating them with wands of woven cane. This could not be done while the family was in residence, so the townhouse maids would have to wait until they had decamped to the country house whose staff would already have taken apart and put the rooms back together before they arrived.

In even older days, the first warm days of spring meant the livestock could finally be turned out of their end of the house and back into the fields. These houses were dirt-floored affairs, full of smoke and straw and, quite often, chickens—not the sort of house that one could ever get spic-and-span, but they could at least be shoveled out and smudged with bouquets of juniper and blackthorn. (*Spic-and-span*, by the way, is a mishmash of Old English and Old Norse words meaning "nail and wood shaving" and originally referred to newness, like the scent of IKEA furniture fresh out of the box, rather than cleanness.)

Of course, the laundry couldn't wait for spring; that had to be done weekly, less often if you were well-to-do and had more clothes. Few household chores are as mystical as laundry. There used to be a taboo against doing laundry during the Twelve Days of Christmas because you were said to be washing your winding sheet and sure to give up the ghost before the New Year. Of course, if the infamous Washer at the Ford decided to take in your laundry, there was really nothing you could do about it. The banshee-like Washer at the Ford haunts the shallows of Irish rivers where she scrubs the bloody garments of those about to die.

Here's another secret third-graders adore: We still refer to bedsheets as "linens," even if they're made of cotton. That's because all bedclothes used to be woven from linen. We also call them "whites" because the linen was bleached in urine, which is, after all, cheaper than bleach.

If your kids still aren't sold on housekeeping, there's help out there. For the very young, Mother Goose would suggest reciting:

When I was a little girl, I washed my Mommy's dishes/
Now I am a big girl, I roll in golden riches.

You might also try this little-known third verse of "Here We Go Round the Mulberry Bush":

This is the way we wash our clothes [etc.]
On a cold and frosty morning.

Personally, I recommend the classic Easter tale *The Country Bunny and the Little Gold Shoes*, which, despite having first been published in 1939, is almost militantly feminist. The title character, an apparently single mother of twenty-one little bunnies, trains her offspring to do all the household chores so that she can go out and realize her lifelong dream of delivering Easter eggs to human children. For slightly older kids, there's the Grimm's fairy tale "Mother Holda," in which the dutiful housemaid is rewarded with gold and the lazy one with a bucket of pitch. Teens can be sat down in front of the sumptuously domestic films *Girl with a Pearl Earring* and *The Scent of Green Papaya*. Cleaning never looked more romantic!

To be clear, Mui, the young heroine of *The Scent of Green Papaya*, is a maid because she resides with her employers. A cleaning lady who comes in once or twice a week is technically not a maid but a charwoman, from Old English, *cierran*, "to turn," as in, to take a turn at working at something. Or is it from the Irish *cear*, meaning "bloody"? I must remember to ask the Washer at the Ford when I finally meet her.

Ostara Ritual: Floral Divination

Elizabeth Barrette

PAGANISM IS A NATURE religion, so it pays to include nature in your celebrations. I like to use flowers at Ostara because they connect strongly to the core concepts of this sabbat, and so many of them are in season at this time of year that it's easy to choose ones with personal or thematic meanings. Consult the earlier essay for instructions on making flower baskets, candying flowers, and floromancy. It also has tips on flower characteristics to help you select the right ones for your ritual.

Preparation: This ritual may be performed outside or indoors. Any number of people may attend and participate, but this rite is best suited for four or five people to fill the roles of leader and designated quarter callers. Other celebrants (and this is nice for the shy ones) may simply join in the common spoken parts. Make your assignments accordingly or ask for volunteers during ritual prep. Describe a basic outline of the ritual so that people understand what will be happening and what they need to do.

Set up an altar covered with flowery fabric. At each of the quarters, place a flower basket suited to that location; you may match the flowers by element, color, themes you wish to evoke with this ritual, and so forth. For the flower divination, you will need a basket with plenty of flower heads for everyone to choose freely, each one wrapped to conceal it and tagged with a folded card to give its name and meaning. For cakes and ale, you will need a plate with enough candied flowers for everyone, and a chalice full of floral beverage such as dandelion wine or lavender soda.

Ostara Flower Ritual

Cast the circle with flowers. If you are working outdoors, you can choose flowers with many petals; pull off the petals and scatter them around to draw the circle. Indoors, flowers with long stems offer a less messy way to cast the circle as you simply lay them out in a line around the celebrants. As you **[the leader]** walk, say:

Flowers bright and flowers sweet, cast the circle as we meet.

The caller for the East should face the eastern basket of flowers and say:

I call to the East and the powers of Air,
which make the flowers dance
and carry pollen from bloom to bloom.
May you join us in our ritual today,
and awaken us to the growing season.
Hail and well met!

Celebrants respond: *Hail and well met!*

The caller for the South should face the southern basket of flowers and say:

I call to the South and the powers of Fire,
whose gentle sunlight beckons the blossoms
to emerge from the warming soil.
May you join us in our ritual today,
and enlighten us this growing season.
Hail and well met!

Celebrants respond: *Hail and well met!*

The caller for the West should face the western basket of flowers and say:

I call to the West and the powers of Water,
the cool spring showers whose touch
waters the flowers so they may grow.
May you join us in our ritual today,
and flow with us into the growing season.
Hail and well met!

Celebrants respond: *Hail and well met!*

The caller for the North should face the northern basket of flowers and say:

I call to the North and the powers of Earth,
which support the plants and flowers,
nourishing them to bring forth fruit.
May you join us in our ritual today,
and enrich us this growing season.
Hail and well met!

Celebrants respond: *Hail and well met!*

Leader evokes the goddess Kore with these words:

Kore, Maiden Goddess
of morning light and spring breezes,
painter of flowers and tender of bees,
bringer of lengthening days,
we call on you to join us today
in celebration of Ostara.
Hail and well met!

Celebrants respond: *Hail and well met!*

Leader introduces the ritual with a statement of intent, saying:

We gather here on Ostara to appreciate Kore, the Goddess of Flowers, and the blossoms with which she has blessed us. May our actions here today aid the turning of the seasons, in this time when day and night are equal and the light is growing stronger.

Leader carries around a basket for the flower divination. To each celebrant, say:

Take forth a sign for the growing season. May this blossom symbolize the things that you can cultivate, or warn you away from hidden dangers.

Celebrants may choose whether to share the omen they have received, or keep it secret.

Leader then says:

Kore, Goddess of Flowers, we offer you our homage in your season of spring. Hear now the work we intend for the months to come.

Leader then goes around the circle and share everyone's plans for the growing season. End by saying:

Kore, Goddess of Flowers, thank you for heeding our plans. Nurture them like seeds as we go about our work, that they may flower and bear fruit.

Celebrants respond: *So mote it be!*

For cakes and ale, serve candied flowers and a floral beverage. When presenting the candied flowers **the leader** will say:

Taste the flowering year.

When presenting the floral beverage, say:

Drink of the blossoming spring.

Then return the plate and chalice to the altar table.

Leader releases the goddess Kore with these words:

Kore, Maiden Goddess
of morning light and spring breezes,
painter of flowers and tender of bees,
bringer of lengthening days,
we thank you for joining us today
and pray you are pleased with our service.
Stay if you will, go if you must.
Hail and farewell!

Celebrants: *Hail and Farewell!*

The caller for the North should face the northern basket of flowers and say:

I turn to the North and the powers of Earth,
which support the plants and flowers,
nourishing them to bring forth fruit.
Thank you for joining us in our ritual today.
Stay if you will, go if you must.
Hail and farewell!

Celebrants: *Hail and farewell!*

The caller for the West should face the western basket of flowers and say:

I turn to the West and the powers of Water,
the cool spring showers whose touch
waters the flowers so they may grow.
Thank you for joining us in our ritual today.
Stay if you will, go if you must.
Hail and farewell!

Celebrants: *Hail and farewell!*

The caller for the South should face the southern basket of flowers and say:

I turn to the South and the powers of Fire,
whose gentle sunlight beckons the blossoms
to emerge from the warming soil.
Thank you for joining us in our ritual today.
Stay if you will, go if you must,
Hail and farewell!

Celebrants: *Hail and farewell!*

The caller for the East should face the eastern basket of flowers and say:

I turn to the East and the powers of Air,
which make the flowers dance
and carry pollen from bloom to bloom.
Thank you for joining us in our ritual today.
Stay if you will, go if you must,
Hail and farewell!

Celebrants respond: *Hail and farewell!*

Leader opens the circle. If you are outdoors, sweep the flower petals out of alignment. If you are indoors, pick up the flowers that trace the circle. As you go along, say:

The circle is open, but unbroken.

Celebrants respond: *Merry meet, and merry part, and merry meet again.*

Notes

Beltane

Beltane: Alone but Not Lonely

Diana Rajchel

IT'S AMAZING THAT BELTANE does not suffer the same backlash as Saint Valentine's Day. By all rights, it should. In some ways, it's worse: the entire holiday celebrates a couple enjoying sex. At least Valentine's allows couples to maintain some illusion of what the Western world considers chastity.

Oh Beltane, sexy, sexy Beltane that sets the hearts and loins of so many Pagans ablaze, much to the irritation of those feeling less than sparky. By May 1st (or October 31st) your influence spreads everywhere a Pagan eye might look: in Pagan book shops, in the gossip of your Pagan meeting, spreading itself around in the high pollen counts that accompany blossoming trees. Online, it gets worse—social media feeds fill up with the eroticized, overidealized, imagined bodies of God and Goddess, and people post erotic poems or vague giggling status updates about how they celebrated. Attending a public sabbat, depending on where you live, could feel like a warped visit to Noah's Ark—seemingly, everyone arrives at a Beltane sabbat in pairs. As if the constant imagery isn't enough, Pagan-oriented blog feeds and magazine articles fill up with love spells and related admonitions about how to fix being single or how to get the most out of your partner.

This unconscious nonacceptance of those living with neither sex nor partner is a social malady instilled post–World War II. Many, many communities faced severe drop-offs in available sexual partners during that war, and part of the subterranean troubles of the 1950s was about re-establishing all that was considered "normal" before the war. Valentine's Day became the popular expression of romantic normalization, although Pagans, often unaware how much mainstream culture still affects them, also transferred many of the meanings associated with Valentine's Day, about the importance of coupling, to Beltane.

The twenty-first century result is the unwitting simultaneous stigmatization and elevation of the single. You're single? That's wonderful! You're sexually available! You're single? That's awful! You're sexually available!

᠃

Even Pagans, for all their bohemian influences, sometimes fail to understand people wanting, let alone enjoying, life without a romantic partner. Pagans soaking up the sexiness of Beltane are not to blame—sex positivity does the world a lot of good by destigmatizing sexual orientation and killing misogyny one double-standard confrontation at a time. Accepting, even embracing, the decision not to pursue sex and relationships is an advanced step toward sex positivity that most people don't even know they need to reach. For those who prefer no partner, who are in a healthy situation where dealing with a partner's sexual needs is too much, or who are wanting a rest break between relationships, it's important to internalize the following messages:

You are not spiritually deficient because you lack a romantic or sexual partner. Having no interest in romance, sex, etc., is not a moral failing. You need not muster up sexual interest for the sake of a holiday. Most animals have a mating season. As the French playwright P. A. Caron de Beaumarchais pointed out, "We drink when we are not thirsty and make love at any time, Madam. These are the only things which distinguish us from other animals." You can also refuse to make love at any time, and this right is sacrosanct. While the biological underpinnings of desire can move us toward or away from human appetites, ultimately we can overcome, or at least manage, desire. In cases of severe health issues, such as cancer treatment, the lack of interest isn't just understandable, it's possibly necessary.

Preferring to celebrate Beltane without involving sex does not make you a bad Pagan.

Beltane energy fertilizes much more than the human body and the land. You can draw on the energy of that fire to fuel relationships and endeavors that have nothing to do with sex.

The only way to counter those Pagans who push coupling the hardest, especially at Beltane, is to set an eroticism-free celebratory example. Rather than sit on the sidelines and feel sorry for yourself while you watch couples pair off to jump a bonfire, consider some different ways to tap into that energy for your own benefit. To do this requires a rethink of Beltane and its associated energies. There are purposes for seeking new friends and enhancing glamour and power that have nothing to do with sex.

Drawing Friendship

Since the Internet came along, more people than ever now know that face-to-face friendships take work. This has become a larger part of cultural consciousness since the Internet allowed people to stay home in lieu of socializing. For a select few, it improved their social lives: those that could not afford to visit clubs, drink, or join bowling leagues might hop on a chat room. It definitely transformed the Pagan world, with those unable to visit occult shops or afford festivals finally able to make their voice heard loud enough that others identifying as Pagans could find them. Yet as society transforms again, new technologies have shifted us back toward contact with people we have met in the physical world. Phones allow people to maintain Internet contacts while retaining mobility, and social media connects us to people we initially met offline. Yet finding and keeping friends is harder than ever before. If you, like many other people, dove too hard into online life, you may need to work some magic to cultivate more local connections.

Personal Mystique

In addition to drawing compatible friends, Beltane energy lends itself to personal enhancement. Many of the same spells and ingredients used to add sexual allure may be mitigated into milder expressions of that energy. For instance, catnip, typically used as a come-hither ingredient, can help you exude a more affable form of attractiveness. Beltane is a good time to work on making yourself seem more charming to people in general, and for reasons far beyond seeking a mate.

Strengthening and Calibrating Friendships

Never take the friends you already have for granted. Plenty of Pagans work spells with an eye toward maintaining and adjusting romantic relationships, especially at Beltane. Relatively few apply similar work for strengthening platonic friendships.

Love, even platonic love, needs feeding. Beltane kindles all types of love. This is an excellent time to take stock of who in your life takes up too much energy in exchange for too little, and, while anathema to those who romanticize friendships as lifelong relationships, root out those who have had too much of a negative impact on you. If you have people in your life who put you in dangerous situations, who start fights with you during crucial professional or creative turning points in your life on a regular basis, or who take pleasure in making you feel bad, cut them out and use Beltane fire energy to cauterize those wounds. The same spells used for smooth romantic breakups also apply to smooth friendship breakups. Beltane, as a harbinger for summer, also wets the ground, making it easy to weed out the choking growth.

Family

Familial love can also need a little magical adjustment. While genetics can bond us, a little magic to make those bonds of joy instead of obligation can go a long way toward creating happiness. If your family will cooperate, introduce ways to turn conflict into transformative communication instead of avoidance. Work healing magic on wounded relationships. In modern times it's less discussed than it once was, but the veil that thins at Samhain also thins at Beltane, though not to as dramatic a degree. If you know of generational trauma that passes down family lines, this season of a thinned veil is an opportune time to invoke your ancestors for help in healing old hurts and breaking generational chains. If you live with a family blessed with freedom from such traumas, use this time to work some harmony magic for everyone in a shared household.

Business Networking

We live in an age where the newspaper classifieds no longer lead to a career. Beltane's extroverted energy can help overcome the obstacles inherent in job networking. A little Beltane-energized magic can help you cut through the sea of people to the ones who share goals and projects compatible to your own. Some of this comes from blending attraction magic with prosperity magic: think catnip and high john as a replacement for more erotic draws like musk and jasmine. In turn, you can use all that Beltane fertility energy to bring the right customers to your business while weeding out the customers who game the system and drain resources.

Healing Magic

In between people who want the sexual energy of Beltane for sex and those who prefer to abstain from it are people passing through a healing phase. Often men and women in treatment for cancer have no desire. Also, people dealing with recent family loss may experience a nadir in the libido. Healing workings at Beltane may not result in a "ready for love" outlook although it might—it depends on the nature of the psychic injury. Fertility energy, while popularly used to make new plants and new babies, can assist a doctor trying to healing already existent illness.

General Health

The fertility energy of Beltane well suits healing needs from people suffering physical problems. The energy of Beltane best serves people who need greater strength to heal, who need to see cell growth happen in their ailment, or who need to be harmoniously readjusted to nature.

For example, if someone has a common cold hit right around Beltane, that person might drink tea, take cold medications, and visit a doctor if it lasts more than three days. With the addition of Beltane energy, you might charge a green candle and call upon the energy of the Lord and Lady's union when you light it to infuse the sick person with refreshed energy and health.

Healing the Heart

Beltane can give a person going through emotional difficulties significant renewal. Beltane's energy allows for a balance of the masculine and feminine wisdom. This is a time to observe how couples in your life interact, starting with your parents and moving outward to the people you spend the most time with. Who seems the happiest? Who seems the unhappiest? Notice how the happy ones take their disagreements to one another. This is also a good time to meditate on past relationships. While the *High Fidelity* scenario (from the classic film starring John Cusack and Jack Black) where you interview all of your exes is usually not feasible and definitely not wise, you could benefit from digging out old diaries, emails, and texts to look at what attracted you to those people and how that went wrong. As you identify the negative traits that attracted and ultimately repelled you from people, you can establish magical practices to help you undo those bad emotional habits and establish new emotional habits to replace them.

Healing the Earth with Targeted Treatment

In the Northern Hemisphere, Beltane's proximity to Earth Day sometimes influences the former holiday's celebrations. Some groups may raise a great deal of energy and then push it into the soil, commanding the energy to "heal the earth." The sentiment is lovely. The practice itself, however, could benefit from tweaking. Beltane is an excellent time to try a few adjustments for environmental magic. After all, the earth isn't dying—it just might kill everyone as a by-product of the way we treat its resources. Rather than awns generic healing energy, pick a specific cause to work magic on. For instance, you might want to send the energy raised at Beltane outward and upward to seed the possibility for cleaner air all over the world. You may use the fire energy to kindle new ideas to make environmental innovation affordable. You might pour libations and add fertility and prosperity herbs to the offering such as carrots, cucumbers, and rosemary. You can direct that work toward clean, potable free water, recycling materials, and making world leaders more conscious of how their decisions affect resources. Magic, like charity donations, has the most effect if you pick one cause and concentrate on that.

🌿

Being single at Beltane does not mean you need to drum up a date or interest in a date. It gives you a way to find a new angle on the energy of the season, and to apply that energy toward love, healing, and connectivity beyond common conception.

Cosmic Sway

April Elliott Kent

THE SUN IN TAURUS in a harmonious trine with Jupiter in Virgo, and Venus in contented Taurus, reinforce Beltane's spirit of feasting and fertility. This Beltane begins with a Last Quarter Moon in friendly Aquarius; the call is to gather with friends old and new to celebrate the height of spring. Gather for a bonfire at the beach or sparklers in your backyard!

Mercury in Taurus will be retrograde through May 22. Mercury's retrograde periods can be aggravating if you are trying to meet specific deadlines or maintain a fixed schedule. Many of us travel at this time of year, and I've found that Mercury retrograde is actually not a bad time for it, provided that (1) you have made the arrangements while Mercury was direct and (2) your itinerary is not too aggressive. Be sure to double-check all arrangements, have backup plans, and build plenty of extra time into your schedule. And it is best to wait until after Jupiter turns direct on May 9 to travel overseas, especially to places you've never visited before.

Mars, retrograde since April 17, will regress into Scorpio on May 27. This is time to review unfinished business from Mars' recent visit in this sign (between January 3 and March 5). If there are old disputes or unfinished work, resolve and bring them to completion; it is hard to make the most of Beltane's fecund promise when your heart is filled with hurts and your inbox is filled with half-done projects.

Neptune turns retrograde on June 13. A retrograde planet generally behaves "against type," so Neptune's qualities of intuition, sensitivity, and imagination are turned inward and we cannot easily read our environment. Generally these are good times for retreat, introspection and meditation. Your perspective on yourself and the truth about your life is actually quite clear to you now, and that can lead to some uncomfortable but invaluable insights.

New Moon in Taurus – May 6, 2016

With the New Moon and Venus in money-oriented Taurus, in a grand trine with Jupiter and Pluto, and falling on Friday (which is Venus' sacred day), this is the Mother of all New Moons for summoning prosperity! If you do nothing else at this New Moon, try this prosperity ritual from my friend Dana Gerhardt, adapted from Caroline Casey's Santería Ritual in *Making the Gods Work for You.* I've performed this ritual many times, with results ranging from impressive to astonishing.

There is one caveat: Jupiter is approaching a square with Saturn, which may limit the results somewhat. Make your wishes very specific and practical; these are the intentions most likely to be rewarded now.

Prosperity Ritual
You'll need a round piece of bread (perhaps a dinner roll), a nickel or five pennies, honey, a yellow candle, a piece of paper, and a source of flowing, fresh water, such as a stream or river.

On this New Moon on Friday, make a hole in your dinner roll and place your coins inside. On a small piece of paper, clearly declare your wishes; fold the paper and put it in the bread, on top of the coin. Pour a little honey on top. Finally, place a small, yellow candle (between a birthday candle and a taper) in the hole and light it. As it's burning, honor Venus with an activity that makes you feel happy, wealthy, beautiful, and pampered. When the candle is completely burned down, take it to the river or stream and toss it in, while calling the Goddess in words of your own choosing.

Full Moon in Sagittarius – May 21, 2016

This Full Moon in Sagittarius is in a tight conjunction with retrograde Mars. It's an emotionally volatile combination, given to expressions of anger, and Sagittarius is a very blunt sign; combined with Mercury stationing to move direct, the impulse is strong to speak your mind and act on your feelings. But that might cause more problems than it solves. Instead, direct your thoughts inward to better understand your own reactions to situations, especially angry reactions. Mars turns direct on June 29, and then it will be much clearer what is really bothering you, and which are the right actions and words to help you resolve the situation.

New Moon in Gemini – June 4, 2016

On the heels of the volatile Full Moon in Sagittarius comes one of the most significant New Moons of the year. Tightly conjoined Venus, the New Moon in Gemini opposes Saturn and squares both Jupiter and Neptune. This combination of planets emphasizes affection, responsibility, idealism, and optimism in nearly equal measure. It also represents the midpoint between the year's eclipses in March and September, triggering significant changes in the areas of spirituality, health, and day-to-day responsibilities.

As this New Moon falls on a weekend in early June, which is a very popular time to marry, it will have a long-lasting impact for a great many people who will carry this energy forward in their marriage charts. The most significant challenge for these couples will be finding a balance between Jupiter and Neptune's optimism and idealism and Saturn's demands that they maintain realistic expectations of each other and the marriage. Luckily, Gemini is an extremely facile communicator, and the ability to laugh together and discuss almost any subject is the great blessing of a marriage that begins with the Sun, Moon, and Venus in this sign.

Full Moon in Sagittarius – June 20, 2016

Coming just hours before the Summer Solstice, this powerful Full Moon is the second in Sagittarius, at the very last degree of that sign. In astrology, the 29th degree of a sign is called an anaretic degree, sometimes referred to as a karmic degree. The energy of a planet at 29 degrees creates a sense of urgency, so at this Full Moon, both the Sun's will and the Moon's intuition demand their due.

Each of them brings along a companion: The Sun in Gemini has Mercury nearby, at its strongest in this sign. Mercury is closely opposed to Saturn in Sagittarius, on the Moon's side of the sky. This Full Moon demands nothing less than our total commitment to communicating with one another, and balancing the need to take responsibility for our own convictions (Sagittarius) while still being willing to maintain a curious, questioning spirit (Gemini).

Jupiter is in a nearly precise conjunction with the Moon's North Node, seemingly tilting the scales in favor of maintaining your own opinions. But Jupiter and the North Node are in Virgo, one of Mercury's signs; there is no breaking of this stalemate. The only solution is compromise, balance, and a willingness to learn from others.

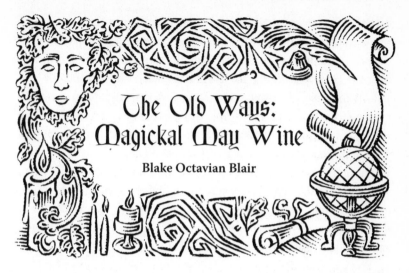

The Old Ways: Magickal May Wine

Blake Octavian Blair

THE FIRST OF MAY is well known among magickal and Pagan folk as Beltane, a celebration of fertility, the blossoming of the land, and of springtime and the coming summer. The consumption of wines and ales at Pagan sabbats and celebrations in general is a long-standing tradition. However, Beltane is graced with having associations with a wine all of its own: May Wine. As will be explored, it is a drink most fit for the occasion!

The tradition of May Wine is long connected to the celebration of May Day, Beltane, and Walpurgis Night. The origins of the drink can be traced back to Germanic origins, where it will be seen spelled as Maiwein or Maitrank. In fact, its signature ingredient is waldmeister, or sweet woodruff, which grows wild in the forests of Germany. Some refer to sweet woodruff by the folk name Master of the Forest, and it is certainly May Wine's "master ingredient"! Recipes for the drink may vary; however, its ingredients always seem to resonate the energies of spring and the qualities of the Beltane holiday. For example, sweet woodruff itself has a masculine energy and is said to be associated with the element of fire—this serves as a nod to the traditional fires of Beltane. Lore also says that the herb is associated with prosperity, which in itself is a type of fertility. Traditional lore says that sweet woodruff should only be used as a flavoring in the month of May, as that is when the leaves are said to be most tender.

Recipes almost invariably include the signature scent and flavoring of sweet woodruff and use a white wine such as a Riesling or Moselle as the base. However, recipes can vary considerably from there, ranging from consisting of simply those two main ingredients all the way to a veritable springtime cocktail-style collection of ingredients. This is not surprising. Like any other holiday dish, different individuals and families develop their own particular recipe or brand of May Wine as the years pass and depending on what is at the ready for use as well as their preferences. However, popular additions to the mix are extra sugar, honey, brandy, fresh strawberries, oranges, and even garnishes of seasonal flowers such as violets.

Strawberries are probably one of the most common of added ingredients. In addition to bringing their wonderfully sweet flavor notes to the drink, they also serve to energetically balance out the fiery and masculine sweet woodruff. Strawberries are both associated with feminine energy and the element of water. This balance serves to further add to the custom tailored energy of May Wine as a perfect drink for a sabbat celebrating the union of masculine and feminine energies and fertility. Love is among the primary magickal properties assigned to this fruit, and it has long been held among many as a potent aphrodisiac. Beltane being the lusty fertility holiday that it is, it's no wonder that strawberries have earned mainstay status as a May Wine ingredient.

Many recipes call for either sugar or honey to assist in bringing out the sweeter notes of the May Wine. In magick, both are associated with luck, prosperity, and celebrating the sweet parts of life. Honey in particular is often a favorite, as some people also tout it as an aphrodisiac and for its golden (prosperous) color. There is an old saying, "You catch more flies with honey than with vinegar," that goes to show how powerfully deep and culturally ingrained honey is as an attractant of things beneficial to us. The occasional citrus addition of oranges by some recipes adds much of the same spiritual qualities as honey, a prosperous golden color, and magickal associations with both prosperity as well as love.

The garnishing of the finished drink with a springtime flower, most popularly violets, may seem simply like a festive cosmetic addition at the surface. However, it too provides a watery feminine balance to the more fiery masculine properties of other ingredients. Additionally, they are associated with healing, protection from evil spirits, and not surprisingly, love, luck, and fertility! (Are we sensing a theme?!) These qualities might be one reason the drink is often traditional fare at weddings.

The earliest recorded mention of May Wine specifically is from 854 AD by a Benedictine monk named Wandelbertus. However, wine in general has far more ancient connections, such as to the gods Bacchus and Dionysus who are celebrated widely at Beltane. (Dionysus being the Greek form and Bacchus being the Roman.) Dionysus led a somewhat infamous traveling band of satyrs and female devotees and was known for teaching agricultural arts, including wine-making, and creating a sometimes chaotic hoopla wherever they went. Our modern Beltane celebrations contain all the elements of Dionysus's contingent's revelries: the making of May Wine, dancing in the form of the maypole rituals, and activities celebrating agriculture, nature, and fertility aplenty (both amorous and otherwise!).

May Wine seems to embody a Venn diagram of qualities associated with the sabbat of Beltane, so much so that you may wish to venture to include a May Wine into your festivities. If you do so, please keep in mind that too large a quantity of sweet woodruff can be toxic to consume. So please exercise caution and research reputable recipe sources for proper instructions on how to safely include it in your May Wine. It is always a good idea to research any ingredients you may be using in any recipe meant for consumption to be aware of their possible toxicity and if/how they are or are not safe for food use. Also, not everybody wants to or can consume alcohol. Have no fear, there are festive nonalcoholic alternative recipes in the spirit of the season to be found as well.

I hope that while you are setting the stage for your Beltane celebrations, bedecking your altars with the flowers of spring and coming days of summer, and dancing around the maypole, that you will raise a glass of May Wine and toast to the qualities that it and Beltane represent. May the blessings of love, luck, fertility, prosperity, and good health be yours as you so desire! Blessed be!

Bibliography

Cunningham, Scott. *Cunningham's Encyclopedia of Magical Herbs.* St. Paul, MN: Llewellyn Publications, 1985.

Encyclopedia Britannica. "Wine," accessed June 11, 2014, http://www.britannica.com/EBchecked/topic/645269/wine/66676/Flavoured-wines#ref110681.

German Culture. "Maiwein," accessed June 11, 2014. http://www.germanculture.com.ua/library/weekly/aa042601b.htm.

Grimassi, Raven. *Beltane: Springtime Rituals, Lore & Celebration.* St. Paul, MN: Llewellyn Publications, 2001.

Illes, Judika. *The Element Encyclopedia of Witchcraft: The Complete A-Z for the Entire Magical World.* Hammersmith, London: Harper Element, 2005.

Illes, Judika. *Encyclopedia of Spirits: The Ultimate Guide to the Magic of Fairies, Genies, Demons, Ghosts, Gods & Goddesses.* New York: Harper One, 2009.

Wigington, Patti. "Bacchus, Roman God of Wine and Fertility." *About.com.* Accessed June 18, 2014. http://paganwiccan.about.com/od/romandeities/p/BacchusProfile.htm.

Yronwode, Catherine. *HooDoo Herb and Root Magic: A Materia Magica of African-American Conjure.* Forestville, CA: Lucky Mojo Curio Company, 2002.

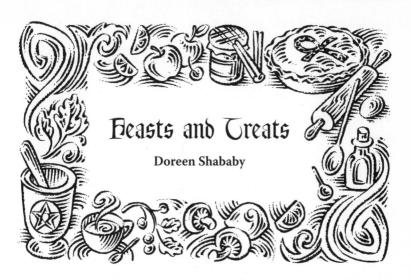

Feasts and Treats

Doreen Shababy

Beltaine inspires us to live large—to make the most of life and love. It is a time to pull out all the stops when attending to romance, and we have all of nature to show us the way. Sweet-scented flowers attract bees who eagerly share their pollen with neighboring blooms. Moths dance on the night sky in a moonlight jitterbug. Sweethearts swoon to the sound of drummers, somewhere. And we know that the May Queen is present. I hope this menu inspires your Beltaine revelry.

Honey-Poached Salmon

The salmon plays an integral role in Celtic mythology, representing wisdom and knowledge. In this case, eating this fresh-poached, savory, sweet salmon brings us healthy fats to nourish our brains, amongst other benefits. Be certain your fish is fresh and firm.

Prep time: 15 minutes
Cook time: 20 minutes
Serves: 6

2 pounds fresh salmon fillet with skin
2 tablespoons butter

1 tablespoon minced onion
2 cloves garlic, minced
2 tablespoons all-purpose flour (or gluten-free alternative)
1½–2 cups dry white wine
¼ cup honey
1 teaspoon chopped fresh dill leaf
Salt and pepper to season

Divide the salmon into 6 pieces and pat dry. Set aside.

In a skillet large and wide enough to fit all the fish (and the wine), melt butter over medium heat. When butter is melted, add onion and cook until translucent, just a few minutes. Toss in the garlic and stir until fragrant, about 5 seconds. Add the flour and stir until well blended. Pour in 1½ cups wine and honey and turn up the heat a little, stirring and cooking until smooth. Toss in dill leaf.

Season the salmon with salt and pepper, then place each piece skin side down in the poaching broth. Add the rest of the wine if needed to cover fish. Return liquid to a simmer, cover, then reduce heat to lowest setting to poach for 15 to 20 minutes, or until salmon begins to flake but is still tender—do not overcook. Check the fish now and again so it isn't sticking. Serve with sauce.

Green Goddess Orzo Salad with Peas

In honor of Beltaine and all things green, this salad is the essence of spring in all her vibrant glory. Beautiful fresh vegetables!

Prep time: 15 minutes
Cook time: 10–12 minutes, for the pasta
Serves: 6

1 package orzo (rice-shaped) pasta
1 cup mayonnaise
1 clove garlic, minced
2 teaspoons anchovy paste (or 3 anchovies, minced)
2 scallions, minced (about ¼ cup)
¼ cup minced parsley

1 sprig tarragon, minced
1 tablespoon lemon juice
1 tablespoon white wine vinegar
½ teaspoon salt
Black pepper to taste
½ cup sour cream or plain whole milk yogurt
½ cup fresh raw peas (or thawed frozen)

Cook pasta according to package directions to serve 6, making sure to use plenty of salt in the cooking water. Drain and let cool uncovered, then cover and refrigerate until serving time.

Combine remaining ingredients in a large mixing bowl until well blended, then refrigerate. This makes about 2 cups dressing.

When ready to serve, combine half the dressing with the orzo, gently mixing so as not to break up the pasta. Let sit a minute or so to absorb, add the peas, then add more dressing as desired to serve.

Strawberry Marlowe

This recipe is fun and everyone will love it. You have to make it early in the morning or the night before to freeze, or you can serve it soft and cloudlike from special dessert cups.

Prep time: 30 minutes, including melting the marshmallows
Chill time: Freeze for several hours, or serve immediately
Serves: 6–8

1 pound sweet ripe strawberries, trimmed and sliced, plus a few for garnish
½ cup orange juice
1 10-ounce bag mini-marshmallows
1 pint whipping cream, cold
1 tablespoon sugar

Combine strawberries and orange juice and let sit for 30 minutes.

In a double-boiler over simmering water, melt the marshmallows until smooth. Remove from heat, mix in 2 tablespoons water, and let cool to room temperature. When cooled, place melted marshmallows in a large mixing bowl, gently combine strawberries, and then refrigerate.

Next, whip cream with sugar until fluffy. Fold into strawberry mixture. If you plan to freeze it, pour into a 2-quart mold and freeze until firm; take out of freezer a few minutes before serving to temper. If you plan to serve immediately, dish into parfait glasses or even champagne glasses and garnish with a fresh berry.

Hazelnut Iced Coffee

We've started out our Beltaine menu with the Salmon of Knowledge and we finish with the nutty fruits that fed said salmon. Feel free to use your favorite hazelnut liqueur in place of the toasted nuts and sugar.

Prep time: 5 minutes
Cook time: 10–20 minutes
Serves: 6–8

½ cup raw hazelnuts
Ground coffee to make one pot (however strong you like it)
¼ cup raw sugar, or to taste

In an ovenproof skillet (or cookie sheet), roast the hazelnuts in a 300 degree F oven for 10 to 20 minutes—do not let them burn. Remove from oven and let cool, sloughing off the skins if possible. Chop coarsely.

Combine coffee and chopped nuts and prepare to brew in your usual way. When the coffee is brewed, pour into a heatproof jar such a canning jar and stir in the sugar. Let cool then refrigerate until serving time. You could also make a separate pot of plain coffee, cool, then freeze as ice cubes to accompany, if desired.

Crafty Crafts

Tess Whitehurst

DIRECTLY ACROSS THE WHEEL of the year from Samhain, Beltane is another time when the veil between the worlds is thin. However, while the world of the spirits merges with our world during Samhain, it is the realm of the faeries that bleeds over into our realm during Beltane. Faeries then infuse us with their unique brand of magic, which includes whimsy, mischief, playfulness, nature wisdom, and the quickening energy of spring.

Of course, faeries are nature spirits, and nature is not all sweetness and light. Those of us who walk the path of nature-based spirituality know that there is darkness and danger lurking in nature, just as it also lurks in the realm of the faerie. Embracing it all—cultivating an awareness and respect of the dark as well as the light—is what keeps our eyes open, our minds clear, and our power strong.

Faerie Wand

Constructing a faerie wand in the manner outlined below is a potent method for aligning with nature and the realm of the Fae. As you choose the wood, crystal, and colors that present themselves and feel right to you, you'll also find that the process of making your wand will help you tune into your unique magical essence, and to embody your very own dynamic dance of duality. Not to mention, once you complete it and consecrate it, your wand will be a powerful tool for directing energy, casting a circle, and instantly accessing that powerful magical place between the worlds.

Time to complete: 1 to 2 hours

Cost: $10.00 to $20.00 (more or less, according to how elaborate you want to make it, as well as many basic craft supplies you have on hand)

Supplies

A relatively straight stick, roughly the length of your elbow to the tip of your index finger (advice on how to obtain it below)

Sand paper

A crystal point that is close in thickness to the end of the stick (this will be attached to the end of the stick, so keep this in mind as you select it: for example, if its base is slanted, it's ideal if the end of the stick is slanted in a complementary way)

A glue gun with glue

Jute twine

Lace or cloth trim, a needle with matching thread and one or two pins (or, optionally, glitter tape)

Scissors

Small rhinestones, in one or more colors that feel right to you

Elmer's glue

Optional Supplies

Pocketknife or athame (this might be necessary, depending on the stick you find)

Essential oil of cedar

Reclaimed or remnant silk

Broken or upcycled crystal jewelry

Find Your Wand

Finding the stick for your wand is likely the most important part of the wand-making process, and it's important to approach it with the proper mindset. Begin with the awareness that you're not going on a shopping trip or a hunting expedition. Rather, you're respectfully opening yourself up to receive a sacred gift from nature, the trees, and the realm of the Fae.

It's best if you're on a camping trip or otherwise spending some quality time in a forest or serene natural setting containing trees, although you can also find a stick from the trees in your own backyard, or even an outdoor arboreal setting in your neighborhood such as a park or a tree-lined street. Don't over think it, but do tune into your intuition and choose the place that feels just right.

Once you've arrived in the outdoor setting, take a moment to relax. Feel your weight on the earth, and notice your breath as it goes in and out. State your intention inwardly to discover, recognize, and receive a naturally fallen stick (ideally without bark on it) that will serve you well as your wand. Broadcast this intention energetically to the earth and trees by silently thinking and feeling it. Continue to relax and breathe consciously. Do your best to remain in a receptive and open state as you hold your intention loosely in your mind and spirit. Go walking, gazing respectfully and lovingly at the trees and earth. In time, you'll find the stick that is right for you. Trust that you cannot choose incorrectly: whatever stick you discover is divinely designed precisely for you. You may find your wand as part of a larger branch, in which case you can cut or break it off at the appropriate length, or you might find it at the desired length.

Please note that while it's excellent if the stick you find is relatively straight, it's great if it has slight waves or undulations along its length, as this is how energy naturally flows anyway. If you're not sure if it's going to help you direct energy in an ideal way, you can test it out by holding it in your dominant hand and pointing it out at a straight line. See if you can naturally feel your personal energy extending out along the length of the stick.

Craft Your Wand

Now that you've located your stick (and cut it to the desired length if necessary), remove any knots, twigs, or remaining bark with a

pocketknife or athame. (Or you could just scrape off the knot, twig, or bark with a sturdy corner, such as on a doorstep, brick, or curb.)

Moving the sandpaper lengthwise along the stick, rub it gently until it's smooth.

Optional step: Anoint the entire surface of the stick with a light layer of essential oil of cedar, and allow it to absorb for at least 15 minutes.

After cleansing the crystal point in sunlight or visualized bright white light, affix it to the end of the stick with the glue gun. Then affix it even more tightly by wrapping jute twine generously around the meeting place of the crystal and stick. Tie it tightly and use the glue gun to hold the knot in place. Then wrap the lace or trim around the jute, hiding the knot. Pin in place and sew tightly.

(Optionally, affix the crystal with glitter tape and tie a little jute twine around it.)

Decorate the length of the wand (or just the end of the wand, closer to the crystal) with rhinestones, in any way that feels right to you, attaching them with Elmer's glue and allowing dry time as necessary before gluing on additional sides.

(Optionally, tie the handle with strips of silk, and drape the crystal jewelry around the end.)

Of course, you can also decorate in any other way that feels good to you, such as by painting runes along the length or attaching naturally shed feathers to the handle.

All One Family:
Secrets for Beltane

Linda Raedisch

YOU NEVER KNOW WITH Beltane, which goes by the name "Walpurgis Night" in our house—it could be like summer, it could be like winter. Walpurgis Night is preceded by a season of nine nights during which the folkloric figure of Walburga is in flight, which is why I thought it an appropriate time for playing Nine Men's Morris. If the weather is bad, you can play it indoors on a board with a cup of tea at your elbow while the rain pours in sheets down the windows. If the weather is fair, you can play it outside with people in place of tokens. (I've been nurturing a fantasy of playing it with giant *kokeshi* dolls—you know, the brightly painted Japanese souvenir dolls shaped like old-fashioned clothespins?—but that's just me.)

You might know Nine Men's Morris by its alternate name, the Mill Game. A "morris" is a kind of English folkdance performed principally by men, while the term "mill" can refer to a folkdance position. I am not a folk dancer, but recently I did learn to play The Mill Game—as it is called on the box—having been taught by my nine-year-old daughter. I really have no excuse for not having learned how to play it earlier. The game has been in the family ever since someone or other picked it up at Siegel's Stationers for the price of $3.00. Inside the box, Wm. F. Drueke & Sons assure me that if we lose any of the pegs, we can purchase additional ones by sending "25c in coin for 9 pegs" to the address indicated, adding, "Mention color wanted." We've somehow managed not to lose any of the pegs over the years, but still I'm tempted to send away to Wm. F. Drueke & Sons to see what happens.

Nine Men's Morris, at its simplest, is Three Men's Morris, a glorified form of Tic-Tac-Toe: you draw a square and divide it into quarters which gives you nine intersections or points. Each player gets four tokens, which can be four of anything, really: bottle caps, chess pawns, or those little china animals that come inside boxes of tea bags. The two players take turns placing their counters on the points with the object of placing three of his own in a straight line: a mill. Now you're ready to graduate to Six Men's Morris. On the board are two concentric squares connected by lines. I'm sure there are diagrams on the Internet that can explain much better than I can here. Offline, my favorite reference is *Board and Table Games from Many Civilizations* by R. C. Bell. You start out with the same object: to place your "men," of which you have six this time, in a mill or straight line of three. Once you do, you're allowed to help yourself to one of your opponent's men, though not one that's already in a mill; mills are safe.

They're also magical. I'm talking about the mill to which you bring your grain to be ground into flour, where you pour an apparently inedible substance in and, by the miraculous actions of the millstones, something powdery and fine and potentially delicious comes out. To us, it's physics, but in the old days, unless you actually worked in the mill, it must have looked like magic. Those prone to deep thoughts began to think of the mill as the universe in miniature, a symbol encompassing all of time and space. One stone is the heavens, the other the underworld. And the grain in the middle? That's us. The millrace is the River of Time which sets the worlds in motion, grinding us all to dust.

The number three is magical also. Set your three men in a row and you have a representation of past, present, and future. Just ask the three Norns of Norse mythology, Urd, Verdandi, and Skuld, who dwell at the center of the square, spinning the threads of fate.

Let's see what they're up to. They've put aside their spindles for the moment, taken a cool drink from the Well of Wyrd and are now relaxing in the shade of the World Tree Yggdrasil, playing a game of Nine Men's Morris. Look through the branches: you can see them moving their pins around in the gravel. Only two can play at once, so Skuld sits dozing, waiting to play the winner.

For Nine Men's Morris, each player gets—you guessed it—nine men. To make the board, all you have to do is add a third concentric square. How do you win? You must reduce your opponent's army to only two men. Three's the thing; two just doesn't cut it.

If, when April 30 rolls around, the sun is shining brightly through the cherry blossoms, you can take the game outside. Depending on how many people you have at your disposal, you can play Three, Six or Nine Men's Morris, chalking the lines on the grass or drawing them on blacktop. Two people can start out as the opposing the players, directing the action from the sidelines, while the rest of the participants serve as the "men," obediently moving where they are told. Once taken from the board, men do not return, so it's up to you how the vanquished should behave: departing the field quietly and with dignity or after thrashing about in dramatic death throes. If it's a hot day, you may want to designate someone to move between the lines, offering lemonade to those who have been standing in a mill for a long time. If you'll be playing after dark, the men can hold colored pillar candles. To claim one of your opponent's men, simply step up and snuff out his candle.

Have fun out there, and may you have better luck than I have. So far, I have yet to beat my nine-year-old.

Beltane Ritual for the Soloist

Diana Rajchel

THIS RITUAL INVOKES BELTANE passion, but not of the sexual variety. This gives you a chance to let the sun—represented by the fire—burn away your negative thoughts, and the circumstantial energies that also hold you back from enjoying life. Once you have burned away the stagnant energies, you rebuild on what you removed with the positive energy raised. The purpose of this is to kindle your passion for life itself. The intent is to rewire your attitude so that you take not a loving, indulgent attitude toward yourself, but a loving, passionate, energetic attitude toward yourself.

While this ritual calls for a small fire, and for you to dance around the fire, it may not be possible. Charcoal incense in a heatproof container can substitute for a fire—just be sure to use it in a well-ventilated area! If you suffer severe asthma and allergies, you can instead microwave vodka, whiskey, or rubbing alcohol in a coffee mug for 30 seconds and float herbs on top of the liquid. If unable to walk around your ritual area because of space or physical limitation, you can instead circle your arms above the fire (or symbolic version) in the prescribed direction.

For this ritual, in addition to the fire/method of producing incense, you will need the following:

Libations: white wine, red wine, and olive oil; if you cannot use alcohol, red and white grape juice also works

Banishing herbs: rosemary, Solomon's seal, lilac flowers, angelica, peppermint, and onion skin

Invoking herbs: St. John's wort, hibiscus, rose petals (any color), lemon peel, a dried avocado pit, almonds, oak bark

Before the ritual, kindle your fire or start your incense.

Circle Casting

The Beltane fires flicker bright
as I feel the warmth of spring sunlight.
God and Goddess joined again;
Seen in lovers, seen in friends.
Kindle in me hope afresh
to buoy my strained heart afresh.
So mote it be!

Quarter Calls

East:
Gentle powers of air in gentle grace
Bless this ritual in time and space

South:
Gentle powers of fire, born in the sun's furnace
Transform me beyond my surface

West:
Gentle powers of water, raise high the tide
Take me to mingle far and wide

North:
Gentle powers of the land
Help me cultivate what I must understand!

Invocation

Hail Athena! Hail Artemis! Hail Vesta!
Virgin goddesses,
open my mind, show me your paths,
lead me to contentment.
Pursuing passions of the mind,
tending well my lands, my hope,
cultivating neighbors and compatriots—
let me be well as you are well
complete as you are complete.
So mote it be!

Pour out a libation for each goddess: Olive oil for Athena, white wine for Artemis, and red wine for Vesta.

Hold your hands above the fire and say:
The fire, the furnace, the sun, the seed,
let me give you dried things for your feed—
and as they burn, I am freed.

Throw rosemary into the blaze and say:
With rosemary, I am freed from bitter memories that hold me back.

Walk counterclockwise around the fire, and then pick up the next herb: Solomon's seal.

Throw the root into the fire, and say:
With Solomon's seal I banish lingering energies that work against my highest good.

Do another counterclockwise circumambulation, toss in the lilac flowers, and say:
With lilac, I banish the wounds I might dig up from my own memory.

On the next time around, throw in the angelica root and say:

Angelica calls to my ancestors and to the divine teachers that protect me—let me get out of my own way, and keep harm from crossing my path!

At the next round, throw in peppermint, saying:

Mint protects, cleanses, and elevates. My wounds are clean and sterilized, and as it burns, I become pure!

On the last counterclockwise round, throw in the onion skin and say:

My old self has peeled away like this onion skin. I find the fresh soul, clean, strong, protected, purified. So mote it be!

Come to stand facing west and spread out your arms and legs so that your posture imitates Da Vinci's "Vitruvian Man." Visualize the old energy as a gray fog that the fire consumes, making invisible. Starting at your feet, send in specific aches, pains, and hidden emotions that you stored in your muscles and bones. Move up to your legs, your hips, your belly, your chest, your neck, and your head. Once you reach the crown of your head, start the process again at your head, and go back to your feet. Pay attention to your body's response to sending that energy into the fire. You may feel lighter, more relaxed, and even relieved. Hold this visual for as long as you can.

Pause for a few moments and breathe, appreciating the sense of relief. Since magic and nature both abhor a vacuum, you must now complete the process of intentional replacement.

This time, throw some St. John's wort into the flames and walk clockwise around the fire and say:

St. John's wort kindles the light within; I see bright blessings everywhere I go.

On the next round, throw in hibiscus and say:

Hibiscus connects me to my passions within: reveal, oh divinatory herb, my hidden talents.

On the next ambulation, throw in rose petals and say:

I am allowed to love myself, as I am, unconditionally. I offer this love in turn to the earth and sky, to the goddesses present, and to the ancestors that have loved me through each step of life.

On the next round, throw in lemon peel and say:

Lemon, by the grace of the Mother Goddess, kindle in me passions to create. By your power let me create peace, let me create art, let me create good in the world.

Next, throw a dried avocado pit into the fire and say:

Lust stirs in more than the body—it stirs in the spirit. Invoke in me a lust for knowledge, a passionate curiosity, a desire for mastery paired with purified humility.

On the next time around, throw a handful of almonds on the fire and say:

Almonds, make me whole in myself—anima and animus together, fused with the creative passion that comes from divine inner union

On the next round, throw white sage into the fire and say:

Sage, bring me together in wisdom. Help the herbal energies now burning within me acclimate gently to my body, mind, and spirit. Let me open my soul to new opportunities, new ways of thinking and let me relish the joy of the Beltane season. So mote it be!

After this, sit and gaze into the fire. After a few breaths to acclimate to stillness and say:

Hail Athena, I begin with this meditation on you!

As you envision Athena, pay attention to her specific qualities. Note that she is a balance of martial arts and education. Athena has qualities of war in her, yes, but she also pursued necessary domestic skills: she could weave, she could write, and she embodied the perfect balance between domestic and martial discipline. She concerned herself with the big issues of the world, what we would now call matters of state.

Pause, and listen for what Athena might say to you.
Pour out a libation to her as thanks.

Next, envision Artemis. As the virgin goddess of the moon, she also appreciated solitary pursuits such as hunting—but she did not always choose isolation. She had her friends, male and female, some of whom hunted alongside her. She also served friends, protecting women all the way up to childbirth and looking after her animal companions as well.

Pause, and listen for what Artemis might say to you.
Pour out a libation to her as thanks.

Next, envision Vesta. This may be more difficult as she had very few tales spoken of her. She embodied the pleasures of the home life, and helped those who honored her maintain happy, prosperous homes. Think of how your home might feel with her in it.

Pause, and listen for what Vesta might say to you.
Pour out a libation to her as thanks.

Ritual Closing

Farewell to Athena, to Artemis, to Vesta
Virgin queens, show me the way
to the richness of life, independent and free.
Blessed be!

(Pour an additional libation to each goddess.)

Quarter Releases

North:
Gentle powers of the north and earth,
I give you sweet release! Blessed be!
West:
Gentle powers of the west and water,
I give you sweet release!

South:
Gentle powers of the south and fire,
I give you sweet release!

East:
Gentle powers of the east and air,
I give you sweet release!

Circle Closing

(walking counterclockwise)
The fire on the ground may fade,
yet more powerful are the longer days.
My heart fed by heat and sun—
Bring on the summer, bring on the curiosities,
bring on the fun!

Notes

Litha

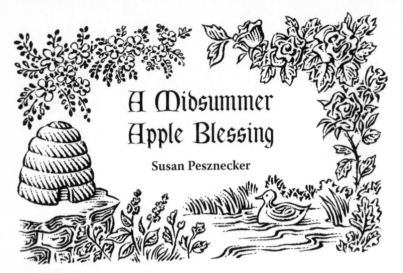

A Midsummer Apple Blessing

Susan Pesznecker

THE APPLE. WHERE WOULD we be without it—without apple pies and apple cider and apple cake and pork baked with apples and apple brandy and… I could go on, but I'm sure you can fill in the blanks with some of your own favorites. Apples make the world go 'round. An apple a day keeps the doctor away. We take our friend the apple for granted because it's available to us year-round in plain sight, filling the grocer's shelves. And yet despite the apple's apparent plainness and simplicity, it has a rich, complex history and is associated with a number of traditions. Let's consider the apple….

If you're Pagan, you already know that many cultures and traditions venerate the apple in myth and story. Norse mythology, which depicts apples as a food of the gods and a key to immortality, tells the story of Loki luring Iounn, the apple keeper, out of Asgard on the pretense of checking out some new apple cultivars. (This didn't work out well for Iounn.) In stories of Avalon, the mythic Isle of Avalon is home to verdant, mystical apple orchards, and the name "Avalon" is said by some to be a derivation of the word *apple* or to mean "Apple Isle." The Roman goddess Pomona is said to have been responsible for the apple harvest in ancient times and for the spring's apple blossoms, while Polish folklore believed apple trees were "dream trees";

sleeping under one could induce prophetic visions. The Greeks share a number of myths in which apples are either a focus of immortality or appear as "golden apples," a treasure of unimaginable worth—everybody wants one. Indeed, the golden apple pops up throughout both myth and fairy tale across many cultures, always as a symbol of wealth, power, and/or immortality. Science fiction genius Ray Bradbury would, in 1953, pen the story "The Golden Apples of the Sun," a futuristic testimony to hubris and the search for power. And, of course, the Christian mythos has its Garden of Eden, with the apple as the forbidden fruit that ruled mortality, casting humans out of paradise and into the realm of finite life and original sin.

Modern Pagan traditions continue to venerate the apple, typically viewing it as a power object. Discordianism recalls "The Apple of Discord," a golden apple belonging to the Greek goddess Eris and used to get Olympus's goddesses mad at each other, which may have led to the Trojan War. To Celtic reconstructionists, the apple is an emblem of transformation. Druid lore tells of carrying apple branches to which were affixed small silver, gold, or brass bells as tokens of office, and many Druids continue this practice today. Wiccans view apples as symbols of fertility and the harvest as well as having a feminine correspondence, with apple blossoms used frequently in love charms and spells. Cut an apple through its equator, and a perfect pentagram appears in the center. Peel an apple so the peels fall in a single piece, and the fallen strip is said to take the shape of one's future mate. In Wicca, apples are also seen as a food of the dead, appearing during the autumn harvest as the year wanes toward the metaphorical death of winter, and they often show up on Mabon (MA-bunn, with the MA rhyming with "cat") and Samhain (SOW-unn) feast tables or in the Dumb Supper.

Apples are also associated with the practice of "Wassailing the Orchards," which involves trooping into orchards in January to sing to the trees (and to drink a hearty quantity of mead!). The singing and loud festivity are aimed at frightening away evil spirits and ensuring the trees' health, while cider and cream are spilled around each tree's roots as offerings for health and fecundity. This is a custom that began as uniquely British but today is maintained in many other places as well—including my own mini-orchard in northwestern Oregon.

Probably the greatest homage to the apple is the autumn harvest festival. Autumn is one of the year's pivot-points: temperatures drop, days shorten as we move toward the Winter Solstice (the longest and darkest night of the year), and most of us feel a fierce drive to prepare for the coming cold months. Harvest festivals are a worldwide phenomenon—every culture has one. It's the time to celebrate the harvest and collectively put away food and goods for winter, a process known as "wintering in" (or in some places as harvest home). Since apples ripen between late summer and early to mid-autumn in perfect synchrony with reaping time, they're a focal point of harvest celebrations. Today there are more than 2,000 apple cultivars throughout the world—with more being developed all the time. A visit to a fall farmers' market is a good opportunity to sample a number of them as well as check out the latest technology in apple-peelers and hand-screwed cider presses.

Overall, apples and orchards are honored throughout the year in a number of ways, beginning with the wassailing of existing orchards in deep winter—January. The wassailing is followed by the planting or grafting of new apple tree stock in early to mid-spring, which is invariably accompanied by spontaneous rituals of nurturing and care as the young tree is fed, watered, and protected from the elements. Skip ahead several months to autumn's harvest home, where the tree's life cycle bear's fruit for all.

A Fruit for Most Seasons

Apple love, ritual, and nurturing in the winter, spring, and autumn. Sounds great—but what's missing? Why, the summer! Summer is the time when fruit is set and the apple trees put all of their energies into producing the bounty of brilliant, crunchy fruit that we'll covet come September. But they're apparently doing that without magickal support from us, the ones who love them. I have a small orchard of my own (and by the way, if you have three or more fruit trees, you have an orchard!), and in terms of the apples, summer had always seemed like a big empty gap in the midst of a year of ritual work among the trees. "What was needed?" I asked myself. And then it came to me. What was missing was a summertime ritual to bless and cheer on the trees during their growth period, appealing to the gods for each tree's life and success as well as raising energy to inspire their bountiful production. And what followed next was me pulling a chair out in the space among my trees and sitting down with pen and paper to draft an apple blessing ritual.

When would be the ideal time for the ritual? I settled on Midsummer—the Summer Solstice, known as Litha (LEE-thuh) in some traditions. The wassailing tradition had gotten the trees off to a good start in the winter, and the nurturing and care had extended through spring. Midsummer is the pivot point between summer and winter—the Summer Solstice features the solar year's longest day and the longest period of daylight, with the days then beginning to diminish in length as the wheel swings back toward the winter solstice. It seemed like the perfect time to give the trees a seasonal boost.

Midsummer Apple Ritual

With that decided, I asked myself what such a ritual would need.

First, it would need people. Since the apple crop leads to the celebration of harvest—traditionally a communal activity—I decided that a proper Midsummer apple ritual needed a number of people: a gathering of magickal friends. The participants would work together to carry out the ritual and to celebrate after.

We'd begin by walking together in procession to the ritual location: the apple orchard. An altar space would be set up in advance, and we'd sing and maybe even dance a little as we walked—getting an early leg up on the energy raising. We might wear apple colors too.

Once at the ritual site, we'd pray to or entreat the gods of choice or the local land spirits. We'd raise additional energy with singing, drums, and bells—frightening out any lingering evil spirits as we did so. We'd sing with joy for the apples and the bounty they'd bring to the world. We'd follow this with care and offerings, allowing the energy to begin to ebb as we worked, and then we'd pause for a moment of shared gratitude. Finally, we'd offer thanks and enjoy "cakes and ale" with an apple focus. Later on, we'd walk quietly from the trees, duty discharged (and full of delicious apple treats!).

The original plans took shape and a ritual was born. I have since done this ritual several times, all but once with my friends. The one time I worked solo was fine, although not as richly ceremonial as when others were with me. But it was all good, and with each year's ritual, I've fine-tuned the proceedings. In response, I have been rewarded each year with healthy, thriving trees and a ridiculously huge crop of apples—so many that I process bushels, give away boxes, and still take a carload to the annual cider pressing in the nearby urban farm store. I'm a believer, and I'd like to share the ritual details with you so you and your trees can benefit as well. Later on in this chapter (starting on page 227), you'll be able to read the entire ritual. I hope you enjoy it!

The Correspondences of Apple

Here is some additional information about the apple—you can use it to work with details in your seasonal or ritual work.

Family: Rosaceae
Genus: *Malus*
Species: *x domestica* (various cultivars)
Other names: Crabapple, Fruit of Avalon, Fruit of the Gods, Fruit of the Underworld, the Silver Bough, the Silver Branch, the Tree of Life, the Tree of Love, Wild Apple, Witch Tree
Gender: female
Elements: air, water
Direction: west

Stones: rose quartz, emerald, garnet

Planetary: Venus

Astrological: primary in Libra and Taurus; secondary in Cancer, Pisces, and Scorpio

Gods: Apollo, Dionysus, Eros, Lugh, Mananan, Olocun (blossoms), Shango (blossoms), Tegid, Vertumnus, Zeus

Goddesses: Athena, Aphrodite, Astarte, Babd, Cailleach, Cerridwen, Diana, Flora, Freya, Gaia, Hera, Idunn/Iounn, Ishtar, Macha, Nemesis, Ochun (blossoms), Olwen, Pomona, Rhiannon, Venus

Day of week: Friday

Modern (Gregorian) calendar: spring (planting), summer (growth), and autumn (harvest)

Celtic calendar*: September

Ogham: Quert

Rune: Ing

Energy: yin

Chakra: brow

Parts used: peel and flesh; the seeds are mildly poisonous if taken in large quantity

Medical actions: treats diarrhea (lots of natural pectin); may ease sleep

Magickal uses: one of the nine sacred woods in Celtic lore; sometimes called a gateway to the Underworld; an excellent wood for making wands; ancient Druids carried bell branches made from apple wood; apples are often used in the "dumb suppers" of Samhain; protection; consecration; contacting the afterlife; known to be a sacred food of the Gods; widely used in spells for love and attraction and to heighten sexual desire; the blossoms' scent is considered intoxicating and bewitching; fertility; marriage; rebirth; wisdom; youthfulness and immortality

***Note:** The "Celtic tree calendar" is a modern invention and was actually neither known nor practiced by the ancient Celts. However, many folks today follow it as a modern convention.

For Further Reading

Drew, A. J. *A Wiccan Formulary and Herbal.* Franklin Lakes, NJ: New Page, 2005.

Kynes, Sandra. *Llewellyn's Complete Book of Correspondences.* Woodbury, MN: Llewellyn, 2013.

Rosenberg, Donna. *World Mythology: An Anthology of Great Myths and Epics.* New York: McGraw-Hill, 2001.

Cosmic Sway

April Elliott Kent

We welcome the Summer Solstice and Midsummer as the Sun enters Cancer at 6:35 p.m. Eastern time. In astrology, the Sun is associated with the sign of Leo, and in a couple of weeks from now, Mercury, Venus, and the Sun will all enter that royal sign. But it's telling that the Sun, the symbol of all that gives us life and a sense of personal importance, reaches the Summer Solstice in Cancer, the sign of family. Without a strong sense of family, of belonging to a safe haven of loved ones who care and look out for us, it's incredibly difficult to embrace the qualities that make us unique.

At this Summer Solstice, we celebrate the Sun, giver of life, and we celebrate the family that nurtures and protects that life. Just hours after an intense Full Moon at the last degree of Sagittarius, the Solstice Moon is in serious, paternal Capricorn, opposed the Sun and Moon. Mother and Father unite to lend us the support and love we need to move forward into whatever the summer wishes to bring.

Ritual to Honor the Ancestors

A few years ago, I visited Stonehenge for the first time, just after Midsummer. What I wouldn't give to celebrate a Summer Solstice at that magical place! But what our own rituals may lack in epic scale, they can make up in creativity and soul.

With the Sun in Cancer and the Moon in Capricorn, let's honor the ancestors who brought us into the physical world and who live on through our DNA. Family ties can be fraught, and you may find this waning Moon Solstice is a good time to disconnect from old family patterns that bring you pain. It is difficult to entirely reject ancestors, though, without rejecting a part of yourself.

At this Solstice, gather family—those related to you by blood, or those whom your heart has chosen for you. Ask each person to bring a photo and a remembrance of an ancestor. In a safe place, create a simple altar and provide a small candle for each participant. Build a bonfire, or light a chimenea or tiki torches to honor the Sun. Include some element of water—a fountain, swimming pool, ocean, lake, pond, or stream—to honor the Moon.

At sunset, have each family member place his or her ancestral photo upon the altar and take a candle. In turn, each can light his or her candle from the common fire source and tell the story of their ancestor. When each is finished, lead a simple invocation to thank the fierce spirits of our ancestors for their positive legacies, and release the fearful, damaged spirit debris to be burned up in the fire. Stick your candles in the dirt and let them burn down while you share a meal together.

Celestial Highlights

Mars moves direct on June 29, ending a long retrograde period (since April 17). Mars retrograde periods are filled with delays and roadblocks, and it will be good to finally feel that we're moving forward again!

It seems summer doesn't really get started until a planet or two moves into Leo, the Sun's own sign. Venus enters this joyful, fun-loving sign on July 11, followed by Mercury on the 13th and the Sun on July 22. Grab your sunblock, call your friends, and head to the beach or the pool—Leo wants to play!

New Moon in Cancer – July 4, 2016

At this Cancer New Moon, the United States celebrates its birth as an independent nation. It is traditionally a time of happy summer barbecues with family, beach parties with friends, fireworks, and music.

This New Moon degree is in opposition to Pluto in Capricorn, though, so the mood is not entirely carefree. Serious matters occupy our minds and hearts. Sometimes we are unhappy with the direction our lives appear to be taking, or even with the condition of the world itself. These are the matters that weigh on us now.

But just as there was a dream that brought men of vision together in Philadelphia in 1776, each of us has the ability to conjure the world that we desire to live in. This New Moon is in a shimmering trine to imaginative Neptune, reminding us that if we dream vividly enough, the dream can become contagious. We can find like-minded souls to share the vision and to help us give it form. With Saturn square to Neptune, this is the New Moon for dreaming a new world, and for taking steps to make it come true.

Full Moon in Capricorn – July 19, 2016

There is a large aviary in the zoo near my home. It is vast and filled with lovely birds. They have a lot of room to fly around. They are safe from predators. But they are not free.

At this Full Moon, the Sun and Moon in the parental signs of Cancer and Capricorn are both square Uranus, the planet of freedom and rebellion. Each of us faces moments when we must choose between safety and security and the glorious independence of living an entirely different kind of life. For each of us, with varying degrees of intensity, this Full Moon represents such a moment.

The Sun and Moon make supportive aspects to Mars, the planet of courage and decisive action, strong in fearless Scorpio. You are ready to make your own declaration of independence. Don't be afraid. You have honored the ancestors this Solstice season, and they will stand behind you now, even as you break away and walk alone in the Full Moon light, down a path of your very own.

❧

As Midsummer begins, a powerful configuration involving Jupiter, Saturn, Neptune, and the Lunar Nodes is triggered by fast-moving Mercury. This combination of planets in mutable signs (Virgo, Sagittarius, and Pisces) is like a windmill—it generates a lot of energy, but it's difficult to harness. The areas most affected will be finances (Jupiter/Saturn), ideology (Jupiter/Neptune), disillusionment (Saturn/Neptune), and tension between faith (South Node in Pisces) and critical thinking (North Node in Virgo). Those born with the Sun, Moon, Ascendant, or Midheaven in one of the mutable signs will be particularly vulnerable to stress and overwhelm, with the influence strongest in the last week of June, and again in late August through early October.

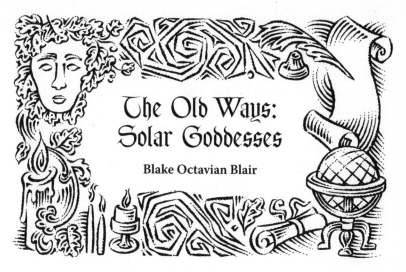

The Old Ways: Solar Goddesses

Blake Octavian Blair

LITHA, OR MIDSUMMER, IS the quintessential solar celebration. It centers around the sun with good reason, as this sabbat marks the longest day and shortest night of the year. The sun is seen to be at the height of its power. For these reasons, it is a sabbat that often celebrates the divine masculine and corresponding male deities. However, the divine feminine also has a foothold on this day. Cultures around the world bring to us a plethora of solar associated goddesses, some who possess an inseparable link with Midsummer itself.

Aine (Irish)

The Irish goddess Aine is the embodiment of protection, love, fertility, and good health. It is said that her power reaches its pinnacle on Midsummer's Day. Her associations with fertility also gained her status as an agricultural deity. She is petitioned for blessings of protection and success of the season's crops. She is often depicted as riding a flaming red mare—which conjures a visual connection to the flaming sun that she is so interconnected with. Midsummer has bountiful lore and a long connection to the fairy realms—and so does Aine. She is so embedded into Irish culture that several modern families claim to have Aine in their ancestral line. She is associated with several sacred sites in Ireland, some of which bear forms of her name within the Irish form of their titles, such as Toberanna, which in Irish is *Tobar Aine*. The goddess Aine has even managed to survive the infiltration of Christianity among the Irish people by being reinvented as a fairy queen! If you honor the fairy folk on Midsummer, remember to give a nod to the goddess Aine as well.

Sol, or Sunna (Norse)

Another goddess of the Sun who is connected with its journey across the sky comes to us from the cosmology of the Norse. The goddess Sol, or Sunna, is viewed as the Sun personified. She travels across the sky on a horse-drawn chariot and rules the daily cycle of light and dark. Sunna's journey across the sky, and rising and setting, became logically very closely associated with agriculture and the cycle of the crops. This continues a developing theme of solar goddesses with a good steed as deities of agriculture. Sunna's constant presence in the sky in the form of the Sun is often said to be a visual reminder of the gods' presence in our lives and reminds us to call upon them for assistance in times of need.

Amaterasu (Japanese)

As we have seen, many of these solar manifestations of the divine feminine often embody many maternal qualities. If we head to the Far East and to Japan, we are introduced to Amaterasu, who is a solar goddess that offers her followers compassionate and nurturing protection. She is actually properly categorized as a Kami. Kami are the indigenous spirits in Japan's Shinto religion and Amaterasu is venerated as the top Kami of the Shinto pantheon. Further reinforcing her image as a maternal figure, the Japanese imperial family claims that their lineage descends from her. Her central mythology revolves around her retreat into a cave in reaction to rude actions on the part of her brother, Susano—a storm god, who defiled the rice fields of which she held dominion over. This in turn plunged the world into darkness as she is indeed considered the sun personi-

fied. This threatened the success of the crops and the health of the
people. One version of the conclusion of the story sees Amaterasu
drawn out of the cave by alluring reflections, including the beauty
of her own reflection, from a mirror placed outside the entrance of
the cave by other Kami. Legend has it that Amaterasu's mirror, called
"Yasakani no magatama," hangs even today in the Ise Grand Shrine
in Mie Prefecture, Japan. The cave in which she is said to have withdrawn into is also nearby. The round mirror's appearance even conjures solar symbolism. The story itself fundamentally shows how the
life giving power of the sun was attributed to the maternal divine
feminine and the importance to and dependence of the people upon
its powers for survival. When cast in that light, it becomes very easy
to see the sun personified as feminine rather than masculine.

Bastet, or Bast (Egyptian)

One popular and very maternal goddess worshiped by many as a
lunar deity, Bastet, in fact has origins as a solar goddess. More simply and popularly called Bast, she is now in many places worshiped
as both a solar and a lunar goddess. Bast is not viewed as the sun
personified; however, her solar links are undeniably strong. She is
commonly considered the daughter, or in some circles the wife, of
sun god Ra. Ra is considered to be the sun himself. Bast's popularity
among magickal folk is really no surprise. She holds dominion over
a wide array of life areas including fertility, prosperity, healing, love,
parenting, childhood, and more. Her dominion over cats is likely a
solidifying factor for her relationship to many modern magick makers—as witches and cats are often an almost synonymous pairing.
Her annual festival, called Bubastis, is a rowdy celebration of sexu-
ality, music, dance, and great joy. Bubastis could be perhaps (and
often is) described as a combination of Beltane and Mardi Gras!

Roman Goddesses of Dawn

The Romans offer us not one but two goddesses of the dawn. One of
them is Mater Matuta. Among her areas of specialty is the protection

of newborn babies. This is not at all surprising when we consider the symbolism of the dawn of a new day, and the growth of the sacred light on the horizon and into the sky, as parallel to the birth and raising of a newborn child. Both ring of the birth of life and new beginnings. Secondly, Mater Matuta falls into good company with the long line of solar goddesses with maternal instincts. The second solar goddess that comes to us from the Romans is Aurora. She is the light of the dawn embodied, and like the Norse Sunna, rides a chariot across the sky. It is important to note that Aurora is not considered as the sun, but rather the spirit of the dawn's light. The sun and the moon are Aurora's brother, Sol, and sister, Luna. A fun bit of lore is that Aurora is associated with the exotic spice saffron. It is said that the bed she leaves every morning for her chariot ride across the sky is made of saffron. Of course, the golden color of saffron is also the color of the radiant light of the shining dawn.

From the goddess-turned-fairy-queen Aine to the chariot rides of Sunna and Aurora, we can see that Litha is the territory of the divine feminine and solar goddesses as much as it is a celebration of the god. This Midsummer's Day may you and yours be blessed with the abundance, protection, and maternal compassion of the solar goddesses!

Bibliography

Dugan, Ellen. *The Enchanted Cat: Feline Fascinations, Spells & Magick.* Woodbury, MN: Llewellyn Publications, 2006.

Illes, Judika. *Encyclopedia of Spirits: The Ultimate Guide to the Magic of Fairies, Genies, Demons, Ghosts, Gods & Goddesses.* New York: Harper One, 2009.

Krasskova, Galina. *Exploring the Northern Tradition: A Guide to the Gods, Lore, Rites, and Celebrations From the Norse, German, and Anglo-Saxon Traditions.* Franklin Lakes, NJ: New Page Books, 2005.

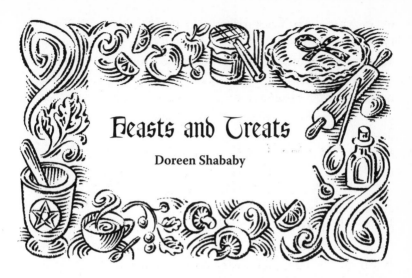

Feasts and Treats

Doreen Shababy

LITHA DRAWS US TO the great outdoors, from dancing the night away under the mantel of the midnight sky to camping out and waiting for it to get dark and seeing that it never really did. The level of activity has switched from busy school days to cruise mode. Let's enjoy the season with picnics, kayaking, farmers' markets... and good summer eats!

Grilled Eggplant Subs

I like to use Italian eggplant for this dish, but if you find another sort that are fresh, firm, and shiny, then use those and portion accordingly. You don't have to use an outdoor grill to prepare this; a grill pan is actually preferred, and a heavy skillet will work as well.

Prep time: 15 minutes, plus 30 minutes rest time for eggplant
Cooking time: 20 minutes
Serves: 6

2 medium Italian eggplants
Salt for sprinkling
Salt and pepper to season
Garlic powder to season

6 6-inch crusty sandwich rolls
Olive oil pan spray
1 24-ounce jar mushroom marinara sauce (I like Muir Glen)
6 ounces mozzarella, grated
Soft butter for spreading

First, trim eggplants and peel. Slice into ½-inch rounds, place in a large bowl, and sprinkle heavily with salt. Set aside for 30 minutes.

While the eggplant is resting, pour the marinara sauce into a pan to heat thoroughly, and keep warm at low temperature. Slice the rolls most of the way through, keeping a hinge on one side. (You can toast these under the broiler for a couple minutes if you have time.)

Rinse eggplant well and pat dry with a towel. Season with salt, pepper, and garlic powder, and coat lightly with olive oil spray. Spray grill pan with olive oil, then heat to medium-high. Place the eggplant in the pan without crowding and grill until it begins to soften and you have some nice grill marks on the bottom. Use tongs to turn over and grill until done, which should take about 10 minutes total. Remove from pan and repeat with the remaining eggplant, wiping out pan if necessary to keep it clean. Keep eggplant warm in a covered casserole.

To prepare the submarine sandwiches for eating, spread some butter on the rolls, then dab a little sauce on each side. Layer a few pieces of eggplant on each, sprinkle with cheese, then a little more sauce, and serve hot. If you can eat this without making a mess, you deserve a prize.

Artichoke Cannellini Salad

I have been taking this salad to potluck dinners for years, and I know I'm not the only one who totally loves it. It takes no planning except to chill, because nearly all the ingredients are already on your pantry shelves. It can be served as is, or on a bed of fresh garden greens.

Prep time: 10 minutes, plus a couple hours chill time
Serves: 6

1 16-ounce can cannellini beans, rinsed and drained
1 6-ounce can whole ripe olives, drained (reserve the brine)
1 6-ounce jar marinated artichoke hearts with liquid
1 clove garlic, minced
1 tiny jar pimientos, drained
2 teaspoons balsamic (or apple cider) vinegar
½ teaspoon dried oregano
Salt and pepper to season

In a large mixing bowl, place the beans, olives, artichokes with liquid (trim off any tough leaves and cut in half if necessary), garlic, pimientos, and vinegar, and stir together gently. Add the oregano, salt and pepper. If the salad seems like it needs a little more dressing add a splash of the olive brine. Chill for at least 2 hours before serving.

Peaches Baked in Amaretto

Peaches are part of what summer is all about. They are a cousin to almonds, with whom they pair wonderfully. The caramelized syrup and crumbly shortbread just add to the allure of this wonderful baked dessert.

Prep time: 15 minutes
Cook time: 30 minutes, plus 15 minutes of cooling
Serves: 6

10 almond (or plain) shortbread cookies, crushed
6 tablespoons soft butter, divided, plus extra for baking dish
½ cup natural sugar, divided
½ cup amaretto liqueur, divided
½ cup chopped almonds
3 large ripe free-stone peaches, halved and peeled
3 tablespoons lemon juice
¼ cup water

Heat oven to 400 degrees F. Butter a shallow casserole dish large enough for the peaches. Stir together the cookies, half the butter, half the sugar, 2 tablespoons of the amaretto, and the almonds until well mixed. Have a little sip of the amaretto.

Brush the peaches with half the lemon juice, then dip in the remaining sugar. Combine remaining amaretto and lemon juice with the water, then pour into prepared casserole. Arrange peaches in the dish.

Sprinkle the cookie-crumb mixture onto the peaches, making sure to pack the cavity where the stone was removed. Dot each peach with remaining butter. Cover dish with foil, turn oven down to 350 degrees F, and bake for 10 minutes. Then remove the foil and bake another 20 minutes or until crumbs are lightly browned and the syrup is bubbly. Remove from oven to cool 15 minutes before serving.

Optional: Serve each peach with a scoop of vanilla ice cream. Summerlicious.

Spiced Lemon Water

This is an incredibly thirst-quenching drink with a little bit of a bite. Just how much bite is up to you. We try to keep a pitcher of it going in our kitchen on a regular basis as a healthful tonic drink, but if you've never tasted it before, you will appreciate the unexpected flavor.

Prep time: 5 minutes, plus 1 hour chill time

Serves: 6–8

1 large, heavy (which means juicy) lemon, juiced
¼ cup pure maple syrup, or to taste
A couple shakes of cayenne powder

In a two-quart pitcher, combine the lemon juice, maple syrup, and cayenne, then fill most of the way full with cold water. I don't usually worry about the seeds, since they fall to the bottom, plus I like the pulp. Taste for sweetness, but leave it on the tart side. Most likely you won't need any more cayenne since it gets a little spicier as it sits. Chill for an hour before serving in small glasses.

Crafty Crafts

Tess Whitehurst

IT'S THE SUN'S PINNACLE: the longest day of the year, and the time when the summer reaches its full expression. Paradoxically, it's also the time when the days begin once again to wane and the sun's journey around the wheel reaches Cancer, a water sign and the only sign ruled by the moon. In the words of author Claire Nahmad in *Earth Magic*, "Cancer, the heavenly Crab, is a creature of the lunar tides that are the breath, in and out, of the great sea of all life, the boundless causal ocean that has ever been the symbol of the Great Mother."

Not coincidentally, imagery related to summer—even in our contemporary, secular culture—is generally equal parts sunshine and water: warm, expansive brightness and cool, watery depths.

The crafts below will guide you to make beautiful, quintessential representations of the elements of fire and water. You can display them on your altar, and they can also be placed around a ritual circle at the south and west cardinal points (for fire and water, respectively).

Flower Petal "Bonfire" Candleholder

Time to complete: 2 to 3 hours (mostly drying time), plus 3 days for pressing the flower petals
Cost: $10.00 to $12.00

Supplies

Flower petals in fiery colors (I chose red dahlia petals and the colored, petal-like leaves of fuchsia and red bougainvilleas)

2 paper towels

A large book

A small, rounded, wide-topped, glass vase (approx. 4–5 inches tall)

Orange and red tissue paper

Flour

Water

A bowl

A paintbrush

Acrylic varnish

A small wreath made of sticks or twigs that will fit around the base of the vase (this can be made or purchased)

A tealight candle

Instructions: Lay the flower petals flat on a paper towel, and cover with another paper towel. Place the paper towels in the middle of a large book and close it, possibly piling a few other books or heavy items on top of it as well. Allow the pressed petals to dry for three days.

In the bowl, make a paste out of one part flour and two parts water. Paint this mixture onto the vase in sections, pasting pieces of torn orange and red tissue paper around the entire outside surface as you go. Allow to dry for an hour.

Repeat this process to paste the flower petals over the tissue paper as desired. (The idea is to create the feeling of stylized flames.) Allow to dry for another hour.

When it feels completely dry to the touch, paint the surface with the acrylic varnish to seal, and allow to dry.

Place the candleholder within the wreath to create the vibe and feeling of a mini bonfire. To use, place the tealight in the candleholder and light. For rituals and simple seasonal décor, you can arrange fresh flowers and herbs in the wreath. (I did this with lavender, geranium, and sage last Midsummer, and it was lovely.)

Mason Jar Ocean "Globe"

The same concept as a snow globe, this homemade jar ocean "globe" will bless your altar with a little splash of a clear tide pool or sparkling ocean wave.

Time to complete: Less than 15 minutes
Cost: $3.00 to $5.00

Supplies

Mason jar with lid (I used an 8 oz. jar)
Distilled or reverse-osmosis water (other water may yellow with time)
Clear, blue, purple, and/or lavender glass marbles
Optional: One or more found seashells (do not purchase unless you trust the source, as commercially available seashells may have been cruelly harvested)

Instructions: Making sure all the supplies are very clean, begin by placing your seashells (if you have any) in the bottom of the jar. Then fill a quarter to a half of the jar the rest of the way with marbles. Pour the water over the top, leaving a half inch to an inch of air at the top of the jar, then seal tightly with the lid. Flip the jar upside down, so that the lid is on the bottom. (That's it!)

Before displaying it on your altar, I recommend placing it on a paper towel for at least 15 minutes or so to make absolutely sure that it's sealed tightly (and therefore not leaking).

Water and Fire Success Ritual for the Summer Solstice

With the sun and summer at their peak, Litha can be an ideal time to work success magic. This ritual draws upon the power of water and the moon to cleanse away any blocks to success, and then the power of fire and the sun to infuse you with the bright, blazing energy of success. It can be done alone or in a group.

After casting a circle, invoke the watery aspects of the moon by saying something like:

Glowing Lady of the night,
Matron of the silver light,
As you attend the ocean's tide,
Please come to us and be our guide.
What does not serve, please clear away,
So that success can light our way.
Just as rushing waves flow free,
We thank you well, so mote it be.

If you're in a circle with others, pass a chalice or bottle of blessed water around the circle in a counterclockwise direction, instructing each participant to cleanse her personal energy and clear out blocks to success by anointing her forehead, throat, and heart center. Complete the circle by doing so yourself. (Or, if you're solitary, just anoint yourself.)

Next, invoke the fiery, life-giving properties of the sun by saying something like:

Bright and blazing God of sun,
Lord of all and everyone,
Please come to us and share your light
That we may shine with all that's bright.
May we walk a road that's blessed,
As you pave our way with great success.
By your rays so heavenly,
We thank you well, so mote it be.

Lift the bonfire candleholder (leaving the wreath on the altar or in the circle). Pass it around the circle in a clockwise direction, instructing each participant to hold it in both hands and visualize a sphere of bright sunlight completely surrounding and encompassing her, infusing her with the lucky energy of success. Finish with yourself.

You may want to continue your Midsummer ritual with songs and chanting. Then give thanks to the moon and the sun, and open the circle in the usual way.

For Further Reading

Nahmad, Claire. *Earth Magic: A Wisewoman's Guide to Herbal, Astrological, & Other Folk Wisdom*. Rochester, VT: Destiny Books, 1994.

All One Family: Midsummer Secrets

Linda Raedisch

IT'S NO SECRET: WITCHES love string. In fact, I think it's safe to say they love it almost as much as their cats do. Medieval witches were believed to work spells with the aid of *aiguillettes*, knotted loops of string. Add a few feathers to a length of string and you have a witch's sewel or wishing rope. You could even steal a person's shadow just by measuring it with a piece of string. So prevalent was this string magic that, as Christianity worked its way north into Europe, the church issued special edicts against the tying and untying of knots. The oldest piece of string we have dates to 15000 BCE and was apparently dropped by one of the famous cave painters of Lascaux. While it might have been used to work magic, it's a little thick to have been used for Cat's Cradle, which is the subject of this article.

It's possible you are not familiar with the term "Cat's Cradle." When I recently came upon my daughter's nine-year-old friend "Natalia" (I've changed her name in the interests of being mysterious) with that familiar web of string between her fingers, I said, "Oh! Cat's Cradle!" And she said, "What?"

"This," I said, inserting my thumbs and forefingers into the figure and attempting to transfer it onto my own hands the way you're supposed to.

"I didn't know you called it that," said Natalia as the intricate figure sagged and lost its shape. (I've never been good at Cat's Cradle.)

"Well, what do *you* call it?" I asked Natalia.

"It's just string."

String figures, as the anthropologists like to call them, are an ancient phenomenon. When we sit down with a friend to make the "cat's cradle," we are engaging in an activity that dates back to the days before there even were cats. Of course, it's not always called Cat's Cradle. The Chukchi of Siberia like to make a "house" while the Australian aborigines make a "drum." Originally, they were used to illustrate stories, much like Hans Christian Andersen's on-the-fly paper-cuts. The Navajo used the same figures to represent the shifting position of the Pleiades in the night sky, while among the Inuit, the time for making string figures is just after the summer solstice, the idea being to trap the sun inside the figure and keep it from disappearing as it will in the winter. (Yes, that's why I've chosen to write about string figures for Midsummer: that and the fact that it's a fun game to play while sitting on the stoop of a summer's evening.)

In Japan, string figures in general are known as *ayatori*. My highly sketchy command of Japanese does not allow me to provide you with a literal translation of ayatori, but one of the signature figures in ayatori is the *neko*, which means "cat." Instead of lying down quietly in its cradle, however, the cat turns into a *nekomata*, a "wild cat," on the next move.

It's clear that the making of string figures used to be, and in some places still is, much more than a game. We've managed to keep the figures themselves here in the west, but what happened to the stories, spells, and lessons that used to go with them? I have a feeling it had something to do with those early church edicts. Like nursery rhymes, our string figures must also have held some deep, dark secrets.

In our house, my sister was the mistress of Cat's Cradle, so I decided to call her up and pick her brain, forty or so years after the fact.

"After the Cat's Cradle," she explained patiently, "you make it into Scissors, and the two players can pull the string back and forth to make it look like the scissors are cutting. Oh, yes, and then there was Water. There were four parallel strings, like a river with the banks on either side. No, wait, wait . . . that was Chinese Jump Rope."

For those of you born after the early seventies, Chinese Jump Rope is a bungee-like band, usually brightly colored (wasn't everything in the seventies?), that one stretched between the legs of two chairs and then jumped in and out of. Like Cat's Cradle, there were all different figures you could make. Is it ancient? Is it even Chinese? I have no idea.

"Why is it called Cat's Cradle?" I asked my sister, for surely she could tell me that much.

"I have no idea."

The name may originally have been "Cratch Cradle," with "cratch" being an old word for "crib," which would give us a meaning of "cradle, cradle," which seems silly to me. Natalia's mother told me later that she had played the game as a child in Nepal. It had no name. "Everybody just knew it. Everybody did it." She was amazed when she found out kids did it here; just as I had assumed it was a seventies thing, she had believed it was played only on the streets of Kathmandu.

If you don't yet know how to play Cat's Cradle, YouTube awaits. If, like me, you'd rather look at archival photographs of children playing it all around the world, I would direct you to search for Cat's Cradle in the Smithsonian Collections Blog. My favorite is "Two Girls in Informal Costume Sitting on a Mat and Playing Cat's Cradle with String on Snow, no date," which shows two little Ainu girls bundled up against the cold, their fingers artfully entwined.

❦

This just in from our old friend Mother Goose: she says if I wanted to give the children something exciting to read on Midsummer Eve, I should have written about "Here We Go 'Round the Mulberry Bush."

But, Mother Goose, there are no "cold and frosty mornings" at Midsummer, not even in England, I would guess.

Nevertheless, she tells me, in England it was customary for girls to dance round a mulberry bush, which is really more of a tree, on Midsummer Eve. Thank you, Mother Goose.

Well, while we're at it, we might as well check in with the Norns. Looks like they've gotten tired of playing Nine Men's Morris: Urd has gone back to her spinning, and what's that Verdani and Skuld are concentrating on so hard? Of course, they're playing Cat's Cradle!

The Litha Apple Blessing Ritual

Susan Pesznecker

AS I EXPLAINED EARLIER in this section, I developed a midsummer apple blessing as a way to support and honor my apple trees during their summer growth period. I had become aware that Pagan traditions had provided a model for celebrating the apple trees in every quadrant of the year except for summer, and I wanted to fill the gap. This ritual is the result.

I've since done this ritual for the last several seasons, all but once with a group of magickal friends: the details and description that follow below are my fine-tuned results. The ritual I'm sharing here has been written for six people, making it perfect for a small magickal circle, coven, grove, or the like. But it would be quite easy to tailor it for more or fewer people.

• **If your group is larger than six**, simply divide out the speaking parts a little further so each person can have an active role. There are twelve individual spoken parts in the ritual below, and there are also spoken pieces when the golden apples are tied to the trees. Theoretically, you could keep expanding this for even a large group by spreading out the speaking parts (one per person) and letting everyone else tie a golden apple to one of the trees and give a spoken blessing. (The more golden apples, the more impressed the trees will be!)

- **If your group is smaller than six**, reassign the speaking parts accordingly so they're all covered. This just means some people will have more to say (and more to do) than in the example I share below. Otherwise, the ritual will still be easy to work with. If any part of it seems a little too cumbersome for a small group, you could shorten it by omitting some portions, provided the omissions don't affect the intent of the process.
- **If you want to try this as a solo ritual**, don't be afraid to do so. As a rule, larger rituals tend to have a more profound sense of seriousness and ceremony, but solo ritual can also be incredibly rewarding. I did this ritual as a solo venture once, and it remained very meaningful. If you choose to work alone, I suggest you start by reading through the entire ritual, making notes of any aspects you'd like to drop or alter in some way.

The ritual is also flexible enough to be adapted to fit your own spiritual preferences.

- It would be easy to switch deities to fit whichever Pantheon you follow. In the ritual below, I refer to the Norse goddess Iounn, who is known as Asgard's apple keeper. You could as easily refer to the Roman goddess Pomona or even to your favorite earthly or agricultural deity or local land spirit. For ideas, see the Correspondences table on pages 202 to 203. If you make changes, you may need to modify some of the wording accordingly, but in many ways, the act of customizing is one of the most fun parts of creating ritual.
- What if you want to do the ritual with your favorite non-Pagans? The ritual can easily be fine-tuned for a non-Pagan audience: simply remove the deity references and substitute words about the bounty of the earth, the changing seasons, the sun and energy of summer, or the like. Perhaps mention Johnny Appleseed's work in place of the prayers to deity. You might also want to remove the reference to the pentagram hidden inside the fruit.

Timing of Ritual

This ritual should be done on or right around Litha. The exact date isn't extremely important, but if it works to do it on Litha, it makes an extra-nice way to celebrate the sabbat. That said, the date can be considered quite flexible: while some rituals really do need to be done at a specific date and time, this isn't one of those, and that makes it easy to carry this out with a group who, for example, may only be available for weekend activities.

While the calendar cycle is flexible for this ritual, the lunar cycle is less so. I feel it's important to do carry this out during the waxing moon phase (between the new/dark moon and the full moon), as this corresponds with growth and the raising of energies, so consider this when planning the date. The closer you can get to the full moon—while still staying on the waxing side of the cycle—the better.

You'll want to think about timing, too. If you're able, I suggest doing the ritual between 10:00 a.m. to 2:00 p.m., when the sun's energies are rising and at their highest. That said, the time is flexible, too, and if you need to vary it to meet the needs of participants, it will still be effective. After all, summer probably doesn't care about our twenty-four hour clock. Traditional correspondences suggest that apple's "day of the week" is Friday—keep that in mind when planning.

Weather is always a variable in outdoor ceremonies. I think it's probably ideal to carry this one out on a sunny day, since we're honoring summer's energies—and besides: most folks prefer a sunny outdoor ritual over one held in the rain. But as far as the ritual's intent, the weather doesn't really matter. Summer is summer.

In conclusion, this ritual is meaningful, enjoyable, has practical applications, and is fairly easy to tailor to your needs. I have loved doing it every year, and the direct results include an orchard of healthy, thriving, disease-free organic trees and a crop of apples so large I can barely keep up with it. My wish is that it works just as well for you! I'd love to hear your results, too. If you have a moment, contact me on my Facebook author page (https://www.facebook.com/SusanMoonwriterPesznecker) to tell me how it went.

Items Needed

An orchard! Or a single apple tree—whatever is available. Perhaps your neighbors will allow you to bless their trees. You might also consider a private orchard—but be sure to get permission first.

A small table or card table to serve as an altar

A tablecloth—either white, like the inside of the apple, or perhaps in an apple pattern (if you can find a cute vintage fabric)

A quilt or blanket to spread over the ground in the central ritual space

Chairs for those who cannot comfortably sit on the ground

Drums, finger cymbals, rattles, and other percussion instruments

Bells

A large, stately red apple that sits upright nicely

A small bowl of granular fertilizer—or baggies or cups of fertilizer for each tree.

A jug of water—enough to offer a good pour for each tree. Or, if there are only a few trees, one small vessel of water for each tree.

Garden shears (providing more that one pair will allow additional people to work with the shears)

A small saw—the kind that could quickly cut off small broken or jagged limbs

Garden gloves—if needed to work with the tools

A sharp knife

Small cutting board

A number of strips of red, white, yellow, or green cotton fabric (no synthetics, please!)—about 1 × 18 to 24 inches

Ink pens (not permanent markers—just regular ink)

"Golden apples" made from yellow or gold paper (one for each tree), with cotton string for tying them to the trees

Cakes and ale made from apples: consider sliced apples, apple pie or cake, scones with apple butter, apple cider, etc.

Optional: Divination tools

Six or more people (This ritual may be done solo or with any number of people if needed.)

Preparation:

1. Set up the table and tablecloth in a central point among the trees.

2. Lay the quilt or blanket on the ground in front of the altar table.

3. Set up chairs around the blanket for those who need to sit.

4. Set up the table with fertilizer and water vessels; garden shears, saw, and gloves; knife and cutting board; cloth strips and pens; golden apples; cakes and ale; and optional divination tools. If you like a more formal altar, feel free to add those materials to the table—or consider having two tables: one for a "formal" altar and the other for everything else.

5. Plan a walking route to take you from a point or origin to the ritual site. If possible, the route should allow you to circle the grove or orchard before entering it or event to circle each tree, working deosil (sun-wise).

6. Assign speaking/acting parts. Spoken parts may be memorized but should also be written on small pieces of paper and given to each participant. It's better to have a script to refer to than to risk forgetting one's words.

7. Have each participant "purify" by bathing or by washing hands and face; ask everyone to dress in apple colors: red, pink, green, yellow, or white.

The Ritual Itself

[**Person 1**] bears the apple in front of her as she leads the processing to the site. Because of apple's traditional feminine correspondence, you may wish to have a woman do the bearing.

[**Remaining participants**] follow behind, singing softly, playing instruments, and swaying rhythmically as they walk. For the processional, use a customary song or chant, either a Pagan version or your favorite song about summertime. (I've sung Beach Boys tunes a couple of times. Seriously.)

Upon arrival at the central space and altar table, [**all participants**] form a circle around the ground quilt with the apple-bearer standing closest to the altar table.

[**All participants**] turn to face each other.

[**Person 1**] holds the apple up in both hands, showing it to all participants, then turns and sets it in the center of the altar table.

[**Person 2**] *See the shape of the apple, its roundness a reminder of the circles and cycles of life which bind us and all the seasons.*

[**Person 3**] *See the color of the apple, its red cheeks reminding us of health and vitality, gifts the apple gives willingly. As it is said, an apple a day keeps the doctor away!*

[**Person 4**] *Let us offer prayers to Iounn, ever-young, keeper of the apples, the rejuvenating one.*

[**Person 5**] *Great Iounn, you who have kept apples since time began, you who watch over the orchards and see to their fertility and fecundity, we ask that you watch over and bless this orchard* (alternative: *these trees*) *so that it may be healthy and heavy with fruit. In exchange, we make these offerings of food and water.* (Option: *of food, water, and tending.*)

As many [**participants**] as appropriate take the fertilizer packets and scatter the granules around the roots and base of each tree. The empty packets should be replaced on the altar when finished.

As many [**participants**] as appropriate take water vessels and pour water around the roots and base of each tree. The empty vessels should be replaced on the altar when finished.

If needed, as many [**participants**] as appropriate take the clippers and small saws could be used to tend the trees, removing broken branches or snags, etc.

[**All participants**] now raise energy by dancing, singing, and/or using drums, bells, or other instruments. If the space is small, this could be done in a circle within or outside of the trees. In a larger space, participants could join hands and do a spiral dance, snaking around and through the trees until an agreed-upon leader returns the group to their original positions. A standard chant like "The

Earth, The Air, The Water, The Fire" would work well, or you might once again select your favorite summer tunes. (Once I even brought our a boom box to play music while we danced—it was a fun variation.) Also note that bells work well to disperse "evil" influences—a double whammy!

Once the energy has been raised and the [**participants**] have returned to their positions, the ritual continues.

[**Person 4**] *See the magick of the apple.* He steps to the altar table and uses the knife to cut the apple in half around its "equator." He holds the halves up so their centers are visible to the participants. *Hidden within is the magickal symbol of the pentagram. May it remind us of the powers concealed deep within this simple fruit.*

[**Person 5**] *See the bounty of the apple.* She steps up to the table and uses the knife to flick a few apple seeds onto the table. She then cuts one of the apple halves into sections and hands one to each participant. *See how the apple feeds us and keeps us well. Let us share in this bounty.*

[**All participants**] eat their sections of apple.

[**Person 6**] *See the promise of the apple.* She steps up to the table and picks up the flicked apple seeds; placing them in one open palm, she faces the participants. *In these seeds are the future. From these seeds will grow new trees, laden with fruit. With the gift of these trees, we shall endure.* She returns them to the table for safekeeping.

(**Note:** If a space exists, the seeds could be planted as part of the ritual, "insuring the future.")

[**Person 1**] *Let us share our good tidings with these wonderful trees.*

Arts and Crafts

Now comes the arts and crafts part of the ritual. The writing could be done before the ritual, but after doing it both ways, I've found it feels best to do this among the trees themselves.

[**All participants**] come to the altar table, where they use the pens to write good wishes and glad tidings—messages and blessings

233

for the apples—on the cotton strips. They then wind the cotton strips loosely around the smaller branches, talking to the trees as they share these tangible blessings with them.

(**Note:** you may knot the strips but should do so very, very loosely, so there is no danger of the strips becoming too tight as the tree grows and damaging the branches. The cotton strips are biodegradable; as they fade and fray, they will compost into the earth or even be used by birds for nesting material.)

[**Some participants**] may wish to do divination at this time.

(**Note:** I suggest divination because in my own Celtic reconstructionist Druid traditions, divination is often part of every ritual. The divinatory work helps intuit whether the Gods have accepted the blessings and intentions of the ritual. Of course, divination may also be done for other purposes, too. Whatever the purpose, it works well under the beneficent apple trees.)

[**Some participants**] then tie golden apples onto the trees—one per tree—[each participant] saying, *May these golden apples join you to your apple ancients and remind you of your brilliance and power! You are a treasure of untold worth!*

[**Person 2**] *Let us all take a moment of silence to offer prayers and gratitude to the trees.*

[**All participants**] take hands (if possible) and share in the silence.

[**Person 3**] *As our ritual ends, we thank Iounn for her stewardship, and we again thank the trees for their grace. So mote it be!*

[**All participants**] repeat, *So mote it be!*

[**Person 4**] *We will now share in the feast of (fill in names of your cakes and ale).*

[**Person 5**] leads all participants in a "Paganized" version of the "Johnny Appleseed Grace": *"Oh the trees are good to me / and so I thank the trees / for giving me, the things I need / the sun and the rain and the apple seed / the trees are good to me."*

(**Note:** There are "Johnny Appleseed" additional verses, if you wish to modify and add them.)

[**All participants**] now pass the "cakes and ale" and enjoy them.

[**Person 6**] *Our ritual is complete. May we go in peace, and may the trees be blessed.*

[**All participants**] repeat, *May we go in peace, and may the trees be blessed.*

❧

I'd like to congratulate you on completing this ritual—and I hope you now feel a stronger bond with the trees you have nurtured and blessed. For the next few months between now and the late summer-early autumn harvest, I suggest you continue to develop your relationship with the trees. Visit them frequently. Talk to them, water them, pick up fallen fruit (watch for the late June apple drop, which is a common occurrence in orchards), and keep the ground under them free of debris—which can breed disease. When it comes time to pick the fruit, remember to thank the trees anew for this gift of life, which they have given freely.

The ritual ends. May your trees bear much fruit and bring you joy!

Resources

"Johnny Appleseed Song." 2008. https://www.youtube.com/watch?v=V_IrdS-zu48

"Ritual Chants." 2014. https://www.adf.org/rituals/chants-and-songs.html

Notes

Lammas

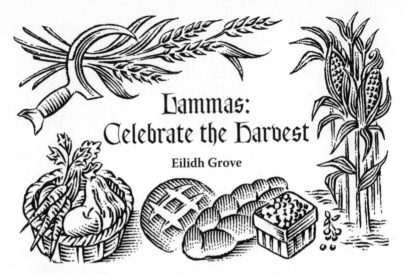

Lammas: Celebrate the Harvest

Eilidh Grove

GROWING UP IN MY very English/Scottish family, any alternative to Anglican religious practices was unthinkable. I followed my family ways without question, until my newly born interest in natural childbirth, ecology, and travels around the country led to an epiphany. A gradual one, to be sure, but it became a life-changing attitudinal adjustment. It was a time of questioning—the place of women, authority, war. We revised it all, or attempted to. I upended my own belief system for one that suited me better—one that took all sorts of roots into account, including my own British ones.

I began to delve into alternative spirituality, looking for an Earth-centered religion. Something I could resonate with. But I was disappointed. The books I found were shockingly lightweight. Fake words pretending antiquity ("be it ardane"), ego, and play-acting, as well as questionable behavior ("Whee, Whoa, Whack!") were wrapped into each book. I didn't want ceremonial magic, either. I had no interest in controlling entities. Was this all? Couldn't there be something else, something deeper and more meaningful? I was in luck! A good friend introduced me to a lovely almanac entitled *Witches All*. A font of information! Just what I needed!

Through this wonderful resource, I discovered a fascinating book based on archeology: *The Silbury Treasure: The Great Goddess Rediscovered* by Michael Dames (Thames & Hudson, 1976). What a revelation! Here was the ancient harvest festival of early August laid out on the land of Britain, land of my ancestors. The Sabbat of Harvest described in the way that my own family may have celebrated it. This changed everything for me.

In ancient times, the "First Fruits" harvest would have been the most important to the individual, and family. The food of the previous year's harvest had likely run out or spoiled. The animals could not be slaughtered until cold weather came and allowed for safe meat storage. Some greens, and a few fruits and berries, were available for picking, but an old name for July was "hungry July." Hay was made for the animals, and they had good grass, but for people there was mostly milk, sour milk, and clabber (curds), and that was only after the calves were weaned. In fact, most dairy products were made into items allowing for several months' storage so they could be eaten in the winter: cheese and butter. Other foodstuffs were pickled, fermented, or dried. The grain harvest is quite often the very first one to be made, as grain is sown either in late winter or early spring.

At a specific time, determined by the priesthood from the phase of the moon, and the state of the grain crop, major harvest activities began. Silbury Hill is a "harvest hill" near Avebury in southern Britain. It is one of many such hills found in Europe. Silbury is part of the huge complex of Stone Age sites comprising a year-long celebratory array, including Stonehenge and Avebury henge. Silbury Hill is a perfectly symmetrical man-made hill, with a shelflike platform on one side and ritual pathways to the summit. There is evidence that water had once surrounded the base. Michael Dames postulates that the shelf area was designed for oversight and ritual, the hill representing the womb of the pregnant Goddess. She gives birth to the moon, and to the harvest. The Full Moon rise would have been clearly visible from the shelf/platform. It appeared to rise from her lower body; she gave birth to it as they watched. Other harvest hills may have served a similar purpose.

Surviving harvest rituals in Britain and Europe, as well, show us that the "Spirit of the Corn" (any grain) was to be found in the last sheaf harvested. This sheaf was often called "the neck" and was carefully kept over the winter, to be sown with the spring grain crop. It was often woven into a corn dolly, a type of wheat weaving. The Spirit was thus perpetuated eternally, each year succeeding the previous one.

When I began to research the topic, it quickly became clear that many significant harvest rituals were performed during the first part of August: harvest dinners, horse fairs, and the ritualized climbing of certain mountains. Croagh Padraig in Ireland is a well-known one of these. Epiphany! Food, celebrated in plenty after privation. Horses, revered as goddess-companions, closely related to the grains they eat. Walking the Harvest Hill as a spiritual exercise often performed on the knees, and as homage to the Spirit of the Harvest, now translated to a beloved saint.

Speaking of "spirit," with the harvest of the grain—oats, wheat, barley, maize—comes the time to brew beer, and stronger spirits, too. Brewing was crucially important in a time when water was not necessarily safe to drink. Alcoholic distilled spirits in many lands and in many languages, is called "water of life." Even the word "whisky" is from the Gaelic: *Uisghe mhath* (pronounced ooshka va) or "good water!" Some aspects of the celebration could be ascribed to the lingering effects of the spirit of the grain.

In learning about ancient practices, I decided that the name "Lammas" or "loaf-mass," although appropriate, was not my choice for this sabbat. "Lughnasadh," in Irish Gaelic, or "Lughnasdahl," in Scottish Gaelic, means "the funeral games held by Lugh" in honor of his mother, Tailtiu. While also appropriate, as many games are held at the end of harvest in celebration, they are not my choice, either. The best, most meaningful name, for me, is "Bron Trogain," the "travail/labor of the Goddess in bringing forth the harvest." This name is found in the earliest Gaelic tales. Finding the connection with the deep past has made all the difference to me. Finally, I could venture into the study of Pagan ways seriously, knowing that I was indeed in tune with earth-ways, as my ancestors had likely been out of necessity.

So. How to celebrate Bron Trogain in the most deeply satisfactory way? I like the pilgrim qualities of a long, contemplative path to the top of a Harvest Hill. I like the feeling of connection to the distant past … a time in which Stonehenge, Avebury, and Silbury were an intrinsic part of the year's round. I have no mountain, but I can construct a ritual path on the ground upon which to meditate and bring forth the harvest: a labyrinth!

There are many sorts of labyrinth forms and designs available, including the beautiful Chartres labyrinth from the glorious cathedral nave. The simplest form to construct is the "seven circuit" labyrinth. It has a logic to the construction which is easy to understand, and simple to draw. There is even some archeological evidence that the seven-circuit form is the one used on Glastonbury Tor in Southern Britain.

A bit of personal history here: in 1984, a group of initiated, elevated witches formed a coven to celebrate sabbats together. We included the children of members in our celebrations, as we disapproved of their exclusion in many groups of the day. We, as Synergy, remained together for thirteen years. In that time, we developed an order of ritual that worked well for us. Each sabbat was written and celebrated by different members, often couples, hosting the ritual and assigning the roles. We were sometimes innovative, sometimes quite traditional. We called ourselves "experimental and experiential." Some ideas worked, and some did not. Over time, everyone was able to host all of the sabbats of the yearly round. The "Bron Trogain" ritual is based on that order, with the addition of the labyrinth as our "harvest hill."

This is the ritual outline: ground and center, ritual washing. (The grounding and centering is an important precursor to any ritual, done to focus intent. Ritual washing serves not only for cleansing but for further focus on changing from the everyday to another reality.) Processional. Make the temple/draw the circle, consecrate the circle with water and incense. Invoke/call the quarters, call the good people, invite the gods. (The previous actions are part of every Synergy circle, and create the sacred space.)

Music/chant. (Performed to raise energy for magics to be done.) Great magic/purpose. (This varies with the time of year, and need.) Cakes and wine. (Grounds the extra energy and provides social time.) Music/song (to unwind from the ritual). Thank the gods, thank the good people, thank the quarters, close the circle. (Do this in reverse to deconstruct the sacred space/temple.)

Ground and center/group hug (to finally "earth" the extra energy, if any). Feast and play.

This form can be as elaborate and complex as you can make it, or simple and quiet. Any words can be changed, or made more appropriate to the season. Space should always be left for meditation or personal introspection. Many decorative efforts can be made, or none. Costume is up to the individual. Experimentation is encouraged!

Cosmic Sway

April Elliott Kent

Lughnasadh is associated with the Irish God Lugh. Legend has it that the feast began as a funeral feast for his mother, who died of exhaustion after readying the fields for crops. Appropriately, this Lughnasadh feast day falls at the Balsamic Moon, with the Moon in Cancer opposed Pluto and square Uranus, and Mars at the last degree of Scorpio. More than just summer is ending.

Mercury is retrograde between August 30 and September 21. Since Mercury will be in Virgo, a sign in which it's especially strong, the effects of this retrograde period may be particularly vexing. Start backing up your computer files right after your Lughnasadh feast!

No fewer than three eclipses fall during this season: a Lunar Eclipse in Aquarius on August 18, a Solar Eclipse in Virgo on September 1, and a second Lunar Eclipse in Pisces on September 16! These will be particularly intense lunations with a great energy of change and unexpected, often critical developments.

Jupiter, the planet of growth, ceremony, education, travel, and adventure, enters Libra on September 9. Jupiter last visited the sign of relationship from September 24, 2004, through October 25, 2005. All important relationships, as well as the Libra house of your chart, are about to experience a period of expansion and risk-taking that you haven't seen in twelve years. It's particularly fitting that Jupiter enters the sign of marriage during Lughnasadh's season, as this is also considered a good time of year for handfasting.

Jupiter Birth Chart

Find the house of your birth chart that has Libra on the cusp. This is where Jupiter will call you to adventure and growth in the coming year:

Jupiter in 1st house: Growing stronger in your individuality, blessings through meeting emergencies with strength.

Jupiter in 2nd house: Expanding your income, blessings through property and possessions.

Jupiter in 3rd house: Enlarging the scope of familiar territory; getting to know more of your neighbors; blessings through sibling relationships and communication.

Jupiter in 4th house: Moving to or visiting a new country. Family growing through birth or marriage.

Jupiter in 5th house: Blessings through creative activities and children.

Jupiter in 6th house: Blessings at work and related to health. Taking on new and more adventurous duties.

Jupiter in 7th house: Blessings through close relationships with others. Growing as a result of compromise and cooperation.

Jupiter in 8th house: Taking on debt, increase in partner's income, blessings through inheritance, tax refunds, or other shared resources.

Jupiter in 9th house: Blessings through travel, foreigners, higher education. Expanding your belief system.

Jupiter in 10th house: Career blessings and earned respect. Expanding your scope of influence. Getting a promotion, earning a new status.

Jupiter in 11th house: Blessings through friendship and social networks. This is the most likely year for significant income from your career.

Jupiter in 12th house: Blessings through spiritual pursuits, quiet times spent alone. An increase in psychic ability and activity.

Eclipse Season

Three of this season's lunations are eclipses. Eclipses signal that some part of your life has reached a turning point. These eclipses will be most powerful for those with the Sun, Moon, Ascendant, or Midheaven within about four degrees of the New or Full Moon degrees. Look to the previous years that eclipses fell near the eclipse point for clues about what the eclipses will mean for you personally.

New Moon in Leo – August 2, 2016

This is a gentle, happy, upbeat New Moon before three eclipses in a row. The Sun and Moon in Leo are trine stable Saturn in Sagittarius; we can play like children, knowing we are safe and have the support that we need. Venus makes an exciting trine to Uranus, and this is a good New Moon to wish for creative breakthroughs and new, exciting relationships. Mars approaching a conjunction with Saturn can be a little frustrating, but remember that slow and steady wins the race; try to slow down and let matters unfold at their own pace.

Full Moon/Lunar Eclipse in Aquarius – August 18, 2016

This Full Moon Lunar Eclipse is at 25.51 Aquarius, a sign of friendship and fraternity, and is sextile Uranus. This could be a time when you must examine the importance of fitting in, and whether or not it matters that you are popular. You may find new friends or admirers, or realize that some friendships have outlived their purpose for both of you. Previous eclipses near this degree occurred on February 16, 1999, and on August 16, 2008; events and feelings similar to those you experienced near those eclipses may recur within a week either side of this Full Moon.

Grounding Ritual for Eclipse Season

Eclipses can be unsettling and nervous-making, particularly in an unpredictable sign like Aquarius. To ground yourself, try this ritual. Gather a black candle, a white candle, and a small bowl of fresh earth, preferably taken from your own garden, mixed with a little salt. Just before sunset the evening before the eclipse, lay some paper on your altar, sprinkle the earth and salt over it, and light both candles. Let the candle burn into the evening until it extinguishes itself.

New Moon/Solar Eclipse in Virgo – September 1, 2016

This solar eclipse at 9.21 Virgo is opposed Neptune and square Mars and Saturn. It falls on the Sabian Symbol, "Two heads looking out and beyond the shadows." This eclipse indicates that it's time to stop seeing things the way you wish they were, and begin dealing with them as they truly are. The square to Mars and Saturn suggest truth telling, often in language that is difficult to hear; Mercury retrograde during this period suggests it is news that has been heard before, though perhaps it's only now that it can be fully understood.

Eclipses near this degree previously occurred on September 1, 1997; February 26, 1998; and March 3, 2007.

Full Moon/Lunar Eclipse in Pisces – September 16, 2016

This Lunar Eclipse at 24.19 Pisces is on the Sabian Symbol, "The purging of the priesthood." Along with Venus opposed Uranus in the Full Moon chart, there is the strong suggestion that some friends or partners must be "purged" from your life. There is the sense that they have proven to be unworthy or unfaithful—not necessarily in a sexual sense, but simply that they have been revealed to be something quite different than you thought they were.

Sometimes, lunar eclipses are simply a time when those who are ill and ready to leave the earth decide that it is time to go. In these situations, it falls to us to be "the good priests" who help them make a peaceful and joyful transition to the next life.

Previous eclipses near this degree occurred on September 16, 1997; March 13, 1998; March 14, 2006; and March 19, 2007.

The Nodes of Influence

The August 18 and September 16 Full Moons occur near the Moon's South Node, a point of release and surrender, while the September 1 New Moon falls near the North Node, symbol of growth and spiritual evolution. The South Node represents the comfort zone that must be abandoned, and the North Node the qualities that must be embraced, if we are to move forward in our development. The South Node in Pisces and North Node in Virgo emphasize the need to critically evaluate the articles of faith that may be keeping us stuck in confusion and disorder. With transiting Jupiter close to the North Node, our harvest will be abundant if we work diligently, plan carefully, and get organized.

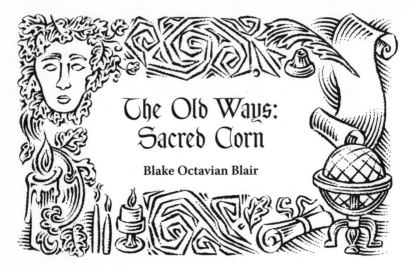

The Old Ways: Sacred Corn

Blake Octavian Blair

LUGHNASADH IS WIDELY REFERRED to as the First Harvest. It is generally around this time of year when corn, wheat, and other grains are ready for harvesting. In modern Pagan circles, this sabbat also commonly goes by the name Lammas, stemming from the Anglo-Saxon term for "loaf-mass," a logical title in conjunction with the season's harvest. While many instantly think of wheat when it comes to Lughnasadh and Lammas, we must not forget the equally important grain of corn. Corn is quite central to many Lammas celebrations and cross-culturally corn plays a role in many other cultural celebrations that occur around the time of the First Harvest. Corn grows on every continent except Antarctica, since it has such a wide growing range, and, being a versatile grain with so many uses, it's no wonder that it has risen to sacred status among so many peoples.

The Green Corn Ceremony, also referred to as the Green Corn Dance, is a prime example of the celebrations that occur around the First Harvest honoring the corn crops. The Green Corn Ceremony has manifestations among many of the North American First Nations, especially in the east and southeast. Ritual customs and procedures vary from nation to nation; however, they share the common theme of honoring and giving thanks to the earth and spirits for the year's corn crop and supplication for continued abundance.

The Corn Mother is a central figure to many Green Corn Ceremonies and Festivals. To North American First Nations, she is a benefic and loving figure. Many versions of her story depict her as a beautiful woman, with her story including variations of a romance with a tribesman. In connection with their union, the Corn Mother provides the people with the information on how to grow, tend, and use the corn crops. Still other versions of the story paint her as an older, almost grandmotherly, loving maternal figure who brought the corn grain to the people through various methods, including rubbing her body and magickally producing grains of corn that would fall from her!

Death and rebirth as well as creation and destruction are common themes for many of the sabbats, and Lughnasadh is no different. Some variations of the Corn Mother stories credit the actual grain of corn with being a child of the Corn Mother, and its harvesting as a death. This parallels the tale from English folklore of John Barleycorn as the grain god, who meets his death at Lughnasadh as well. The planting, growing, raising, tending, harvesting, and eventual replanting of the grain, or John Barleycorn, is symbolic of the cycle of death, life, and rebirth. While John Barleycorn is most often seen as the barley crop personified, in modern times he is very much an applicable personification to other various grains, including, of course, corn.

In a season revolving around the harvest of corn and various grains and celebrations of divine manifestations such as the Corn Mother and John Barleycorn, it is worth visiting a classic Pagan ritual chant that is practically made for this sabbat! The rhythmic cadence of "Hoof and Horn" can be heard in many a sacred circle at Lammas time. Its lyrics succinctly tell the story of the earth at this time of year in an infectious manner perfect for raising energy. There are many variations of the wording; however, one common version is as follows:

Hoof and horn, hoof and horn
All that dies shall be reborn.
Corn and grain, corn and grain
All that falls shall rise again.

Again, we see a call back to the theme of life, death, and rebirth within the lines of the chant. A most perfect chant for raising power at your First Harvest observance!

Due to its sacred nature, corn has without surprise found its way into ritual use as well. Corn and corn meal are a common offering in many different cultures. The Hopi people actually use different varieties of corn as offerings to the sacred directions of their cosmology: yellow corn to the Northwest, white corn to the Northeast, red corn to the Southeast, and blue corn to the Southwest. Due to the sustenance that corn brings and the sacred stories of its origins, it is no wonder that it became a fitting offering to use in sacred ceremonies. An offering is seen as a form of sacrifice in many cultures and a sacrifice must be something of value. Corn undoubtedly has value. In Haitian Vodou, cornmeal is used to draw veves, symbols used to represent and invoke the Lwa (spirits of Vodou). Many shamanic cultures variously use corn as an offering representing fertility, prosperity, abundance, and even the ancestors.

A good deal of the magick and rituals that are performed around Lughnasadh season revolve around giving thanks for an abundant harvest and working toward assuring that next year's crop will be successful. The corn dolly is one of the magickal creations of the season that work toward that end. It was thought by many that saving the last piece of husk from the corn harvest and preserving it would help in carrying the energy of the successful crop to the next year. Traditionally, the corn dolly is made of this last husk to safely house and carry forth the spirit of the corn. At the time of the next planting, the old dolly is ritually disposed of, generally by either burning or tilling it into the fields during planting.

The prominent position of corn in world culture and spirituality has endured the test of time. Cultures across both space and time have a common ground in the magick, abundance, and sacred mysteries of corn. I do hope you'll incorporate some corn lore and horning of this sacred grain into your Lammas and Lughnasadh celebrations! Whether you offer some blue corn to your ancestors, serve up homemade corn bread during cakes and ale, or create a corn dolly, may your First Harvest be blessed with sacred corn!

Bibliography

Cunningham, Scott. *Cunningham's Encyclopedia of Magical Herbs.* St. Paul, MN: Llewellyn Publications, 1985.

Franklin, Anna, and Paul Mason. *Lammas: Celebrating the Fruits of the First Harvest.* St. Paul, MN: Llewellyn Publications, 2001.

"Hopi color Direction Symbolism." West Virginia University. Eberly College of Arts and Sciences, accessed August 26, 2014. http://www.as.wvu.edu/~scmcc/colordirections.pdf

McCoy, Edain. *Sabbats: A Witch's Approach to Living the Old Ways.* St. Paul, MN: Llewellyn Publications, 1994.

Wigington, Patti. "The Legend of John Barleycorn." *About.com.* Accessed September 1, 2014. http://paganwiccan.about.com/od/lammas/a/Barleycorn.htm.

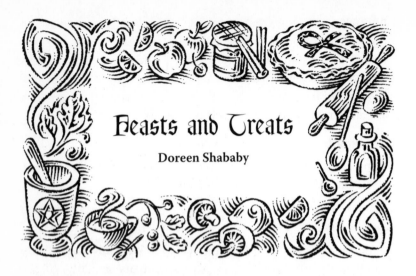

Feasts and Treats

Doreen Shababy

LUGHNASADH IS A HOLY DAY very close to my heart, and not just because I'm a gardener and cook. This is the season of my marriage! My sweetie and I have always celebrated it outdoors, whether on a mountaintop watching the sun come up, at a hot spring, or in a blue-stained huckleberry stampede. Since we love foods inspired by Mexican and Latin American cultures, this menu reflects our northern Idaho sensibilities with a fiesta flavor, for that's what this season is all about: a festive celebration of the harvest.

Fish Tacos

Easily prepared ahead of time and easy to take outdoors, I like tilapia for its firm texture and mild flavor (and cost), but more important is freshness. Figure on one 6- to 8-ounce fillet per person.

Prep time: 10 minutes
Cook time: 20 minutes, including tortillas
Serves: 6

Olive oil for cooking
6 tilapia fillets, fresh or frozen, about 8 ounces each
Seasoned flour for dredging
12 corn tortillas or taco shells

Toppings
Shredded cabbage
Sliced radish
Avocado
Salsa
Grated, or crumbled, cheese such as queso fresco

If using tortillas, lightly brush with oil and salt each one, and heat directly over a gas flame or in a hot skillet until soft and fragrant. Cover until serving time. If using taco shells, heat before serving.

Line a baking sheet with a brown paper bag. Next, heat a heavy skillet to medium and add oil to coat. Split each fillet down the center and then into a few pieces each, so it will fit on a taco. Lightly dredge in flour. Turn the heat up on the skillet, wait until the oil "shimmers," then add a few pieces of fish at a time. Fry quickly until golden brown, then turn to brown on the other side—do not overcook. Place on sheet lined with paper and shake with salt. Continue with the rest of the fish, wiping out the pan and adding more oil if necessary (use as little as possible so it doesn't get soggy).

To serve the fish warm, keep in the oven on low. To serve cold, which is also tasty, just drain on paper, cool, and refrigerate.

Yellow Rice

This festive dish is practically a meal in itself. The unique flavor and color of the annatto is part of its beauty.

Prep time: 10 minutes
Cook time: 30–40 minutes
Serves: 6

¼ cup olive oil
1 tablespoon annatto seed (found in Latin American, specialty and larger markets)
A quarter of an onion
A quarter of a red bell pepper
1 small sweet frying pepper (or green bell)

4 cloves garlic, cleaned and halved

1 plum tomato, halved

Half a bunch of cilantro, washed well

2 tablespoons green olive w/pimiento

2 tablespoons capers

1 tablespoon salt

½ teaspoon black pepper

½ teaspoon ground cumin seed

1½ cups long grain white rice (do not use brown rice)

4 cups chicken broth

1 bay leaf

In a large heavy saucepan, simmer the oil and annatto seed over low heat until it becomes red and fragrant, at least 10 minutes. Keep an eye on it and don't let it burn! When done, remove the seeds, leaving the oil in the pan.

While the seeds are simmering, trim the veggies and toss them and the olives and capers into the bowl of a food processor (or blender) and pulse until coarsely chopped. After removing the seeds from the pan, add veggies to the oil, stirring and sizzling. Add the salt, pepper, and cumin. Turn heat to high, stir in rice, and cook until rice is coated and the grains become opaque, about 5 minutes. Pour in enough broth to cover the rice by an inch, add the bay leaf and stir. Bring back to a boil, cook down for a few minutes, then cover and simmer on low for 20 minutes, no peeking. Test for doneness and add a bit more broth if necessary. Then put it all in a slow cooker to keep warm, and you're turning heads at the sabbat picnic!

Jalapeño Raspberry Fool

This is a treat with a bit of a surprise. Spicy and sweet, cool and creamy. I think it is the perfect accompaniment to the main meal, and very pretty as well.

Prep time: 15 minutes

Chill time: 60 minutes

Serves: 6

1 cup fresh raspberries for puree, plus ½ cup for garnish

1 jalapeño pepper, trimmed and seeded (use a red ripe pepper if you
can find one)

¼ cup powdered sugar

¼ cup chilled whipping cream

2 cups Greek-style vanilla yogurt, stirred

Place 1 cup of the berries into a blender along with the pepper, and buzz until smooth. Pour into a sieve and strain out the seeds, catching the juice and pulp in a small bowl. Add sugar to the berries and stir to mix.

Whip cream until soft peaks form then gently fold into yogurt. Fold in raspberry mixture. Spoon into 6 serving glasses and chill at least an hour. Garnish with fresh berries to serve.

Fruity Red Wine Punch

The nice thing about a "sangria" is if peaches or strawberries aren't available, you can use whatever is ripe and juicy. If you want to make a non-alcoholic version, omit the wine and brandy, and replace with two 1-quart bottles of white grape juice and 1 bottle of cranberry juice. Both versions are splendid.

Prep time: 15 minutes

Chill time: 4 hours

Serves: 6

3 bottles dry red wine (or the above mentioned juices)

1 lemon, washed and thinly sliced

1 orange, washed and thinly sliced

2 ripe peaches, peeled and sliced

1 pint ripe strawberries, sliced

2 tablespoons sugar, or to taste

½ cup good brandy (or omit)

½ cup quality orange liqueur (or omit)

2 bottles of plain soda water

Ice cubes

Combine all ingredients, except soda and ice, in a large punch bowl or other suitable, food-grade vessel, and stir well. Taste to see if you like it sweeter. Cover and refrigerate for half a day before serving, then add soda and ice. Howling at the moon is optional.

⚜

This is an abundant time of year in the garden in many climate zones. After planting seeds of intention earlier in the year, we move forward. At Lammas, we celebrate "first fruits" feast, even though many of us are neither gardeners nor farmers. But we as witches and earth-dancers are aware of the Mother's giveaway—of the fruits of someone's labors and the profusion of good fresh eats. We are filled with celebration and gratitude for the fantastic variety of produce that is available now and work hard again to preserve some of the bounty for leaner times, whether we make freezer pesto, canned green beans, or a simple bunch of dried oregano... it's in our very being to look forward.

And so the wheel turns.

Crafty Crafts

Tess Whitehurst

IT'S LAMMAS: A TIME when we celebrate what we call the "first harvest" or "first fruits." It's that time in the archetypal agricultural cycle when all the hard work of spring and early summer begins to pay off, as that which we have planted and tended begins to mature and flourish, providing tangible and much-needed sources of nourishment.

And, just as the first fruits, vegetables, and grains arrive in abundance, the prosperous, comfortable, life-giving properties of the sun appear to have burnished and nourished the land with those colors that mean wealth and manifestation to so many: green and gold. Indeed, in many parts of the Western Hemisphere, while the grasses and weeds are sun-baked to a gorgeous shade of gold, the trees are at their greenest and most full.

Speaking of trees, when magical rituals call for physical items—such as crystals, feathers, herbs, candles, or anything else—or when we craft amulets, talismans, or charms that we no longer desire to keep around in the physical form, authors and teachers often counsel us to bury the extra ingredients or materials "at the base of a tree." You might say this is because it is a way of respecting the magical energy within the item(s) by returning them to the earth. You might also say that it's a way of assisting the magic we've crafted in merging with the web of life and being assimilated and dispersed upward and outward into the world, like the water and nutrients in the soil.

Many modern witches have problems with this, however. For example, city witches like me may not be able to find a tree where they can safely and discreetly bury a charm. And witches everywhere are becoming more aware of the environmental repercussions of burying a charm containing anything non-biodegradable or otherwise potentially harmful to native flora and fauna. Not to mention, sometimes you don't really need to display or carry around a charm anymore, but you aren't ready to get rid of it either.

For all of these reasons, I created this "base of a tree" box, featuring the image of a tree as well as the golden colors that are so synonymous with magnetizing blessings and manifesting the conditions we desire. In this box, I keep the charms of magic past. Not only does this box represent the earth and hold the symbolic energy of the base of a tree in my subconscious and magical awareness, but it also serves as an enchanted hope chest of sorts, conveniently keeping all my small crafty keepsakes and mystical memorabilia in one place.

"Base of a Tree" Box

With many trees at their fullest expression, and the golden colors of the sun and landscape being so prevalent, this is a great time of year for this summery craft. Also, the alignment of this holiday with the physical fruits of our labor makes it a good time to create a box that holds the enduring physical representations of our magical work.

Time to complete: 4 to 7 hours (mostly drying time)

Cost: $12.00 to $17.00

Supplies

Unfinished wood box with clasp lid (about the size of a shoebox)

Gold craft paint (and up to two additional shades of gold craft paint (such as coppery gold or greenish gold)

Acrylic varnish (optional)

Paintbrush

Tree-shaped cutout (such as you would find in the scrapbooking section of a craft store), sticker, appliqué, or patch

Rhinestones in summery colors such as red, orange, yellow, green, and amber

Flat, dried legumes (such as split peas and lentils) in various colors

Elmer's glue

Optional: small representations of each element, such as a medium-sized sticky jewel in green (earth), yellow (air), blue (water), and red (fire)

Begin by clearing and activating your unfinished wooden box by bathing it in bright sunlight. As you do so, be aware that you're re-awakening the natural aliveness and magical power of the wood. (After all, it may have been sitting in a dark warehouse and then a fluorescent-lit craft store for quite some time.)

Once back inside, open the box and paint the entire inside, including the inside of the lid, gold. (Gold is the color of the light and wisdom of the earth, and it holds the energy of magnetic manifestation.) Allow to thoroughly dry.

Now, paint the outside of the box, allowing it to dry as necessary before painting each additional side. You can use the same color gold, or you can do what I did and use varying golden shades, such as coppery gold and greenish gold.

When the outside paint is dry, paint the back of the tree image with glue, and affix it to the center of the top of the lid.

Arrange the rhinestones and legumes around the tree in an attractive mandala pattern, affixing them with glue. (You can do this in any way you like, but I created a generous circle of lentils around the tree, and then affixed rhinestones and split peas more arbitrarily within this circle. This left me with a pattern that felt like a good, natural balance between random and ordered.) Allow to dry.

If you feel it's necessary, you can paint acrylic varnish over your mandala, or over the entire top of the lid, and allow to dry.

You can also affix rhinestones and/or legumes along the rim of the lid, and generally decorate with them in any way you choose.

Optional: Affix four small representations of each element to each of the four sides of the box. For example, you might place earth on the back side, fire on the side near the opening, water on the left, and air on the right.

Blessing and Consecration

You can bless and consecrate your box in a number of ways. For example, on Lammas or on a full moon, you might take your box to a gorgeous tree and set it down at the base for ten minutes to an hour, allowing it to soak up the tree's energy and to align with it more deeply in your magical awareness. Or you might simply hold it in both hands, relax and center your mind, and say something like:

Box of magic, box of gold
Box that blesses all that you hold,
I see you thus and christen thee:
The base of a sprawling, majestic green tree.

Find a special place for your sacred box, place magical remnants and mementos in it as desired, and enjoy a little touch of Lammas all throughout the year.

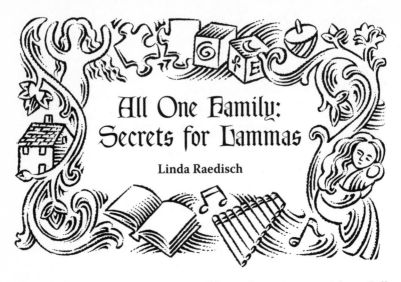

All One Family: Secrets for Lammas

Linda Raedisch

WHEN PRESENTED WITH THE problem of coming up with an "All One Family" piece for Lammas, my first impulse was to write about bread. After all, the name Lammas comes from the Old English *hlaef maesse*, "loaf mass." That's loaf as in bread, not meatloaf, thank goodness! (Interestingly enough, our word "mass" as it is used in physics comes from the Greek *maza*, meaning "barley cake." Who knew?!) Of course, the first peoples to celebrate this festival of bread baked with the fruits of the first harvest did not do so with a church mass but in their own homes and fields, as many witches do today.

Look up Lammas in any halfway-decent dictionary and you'll eventually come to "Lammastide." That's right: Lammas used to be a whole season. Nowadays the early days of August are a sort of non-season. It's still summer, but fall clothes and school supplies are already on sale, and those of us who have not yet gone away on vacation are realizing it may not happen this year. And yet this is a deeply rooted festival, old already in Shakespeare's time. When the Nurse remarked that Juliet's birthday was coming up "on Lammas Eve at night," everyone in the audience knew which date she was talking about. Country folk especially would have looked forward to

Lammastide because it meant the privations of summer were ending and there would be bread on the table again.

If your children are used to having bread on the table every day, not to mention milk, fruit, vegetables, enriched pasta, and maybe even dessert, you might find it hard to help them build up a sense of anticipation for Lammas. So let's see what secrets the ancient festival might be hiding: there must be something in there to awaken the imagination of twenty-first century youth. In medieval England, Lammastide was when everyone was allowed to bring their sheep and cows to graze on the Lammas lands, communal fields whose crops had already been harvested. Okay, not so interesting. The tenth-century *Leechbook of Bald*, a medical text, counsels against bleeding the patient at Lammastide, though it is presumably good practice at other times of the year. Still not sold? Let's turn to the Celts for help.

Late in its history, Lammas' Celtic counterpart, Lughnasadh, was transferred to the last Sunday in July so it would fit more neatly into the Christian calendar. On this day, sometimes called "Garland Sunday," people flocked to the nearest hilltop to enjoy the sunshine, share a meal and have a bit of fun. South of the Firth of Forth in Scotland, the festivities were centered around a flag stuck in the top of a tower of sod. Each village had its own tower upon which to flaunt its own colors.

If you've read Rick Riordan's young adult novel *The Lightning Thief*, you'll already be familiar with the game of Capture the Flag as it is played at Camp Half-Blood. I haven't, so I wasn't; I had to look it up. Basically, there are two teams. Each team has a base with a flag. The object of the game is to capture the other team's flag and bring it to your team's base, with a lot of rough and tumble in the process. So where does the fun come in? In making your team's flag, of course!

It doesn't have to be fancy. The famous—no, make that *sacred*—Fairy Flag of Dunvegan Castle is actually quite plain. Why is it sacred? Because it was presented to Clan MacLeod by an actual fairy, or so the legend goes. It's well known that fairies are especially good at needlework, as were the daughters of the Danish Viking Ragnar Lodbrok. They wove a magical banner that could predict the outcome of a battle by either snapping proudly in the wind or drooping pitifully on its post. The name of this banner was *Hrafn*, meaning, "raven," so I think it's safe to assume the girls had stitched the image of a raven upon it. (In a real-life game of Capture the Flag, Hrafn was seized by the Anglo-Saxons, but of course the Danes were expecting that.)

Your Capture the Flag flag doesn't have to be a work of art, but it should bear some symbol that the team can rally round. It should also be durable, since it's going to have to withstand some scuffling. The Vikings had always been fond of ravens, maybe because the sight of one fluttering on the battlefield reminded the enemy that they might soon be making a meal for these feathered scavengers. Wolves and dragons are also good for striking fear into the hearts of the other team.

If you, like me, are no fairy seamstress, or even Betsy Ross, you can make a passable banner out of colored felt. Once you've chosen an image, you can cut it out in silhouette and appliqué it onto a contrasting ground with a simple blanket stitch, no hemming needed. It's true that felt won't hold up in a rainstorm, but who wants to play Capture the Flag in the rain anyway?

Lammas Ritual: Bron Trogain

Eilidh Grove

THE SABBAT OF BRON Trogain is held to celebrate the harvest of the first fruits and grains. Others call it Lammas, or Lughnasadh. I call it Bron Trogain because it is a pilgrimage to commemorate the travail, or labor, of the Great Goddess in bringing forth the harvest child. The Harvest Child is the Harvest, personified. Her consort is present as her support, as a husband supports his wife in her labor.

In British antiquity, the ceremonies were held on a harvest hill such as Silbury Hill in Wiltshire. I have no hill, but I can construct a ritual pathway to serve the same function. I can make a labyrinth for my pilgrimage.

Advance Preparation

First! Construct your labyrinth! The best, and even very appropriate material to use for the season and not permanently mark the ground was determined to be flour. What better? Any visible grain would also work: wheat flour, cornmeal, barley flour, oat flour, etc. Good directions for making a seven-circuit labyrinth can be found online at the Labyrinth Society (http://www.labyrinthsociety.org).

The center of the equal-armed cross, the original beginning point for constructing the seven-circuit labyrinth, should be set up with an altar, either on the ground or on a table or stump. If another labyrinth form is used, the altar should be in the center. A seasonally colored and decorated cloth may cover the altar. Lay out the ritual implements on the cloth: pentacle (a vessel with an inscribed star form) or dish for the bread or cakes, incense with thurible or other incense holder, candles, a wand or athamé, and a vessel or shell of water. Salt or sea water is always lovely for the season. Place crystalline salt, for the earth, in the dish or use stones or dirt. Think about the colors for the candles: deep gold, orange, yellow, green, and white are right for harvest. Indeed, consider every element, each facet of setting out the circle. In this way, you will satisfy deep connections between yourself and the spirits of the celebration. The correct orientation to the compass points should be maintained. Earth should be to the north, incense to the east, candle in the south, and water in the west. Other candles should be set on either side of the center of the altar. Flowers of the season, such as sunflowers, dahlias, Queen Anne's lace, wildflowers, and early fruits and vegetables are placed on or around the altar. A loaf of bread or cakes, and a chalice of ale/beer, wine, or water should be there as well. A "neck," or corn dolly, would be a lovely addition to the altar.

The Quarters are located, and candles or lanterns placed at the periphery of the labyrinth, along with flowers. Again, the elements of the directions are placed at the Quarters, as on the altar. A basin of pure water and a towel should be put outside of the labyrinth circle for ritual bathing before the ceremony begins. We placed ours in the roots of a grand old beech tree.

Our coven, Synergy, developed an order of ritual over the thirteen years we celebrated together. It was quite basic, but could be elaborated upon, to make a very complex ritual, or kept simple and quiet. The order ensured that no important element was forgotten, and that the ritual built toward the climactic point, then reversed to ground the energies raised. ("And as for witches, this be the Law, from where they enter in, from *there* they must withdraw!") This ensured that all members, especially the High Priestess (HPS) and

High Priest (HP) remained well. Illness can occur if the energies are not properly released. This is a crucial point! A group hug is excellent for grounding energy at the finish of the ritual.

The Ritual Begins

All participants ground, center, and then line up for ablutions or washing of hands. The third eye can be laved with water too. Grounding and centering is a practice common to most Pagan rituals. It involves making yourself quiet, without and within. A mental connection is made with the Earth through the feet, bare if possible. Touching the Earth with the hands will accomplish the same thing. Any extra energy is channeled into the earth until you feel the stillness. Now you're ready for ritual.

Led by the High Priestess and High Priest (we took turns being in charge; that was part of the Way of Synergy), the celebrants circle around the outside of the labyrinth, and stop. Music can be played or sung for the procession, or it can be done in silence. The circle is drawn, asperged, or sprinkled with salted water, and censed with incense and fire.

HPS: *I call forth this circle, to preserve and contain the power we shall raise within its blessed sphere.*

Repeat three times while walking around the circle.

The **HPS** draws the circle around the outside of the labyrinth with a wand or athamé. The circle is then blessed with water and incense. These actions can be performed by the **HPS**, or by others.

We set up the roles each member was to play beforehand. The Quarters are acknowledged, saluted, and welcomed, East first and last.

East: *Powers of the East, we welcome you to our circle! Bring us your wisdom and understanding! Hail!*

South: *Powers of the South, we welcome you to our circle! Bring us your warmth and joy! Hail!*

West: *Powers of the West, we welcome you to our circle! Bring us your love and peace! Hail!*

North: *Powers of the North, we welcome you to our circle! Bring us your ingenuity and determination! Hail!*

Salute East again to close the circle. A salute is usually kissing the hand, or pointing the wand or athamé.

The Good People are called and welcomed. This practice was unique to us, as far as we know. We based it on a verse in *The ABCs of Witchcraft* by Doreen Valiente:

Black Spirits and White, Red Spirits and Gray! Mingle, mingle, mingle, ye that mingle may! Firedrake and Pucky, make it lucky! Liard and Robin, ye must bob in! Around, and around and around about… all Good come running in. All ill—keep out!

Stamp feet!

The Goddess and God are invited and welcomed. The family or couple in charge of the sabbat chose the deities for Synergy rituals, often Cerridwen/the pregnant Goddess and Lugh for the Harvest ritual. (There are many possible choices—research!)

HPS holds arms up to the heavens, and says: *Great Goddess of the Harvest, Cerridwen (or your choice), Mother of the Harvest Child, we welcome You to our circle! Be with us and lend us Your Grace and Wisdom this day (night)! Hail!*

HP hold up arms to the heavens, and says: *Great Lord of the Harvest, Lugh (or your choice), Father of us all, we welcome You to our circle! Be with us and lend us your strength and benevolence this day (night)!*

After a chant (*All that dies shall rise again!*) or dance to imbue the labyrinth with the energy of the Harvest season, there is a period of magical working, concentrating on bringing forth the harvest through labor. All point, with finger, wand, or athamé, to send the energy that was raised in the chant or dance into the labyrinth.

The labyrinth is now walked, slowly, in contemplation of the Goddess's birthing of the new grain and first fruits. All achieve the Center, one at a time. Each celebrant blesses the food and drink there, welcomes the Harvest Child with whatever words come to mind, or in silence. When done, the celebrant slowly retraces the labyrinth to the outside. Children can then be encouraged to walk/run/dance the labyrinth again, as many times as they might wish…and cross it too… no harm done.

The **High Priestess** and **High Priest** walk the labyrinth again, to the Center, to ritually consecrate the bread/cakes and ale/wine/water. One holds the Cakes and Cup; the other, the Wand or Athamé. They speak together:

Blessed be the New Grain! Blessed be the Harvest! Blessed be the Gods whose fruitfulness provides Life!

They carry the "cakes and wine" out to serve the members. Each person makes an appropriate libation, or toast, to the Harvest, the Goddess and the God. All then are seated on the grass to enjoy their repast.

After the pause for cakes and wine, a lively circle dance is done to show happiness and joy for the birth of the Harvest Child. Gwyddion Pendderwen wrote a lovely "Harvest Dance," perfect for the occasion. This can be found on YouTube: (https://m.youtube.com/watch?v=bMDffg9E_WA)

The circle is withdrawn, in reverse, of course, starting with thanking the Goddess and the God for their presence:

Great Goddess, and Loving Lord, we thank You for bringing us Your Wisdom and Strength. Hail, and farewell!

Then the Good People are thanked:

Black Spirits and White, Red Spirits and Gray, we thank you merry spirits well! As you depart to your pleasant and lovely realms, we bid you Hail and farewell!

Finally the Quarters are thanked, moving in the opposite direction: East, North, West, and South. And then East again:

Great (Eastern) Powers, we thank you for bringing us your (wisdom and understanding). Hail and Farewell! Salute, as before.

The circle is withdrawn by the person who cast it:

The circle is no more. (Repeat three times) *All things are as they once were, from the beginning of time.*

All participants ground, center, and hum together. All energies raised by the ritual are carefully grounded and balanced, usually by the **High Priestess**:

All energies are grounded, and in healthful balance.

The feast is served! Potluck! Outside, if the weather permits.

Notes

Notes

Mabon

Mabon: The Pagan Thanksgiving

Magenta Griffith

WHETHER YOU CALL IT Mabon, Autumn Equinox, or Harvest Home, it's one of my favorite times of the year. It's the second of the three harvest festivals: Lughnasadh/Lammas, Mabon/Equinox, and Samhain. The heat of summer is over, and cooler weather is coming. The bounty of the harvest is all around us, from apples to corn, from peppers to squash. It's sometimes called "the Pagan Thanksgiving," a time of giving thanks for what we have—abundant crops, a good job, a healthy family. Most of us live in cities or suburbs, and our crops, if any, could not sustain us through the winter. But someone, somewhere, is growing the food we need, and we can use this occasion to be grateful to the farmers. It is also a time to consider what we have sowed this season, and what we have reaped, what projects have come to fruition, and which have fallen by the wayside.

Because this holiday is determined by the movement of the Earth in relation to the Sun, the exact date and time varies from year to year; it is usually either September 22 or 23. This occurs when the Sun crosses the equator on its apparent journey southward. Astrologically, it occurs when the Sun crosses into Libra.

The word *equinox* comes from Latin and means "equal night," the time when the hours of night are equal to the daytime hours. It is a time to remember that we need both light and dark, heat and cold. If we didn't have the warmth in summer, we wouldn't notice that it's cold in winter. We need the light to see, to grow things, but if we never had the darkness, we wouldn't be able to sleep, or have times of repose. Everyone has to figure out for themselves the proper balance between animation and idleness, work and rest, and this is an excellent time to consider the question of balance in your life. Therefore, think about how you wish to bring things back into balance. This could involve large changes, or might be as simple as returning items you have borrowed, paying back small sums of money you owe friends and coworkers, apologizing for rudeness. Winter is coming, and it's good to be in harmony with your surroundings and community before the harshness sets in.

Mabon, or more precisely, Mabon ap Modron, is a Welsh mythological figure, whose name comes from the Mabinogion, the Welsh national epic. The name translates "the Son of the Divine Mother." In some versions, he was a young hunter, in others, a baby just three days old, when he was kidnapped and taken to Annwn, the land of the dead. He was rescued by Culhwch, and stayed young forever. The name was first applied to this holiday by Aidan Kelly in 1970, to give the holiday a more imaginative name than Autumn Equinox, and to balance the feminine name of Ostara for the Spring Equinox. It became frequently used, in part, because the legendary *Green Egg* magazine used Kelly's names for the holidays for issue names.

Another mythic figure connected to the Fall Equinox is Persephone. Her mother, Demeter, was the Greek Goddess of grain and of the harvest. Persephone caught the attention of the God of the underworld, Hades, who abducted her and took her back to His realm. Demeter wandered the Earth looking for Her missing daughter, and her grief caused the crops to die. During her time in the underworld, Persephone had eaten six pomegranate seeds and therefore had to spend six months of the year in the Underworld. Therefore, six months of the year, the earth is barren while Demeter mourns her daughter. When Persephone returns, at the Vernal Equinox, spring begins.

Harvest Home was applied to the holiday by Fred Adams, who in 1967 founded Feraferia, one of the earliest non-Wiccan Pagan groups in the United States. Harvest Home is an old English term for the celebration of the harvest. The traditional ritual would be a feast, perhaps with songs, since there are a great many traditional folk songs about harvesting grain, and drinking (since some of grain would be brewed into beer). People would decorate the village with boughs. The cailleac, or last sheaf of grain, which represented the spirit of the field, was made into a harvest doll, wrapped in swaddling cloth like a baby and sometimes drenched with water as a rain charm. This sheaf, which would sometimes be made into a wheat dolly (sometimes called a corn dolly), or some other construct, was saved until spring planting. This wheat would be the first seeds sown the next year. If you want to try your hand at weaving wheat, there are instructions online if you search for "corn dolly" or "wheat weaving."

The Autumn Equinox is celebrated in China and Japan, as well as among some Native American and other indigenous groups. It's a natural time for a holiday, since it's determined by an observable event. In China, it's called the Mid-Autumn Festival, and is a celebration of the harvest. The nearest Full Moon is considered the Moon's birthday, and celebrated with round Mooncakes. In Japan, it's called Higan, or Shubun, and is a national holiday, as is the Spring Equinox. Chuseok is the Korean festival at the Autumn Equinox, and is also a harvest festival, when people visit their hometowns, if they are able, and share a feast of traditional foods.

Since this is a harvest festival, it's a time for activities that help you share in the bounty of food available at this time. If you can, go to a "pick your own" farm, especially if you have children, so they can see where their food comes from. There's nothing like an apple you just plucked from a tree, or corn picked an hour before you cook it. Sometime near the Fall Equinox would be a good time for a nature walk. Notice the changing sights and sounds of the outdoors. Listen for geese honking in the sky above you, observe the changing in the colors of leaves, and watch the ground for dropped items like acorns, nuts, and seedpods.

This is the time for gathering and preserving foods, whether you do it by drying, salting, canning, pickling, or freezing. Pickling can be easier than you think: slice cucumbers, put them in jars, and cover with vinegar and herbs like dill. Cold-packed pickles will be ready to eat in a few days and must be stored in the refrigerator; they must be used within a couple of months. If you are adventurous, you might try brewing beer or cider, or if you live where grapes are harvested, making wine. (Of course, wine can be made from other fruit as well.) I've always thought that this should be the time when Pagans exchange gifts, not going with the prevailing culture and exchanging them at Yule. (Guess how much luck I've had with getting people to go along with that.) I tend to give gifts from my garden, and so do a number of friends—pesto, salsa, pickles. Also, in many areas, the Renaissance Faire is going on, a great place to get Pagan gifts.

We know we'll be spending more time indoors in just a few months, so now is the time to do the fall version of spring cleaning. While you still can, open all the windows to air out your home. Go through the house and get rid of anything that needs to be recycled or put in the garbage. (It's sometimes helpful to get friends in to help, and help them in exchange. If nothing else, they will see that box that has been sitting on the porch ready to go to recycling, or that jar that needs to be put away but has effectively disappeared because you have been looking at it for such a long time.) Physically clean from top to bottom, starting with cobwebs on ceilings or in corners—"early Addams Family" is so last century. Dust, then vacuum, then mop the floors. Launder seldom-washed items like bathmats and washable curtains. Clean windows—come December you'll want every bit of sunshine you can get. If you have anything that needs to be repaired, fix them now so you don't have to do them during the winter. While you are doing your cleaning, see if there is anything you want to contribute to the food shelf, or send to Goodwill or a similar agency. In fact, a collection drive for the local food bank is a very appropriate coven or group activity for this time of year. Finally, go through the house and bless every room, sprinkling water and purifying with your favorite incense.

If you keep an altar, this is a good time to clean it and, if you wish, change it. Take everything off the altar and clean the surface. Dust or clean anything that needs it. Put away items connected with summer or before; compost those flowers from the May Basket, or the daisy chain you made at Midsummer. Decorate instead with leaves in autumn colors, nuts you have gathered, and decorative squash. If you decide to try making a corn dolly, it can repose on your altar until spring. I change the color of the candles on the altar as well, but not everyone is as fervent as I am.

This is a busy time of year, and always has been. Gathering crops, winnowing, threshing, and storing them for the winter, preserving with drying and canning, all take a lot of work. We are so lucky to have machines to help, and most of us no longer do the back-breaking work of picking and carrying food from the fields. We can celebrate the food and those who produce it and bring it to us, those who cook, and those who clean up afterward. This is a time to be grateful to the Earth, and to one another.

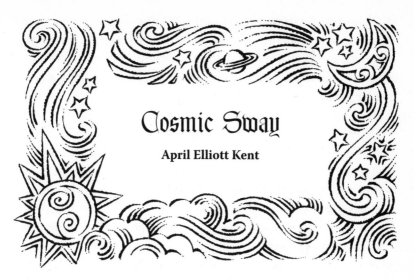

Cosmic Sway

April Elliott Kent

At Mabon, the harvest high season, the fields and our summer labors yield the bounty that will sustain us through the long winter months. There is satisfaction in enjoying the tangible and literal fruits of our hard work, lining the pantry shelves with canning jars full of colorful vegetables. There is a pleasing symmetry to concluding the cycle that began at the Ostara planting season.

Mabon begins at the Autumn Equinox, the day when the Sun moves into Libra (at precisely 10:21 am, September 22, EDT), the sign of balance and partnership. The Sun in Libra is conjoined extravagant Jupiter now, and Venus is sextile Mars; together, they symbolize that this harvest season's greatest bounty lies in the rich joy of relationship. Venus in opposition to Uranus suggests that the recent past has brought a culling of relational dead wood. The people who remain in your life are the ones who have earned the right to be there.

The Disseminating Moon in Gemini is locked in a powerful configuration with Mercury (newly direct after its recent retrograde period), Saturn, and Neptune. Perhaps you have been overanalyzing your feelings, feeling emotionally blocked and a bit lonely or sad. The time is coming to speak from your heart.

Pluto turns direct on September 26, after six long months in his retrograde, underground kingdom. Vast reserves of emotional power are released, and things don't really return to steadiness until after the Sun squares Pluto on October 7; be gentle with yourself and with others.

Mars in Capricorn

Mars enters Capricorn, one of its strongest signs, on September 27. The path to direct and productive action is cleared, though there will be lessons about the limits of power and control when Mars conjoins Pluto (October 19).

While Mars was in Sagittarius, it was time to explore, to try new things without committing to any particular course of action. With Mars in Capricorn, however, we are ready to decide upon a plan and begin slowly, steadily, and methodically working toward our goals.

Mars is considered to be "exalted" in Capricorn, meaning it works particularly well in this sign. Capricorn, ruled by Saturn, is the sign of discipline and structure. It is a sign that gives form and direction to Mars' energy without extinguishing its fiery drive.

Through November 8, Mars in Capricorn will be like a graduate course in business and management—in particular, the business of managing our lives. It's an especially good transit for the self-employed and for those who manage others for a living, but anyone can reap its benefits. We can all benefit from setting realistic goals for ourselves and pursuing them diligently, resourcefully, and persistently.

New Moon in Libra – September 30, 2016

This is the most powerful New Moon of the year for setting intentions concerning relationships—finding them, mending them, releasing them. At this New Moon, the Sun, Moon, and Jupiter are conjoined in Libra, a happy and beneficial message that we are growing through our relationships. They are approaching a square with Mars and Pluto, however, so while the road to a deeply satisfying relationship is opening up, reaching your destination requires that you assert yourself, insist upon the truth, and abandon any hope of completely controlling the situation. Venus in passionate, determined Scorpio makes sextiles to Mars and Pluto and a nearly exact trine to romantic Neptune, so attracting a compelling relationship is entirely possible. But it's important that your New Moon rituals call not for a specific person to respond to you in a particular way, but rather for all relationship situations to work out for the higher good of all.

Summoning Love

Years ago, after a series of disappointing relationships, I decided I was truly ready to find a partner. So I composed a ritual. It began with a step I think was the most powerful—creating a list of the five essential qualities I wanted in a mate. That took some doing; it's probably the first time I had stopped to really think about what I wanted rather than what I *didn't* want. I folded up my list and tucked it under a dish with a pink (Venus's color) candle on it. In a small pink handkerchief, I wrapped a tiny cloth doll that I had picked up at a fair years before. "This is my mate," I declared. I lit the candle, sealed the cloth with some of the wax, and left it on my altar until the candle burned all the way down.

The next day I stowed the little figure and the list in a box and completely forgot about them—until about a year later, when my soon-to-be husband and I were packing up my apartment just before we were married!

Full Moon in Aries – October 15, 2016

This is an explosive Full Moon in Aries conjunct unpredictable Uranus, with the Sun and Moon square Mars and Pluto. The Sabian Symbol for this Full Moon degree is, "An open window and a net curtain blowing into the shape of a cornucopia." When you leave a window open in your life, all sorts of things can come your way, often at great speed and from an unpredictable direction. If you have laid your Mabon groundwork carefully and consciously, and have centered yourself emotionally, this can be an opportunity to release yourself from a variety of difficult entanglements and leave room for fresh bounty.

New Moon in Scorpio – October 30, 2016

Coming just before Samhain, this Scorpio New Moon is trine enchanting Neptune. After the turbulence of the Full Moon in Aries, this lunation calls for tranquility and reflection. Relationships that began with much promise at the Libra New Moon are now at a moment of stasis. They are not necessarily over, but with Venus and Mars conjoined Saturn and Pluto, greater forces are intervening in the affairs of mere mortals.

Scorpio is considered one of the financial signs, and this is one of the most powerful New Moons of the year for rituals related to money and general prosperity. This New Moon is especially favorable for this work with Jupiter, the most benefic planet, in a dynamic aspect to Pluto, who in myth was the wealthiest of the gods. With Venus conjoined Saturn and square Neptune, there is a need to be extremely realistic about the behaviors and beliefs that have created your current financial situation and make a pledge to face it all, forgive yourself for past mistakes, and allow yourself a new vision of prosperity.

The Old Ways: To the Underworld

Blake Octavian Blair

THE SABBAT OF MABON, being the Autumn Equinox, marks a pivotal turning point in the wheel of the year. Today is one of the two days in the year where day and night are of equal length, and from here on out the darkness will outmeasure the light until the Vernal Equinox. The descent into the dark half of the year mirrors the classical descent into the Underworld found in various spiritual systems as well as world mythologies. The Underworld is a rich tapestry upon the spiritual landscape with vast lore filled with gods, goddesses, romance, adventure, power, challenges, fantastical creatures, and noble guardians. Throughout world cosmologies, we see various accounts of descent into and back from this mysterious lower realm, bringing wisdom back to our world along with spiritual gifts, and even, by some accounts, seasons.

Probably one of the best known stories among modern Pagans regarding descent to the Underworld involves Greek goddess Persephone. Her story is intimately tied to the seasonal shifts that occur at the equinoxes and is heard inside many a Mabon sabbat circle. A highly synopsized version of the tale is as follows. Persephone, daughter of Demeter, was strolling along enjoying nature's beauty one day when she finds herself drawn to the unique beauty of a particularly dazzling flower. Upon picking the flower, set as a trap, Hades swiftly appears and whisks her away to the Underworld, of which he is ruler. Demeter, logically being not only concerned but angered that her daughter was nabbed, becomes scornful and withholds growth and fertility from the earth, causing crops to wither and darkness to fall upon the land. (If Mama isn't happy, nobody's happy!) Eventually, all the gods decide that enough is enough and hold council. A deal ends up being struck with Hades for Persephone's return. However, before she leaves the Underworld, Persephone consumes an enchanted pomegranate. This enchantment from Hades insured that she'll return to spend half of each year with him. Each year at the Autumnal Equinox, Persephone descends to the Underworld to spend her time with Hades, ushering in fall. Hades releases her at the Vernal Equinox, ushering in spring.

Perhaps another of the notable tales of descent to the Underworld is that of the Mesopotamian goddess Inanna. While the reason for her descent isn't definitively determinable because accounts vary, some cite her original attempt to pass through the gates of the Underworld as stemming from a desire to attend the funeral of her sister Ereskigal's husband. Ereskigal also happened to be the presiding goddess of the Underworld. A lot of focus is given in Pagan culture to Inanna's descent through the seven gates of the Underworld. It is this that Inanna is predominantly known for. Modern Pagans equate the symbolism of these seven gates with the seven chakras and levels of consciousness. We can pass through gates of consciousness just as Inanna passed through the gates in her descent. Of course, part of Inanna's Underworld tale also includes a seasonal connection. When she left the Underworld, Ereskigal sent demons to follow her (the two sisters were not on great terms), and the demons would not allow Inanna to leave unless someone was offered up to take her place. After several candidates were explored and rejected, they came upon Inanna's husband, Dumuzi. Dumuzi was caught dressed in finery and enjoying himself, instead of mourning the absence of Inanna like others were. This of course did not go over well with Inanna, and Dumuzi's fate was sealed. Dumuzi was offered up to the demons to take her place in the Underworld. To Dumuzi's credit, he did have his sister in his corner, who loved him so much that she arranged for herself to be Inanna's replacement for half the year, and for Dumuzi to take the other half of the year. Despite casting Dumuzi to the Underworld in her fit of frustration, Inanna mourns the half of the year they are now separated. During this time, she withholds her power of fertility from the land, resulting in the arrival of autumn and the darker half of the year.

⚘

Of course, deities are not the only beings who make descents to the Underworld. Practitioners of shamanism make regular journeys to these realms. In shamanism, there is a near universal cosmology that includes three worlds, the Lower, Middle, and Upper Worlds. The Lower World is but another term for the Underworld. The Middle World is the alternate or Non-Ordinary Reality version of the plane we live in now, and the Upper World is yet another geographic layer of existence in the shamanic Otherworlds. As mentioned, all three of these worlds are seen to exist in an alternate reality, accessible through altered states of consciousness. Practitioners of shamanism have been visiting and traversing these realms for thousands of years. While details and accounts of the spirits and landscape of these worlds vary from culture to culture, the similarities between the accounts are too alarming to deny. Additionally, because of this, many differences are thought not to be contradictory, but rather accounts of different areas or locations within these worlds. The Lower World is often seen as a place of healing, lush natural landscapes, and home to powerful personal guardians—often in animal form. It is said the spirit of all species that ever existed—living, extinct, or so-called mythological—can be found in the lower world. Some cultures prescribe the realms of the ancestors and the dead to the Lower World, while others attribute them to the Upper World. Those who journey to these lower realms often do so to glean spiritual wisdom and bring back answers to questions relevant to the their own lives and those of their people. Gloriously, through shamanic techniques, if desired, we can all learn how to visit these realms for ourselves.

It is worth addressing the rather bleak and dark reputation that has been painted about the realms of the Underworld, which has seemed to permeate a lot of Western mainstream thought and culture. With the influence of Abrahamic religion came the permeation of those faiths' concept of "Hell." Most of us are familiar with the concept of this place being less than hospitable to say the least—a fiery realm of punishment, torture, despair, evil malicious entities, and a point of no return for those cast into its bastions. The good news is, as we have seen already in this essay, those viewpoints don't hold the monopoly on perspectives of the Underworld. Earlier we visited the story of Persephone, Hades, and the Greek Underworld. The Greek perception of these realms, in fact, was not at all a place of punishment or torturous despair. This realm that Hades ruled was in fact the afterlife, where all souls went after death. As just examined, the various views of the shamanic Lower World also have almost no resemblance to the Abrahamic view of "Hell." In fact, many shamanic peoples will tell you that all three worlds are Heavens in their own right and are realms of great spiritual healing and wisdom. So, in my opinion, when we speak of the Under and Lower Worlds, we are not speaking of the place that the Abrahamic traditions are speaking of as "Hell." Therefore, feel free to cast any undue apprehensions or anxiety about these realms aside!

The Underworld is a celebrated cosmological location with its own rich lore, beauty, and power worthy of our explorations. As we slide into the unique energetic current of introspection and contemplation following the equinox where the darkness each day outweighs the light, I'm reminded of an old piece of shamanic wisdom: "The darker it is, the better you see." This Mabon, won't you join me in the growing darkness, and descend to the Underworld?

Bibliography

Dugan, Ellen. *Autumn Equinox: The Enchantment of Mabon.* St. Paul, MN: Llewellyn Publications, 2005.

Grimassi, Raven. *Encyclopedia of Wicca & Witchcraft: 2nd Edition Revised & Expanded.* Woodbury, MN: Llewellyn Publications, 2000 & 2003.

Hamilton, Edith. *Mythology.* Boston, New York, and London: Little, Brown and Company, 1942.

Illes, Judika. *Encyclopedia of Spirits: The Ultimate Guide to the Magic of Fairies, Genies, Demons, Ghosts, Gods & Goddesses.* New York: Harper One, 2009.

University of Pennsylvania. "Open Richly Annotated Cuneiform Corpus. Ancient Mesopotamian Gods and Goddesses—Inana/Istar." Accessed September 12, 2014. http://oracc.museum.upenn.edu/amgg/listofdeities/inanaitar/.

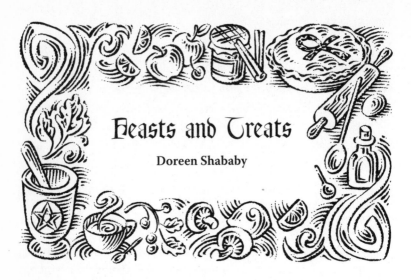

Feasts and Treats

Doreen Shababy

MABON IS MOST RECOGNIZABLE for the change it brings to our daylight hours. So, whether you live in International Falls, Minnesota, or Orlando, Florida, you'll be getting less than twelve hours of daylight now, and even that will dwindle away quickly. The Autumn Equinox reminds us of balance and of nurturing ourselves and each other as we get ready for the even shorter days ahead. Getting together with friends, family, and coven-mates on these fun, bonfire-lit evenings makes for shinin' times to look back on.

Beer-Braised Smokies

My dad taught me how to make homemade sausage when I was still a teenager, and I have been making it ever since, with venison if we have it. For this recipe, you can also use kielbasa or brats. Our local butcher makes nitrate-free smokies and they're awesome.

Prep time: 15 minutes
Cooking time: about 40 minutes
Serves: 6

3 pounds smoked sausages
2 tablespoons butter

4 small onions, thinly sliced

2 12-ounce bottles of beer, preferably a German lager such as St.
   Pauli Girl

In a large heavy skillet or stovetop casserole dish, brown the sausages over medium-high heat, remove from pan, and set aside. In the same skillet, lower heat to medium, melt butter, and sauté onions until translucent, about 5 minutes. Return sausage to skillet, pour beer over all, and reduce heat to simmer. Cook, uncovered, for about 30 minutes.

Remove sausage and onions from pan and place on a serving platter, and cover to keep warm. Cook braising liquid over high heat until reduced by half, then pour it over the smokies and onions on the platter. Serve piping hot.

Green and Bleu Slaw

This slaw, which has a different and very addicting flavor, is a nice contrast to the rich entrée. Cabbage and apples are plentiful this time of year, and combine nicely whether cooked or raw. There is a widely known manufacturer of salad dressings near my home, and they even make their own bleu cheese—thus the inspiration for this slaw. Look for local in your area!

Prep time: 15 minutes

Cooking time: 15 minutes to toast walnuts

Serves: 6

4 cups (about ¾-pound) shredded cabbage

1 large Granny Smith apple, thinly sliced

2 stalks (ribs) celery, thinly sliced

½ cup walnuts

½ to 1 cup Roquefort salad dressing, all-natural style if possible

Spread walnuts evenly in an ovenproof dish and toast at 300 degrees F for about 15 minutes until toasted; do not burn. Remove and cool.

Combine cabbage, apple, and celery in a large salad bowl and toss to combine. Add dressing to your liking, sprinkle with walnuts, and serve cold.

Tea Brack

Reminiscent of the dense fruited breads of yore, raisins were a prized commodity to see the household through the winter months. They also pack a lot of energy into a little package.

Prep time: 15 minutes, plus several hours to soak the raisins
Cooking time: up to 1 hour 45 minutes
Serves: 6–8

2 cups raisins
1 cup brown sugar
1½ cups strong hot black tea
1 egg, beaten
2¾ cups all-purpose flour
1 tablespoon baking powder
¾ teaspoon salt
½ teaspoon cinnamon

In a large bowl, stir together the raisins, brown sugar, and tea until the sugar is dissolved; let soak several hours or overnight.

Heat oven to 300 degrees F. Grease a bread loaf pan and line the bottom with parchment paper. After the soaking time, stir egg into the raisin mixture. Whisk flour, baking powder, salt, and cinnamon in a separate bowl, then stir into the raisin mixture. Pour batter into prepared pan and smooth the surface evenly. Bake for 90 to 100 minutes or until firm to the touch. Leave to cool in pan for 10 minutes before removing to rack to cool completely.

Equinox Stout & Lager

It will be fun to see if you can pour so as to see the two different layers, as a reminder of the beautiful balancing dance we celebrate tonight and always on our journey as witches and magickal beings.

There is even a special spoon made to balance on the glass rim to make what the Irish call a Half and Half.

Prep time: 5 minutes
Serves: 2

1 bottle Harp Lager beer, cold
1 bottle Guinness Extra Stout beer, cool but not cold

Set up two sturdy beer glasses. Pour half the lager into one and then into the other. Next, take a teaspoon (the kind you stir with) and, resting it on the rim of the glass with the back side facing up, slowly pour the stout over the spoon so it doesn't splash up and mix in with the lager. Pour half in one glass, then in the other. Stand back to admire what should be light beer on the bottom half with dark beer on the top half, consider what balance means to you, then enjoy the evening.

Crafty Crafts

Tess Whitehurst

You might say that Mabon is a celebration of the earth element many times over. In addition to celebrating the earth's bounty in the form of the foods and grains that provide our very sustenance, as day and night reach equal length, we celebrate the earth element's associated qualities of divine harmony and balance. And naturally, the deities that we commonly invoke at this time are very intimately tied to the earth and the cycles of the harvest: beings such as Demeter, Gaia, Ceres, Cerridwen, and the Green Man.

Mosaic Harvest Pentacle

All of this means that it's the perfect time to create this potent earth symbol for your altar and magic circle: a mosaic pentacle, created with dried split peas and legumes. As you may know, pentacles are placed on the altar and at the northern cardinal point in magic circles to represent the earth element. The pentacle can also be used as a magical tool of protection, grounding, blessing, and drawing off negativity. In the words of author Ruth Barrett in *Women's Rites, Women's Mysteries,* "The pentagram becomes a pentacle when enclosed within a circle and inscribed on a disc or stone. The pentacle represents the 'great round,' the planet Earth herself, the great cauldron-womb of the Goddess that contains all the elements symbolic of the wholeness and oneness of life."

This project is so simple and inexpensive to make, and yet the finished product has such a rustic and enduring beauty.

Time to complete: 1 to 2 hours

Cost: $3.00 to $7.00

Supplies

An unvarnished terra cotta or cement saucer (such as something that
would go under a potted plant, although I used a cement holder
for a pillar candle)

Dried green split peas

Dried green or yellow lentils

Optional: more varieties of dried legumes (if you want to get fancy)

Elmer's glue

Pencil

Ruler

Protractor

Instructions: Using the protractor and pencil, mark five points around the outside of the inner area of the saucer, each 72 degrees apart from each other. Using the ruler and the pencil, connect each dot to the two dots directly across from it to form a 5-pointed star.

Cover one of the lines with a line of glue and neatly arrange a single row of split peas along that line, flat sides down. Repeat with each line until you've formed a five-pointed star out of split peas.

Optional: Add a single split pea to the center of each of the five outside areas of the star, or otherwise add detail as desired.

Allow to dry.

Section by section, fill in the remaining area of the inside of the saucer with glue and then lentils. (You may need to crowd them together a bit here or there, or select smaller or larger lentils according to the space you have to work with. Lentils are good for this part of the project because you can angle them slightly to fit them together if necessary.) Allow to dry.

Pentacle Blessing and Consecration Ritual

To bless and consecrate your new magical altar addition, begin by bathing it in white sage smoke. On the day of a full moon, when the sun is high in the sky, take it outside to a serene natural setting. Spread a white cloth on the ground—perhaps at the base of a tree or in another location that feels particularly powerful to you—and place the pentacle on the cloth. Leave it for 30 minutes to an hour to absorb and align with the energy of the earth.

Repeat this in the evening when the moon is out so that it can absorb the energy of both sun and moon, night and day.

How to Use Your Pentacle

Pentacles are attractive altar additions, but they are so much more, and their magical usefulness is often overlooked! Here are a few ways to use your pentacle as a potent magical tool.

For protection, first charge your pentacle with protective energy. Do this by setting the intention to infuse it with proactive vibes while simultaneously bathing it in very bright sunlight or visualized bright white light. Then, simply walk in a clockwise direction around anything or anyone you'd like to protect while facing it outward like a shield. Or, if you'd like to protect yourself, again face it outward like a shield and then spin one full circle in a clockwise direction. Or, if you'd like extra protection from one or more unwanted visitors, place it on your doorstep or just inside your front door.

For grounding, sit comfortably on the floor or the earth while holding the pentacle flat on your right hand. (Alternatively, sit in a chair with your spine straight and your feet flat on the ground.) Rest your left hand over the top of it. Consciously relax your body and take some deep breaths as you focus on the solidity of the earth beneath you.

To clear negativity from a room or area, place the pentacle in a central location and charge it with the intention to absorb and neutralize any excess negativity. The next day, take it outside and lay it on the earth in bright sunlight for at least 5 to 10 minutes to clear

and neutralize it. (Or, if bright sunlight is nowhere in sight, bathe it in white sage smoke.)

To clear negativity from yourself, place the pentacle under a chair and then sit comfortably in that chair with your spine straight and your feet flat on the earth. Breathe deeply and relax. Then imagine very bright white light coming down from above. See it moving slowly but steadily, like caramel or honey, and moving through your entire body and aura, pushing negativity down as it moves toward the earth. Envision this negativity being magnetized and absorbed by the pentacle. Stay with this visualization until you feel sufficiently cleared. Then take the pentacle outside and rest it on the earth in bright sunlight or white sage smoke, as above.

To use your pentacle to bless a small object and infuse it with powerful magical energy, on the full moon, clear 4 to 12 white quartz points with sunlight and/or white sage smoke. Then place the object on your pentacle and arrange the crystals around the outside of it, pointing toward the item. Leave it until the next day.

All One Family:
Secrets for Mabon

Linda Raedisch

THE BULK OF THIS series of articles were written in the month of September, that wonderful time of year when desks creak, book spines crack, and the air is filled with the sweet fragrance of pencil shavings. I may have allowed myself to get carried away by the excitement of the season, which is why, as you may have noticed, I've tried to force so many books and reference materials on you. I'm afraid it's just what comes naturally to me. You've probably already guessed that there are books in every room of my home, but I'll go one further by telling you that I keep my *Webster's New Twentieth Century Dictionary, Unabridged, Second Edition* on a stool in the kitchen. Why in the kitchen? Because that's where questions requiring the aid of a dictionary are most likely to come up.

So now you're wondering what secrets this old school marm has saved up for Mabon. Well, I could tell you why pencils are yellow (hint: it has to do with the Chinese emperor) or why a pen is called a pen (think swans), but I'd rather take you all the way back to something more basic: the alphabet.

If you're reading this almanac at all, then you may be the sort of the person who reaches for the runes when feeling mystical, and that's not surprising. I once taught a course on runes and other "secret scripts" to some decidedly non-mystical children, and it didn't take long for them to get hooked. I don't know what would happen if I took a roomful of grown-ups with no knowledge of runes, handed them a stack of name tags written in the Elder Futhark, and told them to find their names in the pile, but kids take to runes like ducks to water. Ten minutes in, they have not only found their name tags, but they're writing secret messages to one another. The "Secret Scripts" class was born out of an earlier class I taught, "Fantasy for the Holidays," in which I developed crafts and activities inspired by the Halloween chapters of Harry Potter, the entry of Father Christmas into Narnia, and the observance of Durin's Day in *The Hobbit*. Actually, we never got to Father Christmas in Narnia, because as soon as I introduced my young students to Tolkien's "moon letters," all they wanted to do was take turns writing and decoding runic messages on the whiteboard.

Runes have always been more magical than practical. M. T. Anderson's young adult fantasy novel, *The Game of Sunken Places*, features a runic newspaper, but no such thing, to my knowledge, has ever existed. Runes form a bridge between the living and the dead in the form of memorial stones, proclaim ownership when scratched on a comb or sword, and, when used in a ritual context, can offer a glimpse of the future.

The alphabet, on the other hand, is a workhorse. No sooner had the Phoenicians invented the alphabet than the Greeks, Hebrews, Etruscans, and Romans took it and bent the letters to their own tongues, turning them, reshaping them, even assigning them new sounds without regard to their origins.

The rune Fehu betokens wealth, Uruz a shaggy ox, Thurisaz a giant, and so on. The workaday letters of the alphabet have no such correspondences. Or do they? The earliest version of the alphabet was probably scratched out by speakers of a Semitic tongue who were in the employ of the Egyptian empire. They had seen the Egyptian scribes bowed over the wickedly complicated hieroglyphs and said to themselves, "There must be a better way." They would have been unlettered folk, concerned with such basics as the welfare of their flocks, with keeping a roof over their heads, and with getting away to the hills from time to time to hunt. In a way, they were not unlike the first runesters who would be inspired by that alphabet, via the Etruscnas, several thousand years later.

That first Proto-Sinaitic alphabet, as it has come to be called, was not just a means to communicate a language that had never been written down before; it was a representation of its creators' world. Turn the letter "A" upside down and you see the horned head of one of their oxen. Tilt the letter "B" and you have a diagram of one of their mud-brick houses, while "D" is the door to that house. "C," which originally expressed a hard "g" sound, is a corner in that house, or else the curved stick you throw to bring down your prey.

Ah, so now you want to know what "E" is! Well, you don't expect me to give you all the answers, do you? And you didn't really think I was going to sign off for the year without recommending just one more book? To unlock the secrets of the alphabet, see *Ox, House, Stick: The History of Our Alphabet* by Don Robb. It's only forty-eight pages long, so go on, do your homework!

Mabon
Thanksgiving Ritual

Magenta Griffith

FOR ME, THE MOST enjoyable Harvest Home celebration is a large feast with friends and family. This takes a certain amount of work, and a circle of people around you who wish to join in celebration. Even if you usually work alone, this holiday does not lend itself to a solitary ritual, so try to find a few people to invite. You can put it in terms of a harvest feast to thank the earth rather than a witch's ritual if some people might be put off by that wording. A potluck where everyone brings something to eat or drink will help to share the effort. It can be held at the house of whoever has the largest dining room table, or the most chairs, or whoever is most centrally located. If it's at someone's house, who you invite may depend on who they feel comfortable having there. If your group is small, invite spouses and partners, and friends who might be interested in this ritual. This is a very family-friendly ritual, since everyone is seated during most of the time, and kids can appreciate a feast. If you will be indoors and there will be children attending, having a corner with a few toys they can play with will provide a place for them to go when they get bored with the adults. An outdoor feast is also possible, weather permitting. If you are doing this celebration at a park or some other public place, it is an excellent time to invite people beyond your coven or usual circle. Check ahead to see if you can reserve space, and consider alternate plans in case the weather turns bad.

Use fresh, locally grown food as much as possible for this feast. If you don't have a garden to provide at least a token amount of harvest, you could visit a "pick your own" farm or orchard, or get some of the food from a farmers' market. This will enable you to be able to follow the food from ground to table.

This is a ritual that needs a leader, whether you call them priestess or priest, or whatever else, to keep the ritual moving. Emphasize that people choose one thing to be thankful for, one harvest from the season. Otherwise, this can take too long, people will get hungry and bored, and it may not be a pleasant experience. Also, the leader may need to gently intervene if one person is going too long or into more detail than others might find comfortable.

If you will be inside, decorate the dining room and the table with seasonal fruits and vegetables and other tokens of the season. If you will be outside at a picnic table, bring a tablecloth as well as items to use for decorating the table. Children can help with this, gathering leaves that have turned orange and yellow, arranging squash in a basket, putting bowls of walnuts on the table. Whether you are indoors or outdoors, the centerpiece can be an arrangement of fruit, nuts, squash, and other seasonal food. Fall flowers, like mums, and foliage can be displayed on the table.

Harvest Home Ritual

This ritual needs three courses: soup or salad, main course, and dessert. If you are doing a feast alone or with just a few people, a few seasonal dishes are enough. If it's still hot, a cold vegetable soup like gazpacho would be perfect; if it's gotten cool enough to want hot soup, try butternut squash or pumpkin soup. Some possible main dishes are stuffed peppers, cabbage rolls, roasted root vegetables, and squash or corn soufflé. Try a new dish like ratatouille, a French vegetable dish, typically containing eggplant, zucchini, onions, green peppers, tomatoes, and garlic; many of these are in abundance right now. For dessert, apple crisp or apple pie, zucchini bread, or just fresh fruit.

To begin the ritual, everyone is seated around a table. Ring a bell or chime, or blow a horn to begin. The leader starts by holding out her or his hand to the person to their left, and saying,

Hand to hand, the circle is cast.

The person on their left takes the leader's hand and says, "*Hand to hand the circle is cast,*" and holds out their left hand to the person on **their** left, who then takes it and says, "*Hand to hand, the circle is cast,*" and so on around the circle.

When all hands as clasped, the leader says,

The Circle is cast, may it hold fast.

Next, call the directions. My coven likes to do this geographically, which means they are not associated with the traditional elements. If there is a large body of water or a sacred mountain, or other important natural feature nearby, you could incorporate that into your calling. For example, we are in Minneapolis and sometimes invoke water to the east, because we live on the west bank of the Mississippi. We have also been known to call quarters by invoking Wisconsin to the east, Iowa to the south, the Dakotas to the west, and Canada to the north. Modify this to suit your location; Paganism is, if nothing else, local, of the earth where you are.

You could sing a song at this point. The hymn many of us learned as children can be changed just a bit to fit in perfectly:

Come ye thankful, people come,
Raise the song of Harvest Home
All is safely gathered in
Ere the winter storms begin.
Earth our Mother does provide
For our wants to be supplied.
Come to Her own temple, come,
Raise the song of harvest home.

First Course

Before the first course of dinner, go around the table deosil (clockwise) and have each person who brought something to eat or drink talk about that item. It could be a little about the history of that food or the farm it came from. It could be the recipe that was handed down from their great-grandmother who came from the Old Country. If this is a large group, there might need to be an informal time limit on how long each person should speak. This is also a good time to let people know ingredients, so that people can avoid allergens, and vegetarians and vegans know what dishes to avoid.

Before eating anything, the leader should give a blessing on the food, for example:

Lady of the Fields and Orchards, Lord of the Animals and the Hunt, bless this food and drink.

People may want to stand for this, or not.

Then serve the first course, soup or salad or both, and allow time to eat. Clear away dishes as needed before you proceed.

Second Course

Go around the table again, and have each person talk about just one thing they have—or have not—accomplished in the season past. What have they sown, and what have they harvested, on the physical plane, or the intellectual, or the spiritual. People should have the option of passing, and not saying anything aloud. If you wish, sing a harvest song at this point, like "The Ripe and Bearded Barley," "John Barleycorn," or "The Reaphook and the Sickle." YouTube is full of recordings of songs like these, by groups like Steeleye Span, Clannad, Pentangle, Fairport Convention, and the Watersons, to name a few.

Serve the second, main course, and after everyone is finished, clear the table again.

Third Course

Go around the table a third time, and ask everyone to say one thing they are thankful for. Everyone should come up with an answer for this; if nothing else, they are thankful for the feast. Children who may not have answered the first round because they didn't bring any food themselves, and didn't answer the second round because they preferred to pass, should be encouraged to say what they are thankful for.

Serve the third course, usually dessert. If people want to sing another song, after dessert would be a good time.

ᴥ

End the meal with the secret of the apple. Get the best large apple you can find. One person holds it up, cuts it crosswise—across the "equator," so to speak—and holds the cut surfaces to show everyone, saying "*Out of death, comes life.*" There is a five-pointed star, a pentagram, formed by the seeds in the center of the apple. Pass the cut apple around so that everyone can have a bite. (If you have never cut an apple this way before, practice on a few apples ahead of time.) The apple is one of the symbols of witchcraft because of the hidden pentagram.

Finally, thank the directions as you called them, and thank the Earth for Her bounty:

O beautiful and generous Earth, we thank you for your gifts to us at this season of Harvest.

To end, ring the bell or chime or blow the horn you used to start.

So mote it be!

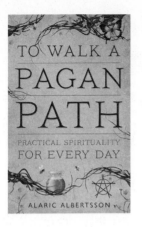

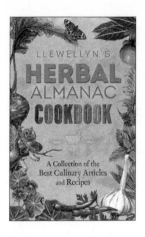

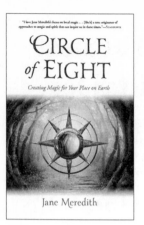

Circle Magic to Celebrate the Festivals of the Wheel

An exciting new approach to magic that is based on your geography, climate, and experiences, *Circle of Eight* can be used to celebrate the Festivals of the Wheel of the Year, create an ongoing ritual group, and explore and develop magical relationship with the land around you. Providing instructions on how to set up your own Circle of Eight and stories illustrating important magical principles, this author radically re-invents our relationship to traditional circle magic. Suitable for beginners seeking ritual and magic as well as advanced practitioners, this book helps you step deeply into the powerful magic of the directions and the great Wheel of the Year.

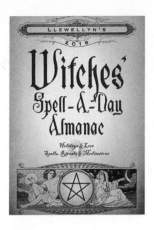

Notes

Notes